Memoirs of a Minotaur

Memoirs of a Minotaur:
from Merrill Lynch
to Patty Hearst
to Poetry

by
Robin
Magowan

STORY LINE PRESS
1999

Published by Story Line Press, Three Oaks Farm, PO Box 1240, Ashland, OR 97520-0055
www.storylinepress.com

This publication was made possible thanks in part to the generous support of the Nicho-
las Roerich Museum, the Andrew W. Mellon Foundation, the National Endowment for
the Arts, and our individual contributors.

Book design by Lysa McDowell
Front cover sculpture by Virgil Burnett

Library of Congress Cataloging-in-Publication Data
    Magowan, Robin.
        Memoirs of a Minotaur : from Merrill Lynch to Patty Hearst to Poetry / by
    Robin Magowan.
            p.   cm.
    ISBN 1-885266-80-4 (alk. paper)
        1. Magowan, Robin. 2. Poets, American— 20th century Biography.
    3. Merrill Lynch, Pierce, Fenner & Smith, Inc.—History. 4. Children of the rich—
    United States Biography. I. Title.
    PS3563.A3527Z47   1999
    811'.54—dc21
    [B]   99-14959
                                                                  CIP

for
Susan Hesse

YOU CAN'T TAKE FROM ME

NO SE PUEDE QUITARME

WHAT I'VE DANCED.

LO QUE HE BAILADO.

— MEXICAN PROVERB

David Jackson and James Merrill seated in front of a Larry Rivers painting.

Team Magowan: Robin, Stephen, Mark, Peter, Merrill

Contents

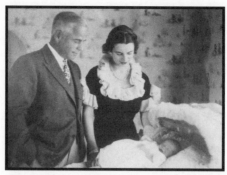

The author's grandfather, Charles Merrill, his Mother, and Robin.

Father in Rapallo, 1949

THE
PATERNAL
OCEAN

The first thing I remember about the ocean is my father. On several occasions, long before I was ready, I recall him yanking me up and dragging me, screaming, into the surf. But when I was seven, the Beach Club lifeguard began teaching me how to cope with the surf. Soon I had a rubber mat, with a rope so I could haul it. The mat's surface consisted of five inflated cushiony rills. I'd stick my chin in the middle and let my arms hang in the water. Then when the right wave appeared, I kicked and paddled hard as I could.

Entering that world I would stand, green as that beginning when wave first flowered into child and I ran away, my home those white umbrellas out there among the tumbling casks. Those waves may not have been the night, but they came crying with the night's full fire, and it was that fire I felt compelled to ride, hurtling onto foam, sand.

Best were those days honored by a red flag when the waves towered high as steeples, spuming into ashen stains. When they rolled me, it felt prehistoric, as if I were whole eons ago: fish swam in my eyes, pebbles scraped me red, and sometimes my head bounced off the bottom, stunned, gangplanked. When I struggled up from the churn, there might be another bearing down, and I'd have to gather my breath and dive and make sure I stayed flatter than a shadow until the whole train's length had thundered past. By the time I surfaced, I was out over my head, and fearful lest the backwash, and my diving momentum, should propel me into the grip of a sea-puss.

In that wrack insanity glittered. "Having crawled out of you, wave, here I am crawling my way back." I was under the world; or more precisely, the breaker was over me as I turned, lifted, and, with my mat held high like a trolley, hastened across the surf's receding slack. My concentration was all on my instinct, this voice directing me out through the successive slits in the breaking wall. I was coming home, home where I had once belonged. Ahead I saw a path opening. I must, I will! Chin down, I hopped on and, paddling furiously, flailed my way out of that vast sunken cathedral.

Once out, a different fear surged as I found myself a good house higher than the shore. But at first I'd be too tuckered to do anything but savor the relief of being afloat in the frothmill, feeling the wind behind the shadow behind the waveblade. Everything was teeth: savage, distant, Saturnian. Mine were chattering, but as I hung on, blue-lipped, I experienced something of what holds the downhill racer poised above a run, the lover as he maneuvers his bulk until it locks onto that tumbling, down-shooting ecstasy when, like sheep, the waves scattered and I shot forth, alone into that night.

As a mat-rider, I wanted nothing more than to be the arc in that fire spume, and it was to that end I waited until finally the right breaker loomed, long armed and maniacal enough to ride. "If not for this, why have I been out here?"—Words to set me paddling ahead of the wave's racing engine. Then the wave and I collided and it was "Diamonds out" as the mat catapulted forward and I took it, this wave-house jelly-spattering me forth, barreling me on a cushion of foam onto land in a ride I never wanted to see end.

The ocean again. My father's weekend arrival in Southampton seemed one continuous motion towards it: the tearing out from Wall Street on the Long Island Cannonball Express; the ritual changing at home into polo shirt and shorts; then, driven over with my brother Merrill and me to my grandfather's "Beach House" and changing into a pair of floppy swim trunks, the long run down over dune and beach and into the incoming surf as he hurled himself with a great crack out through the last wave. There, for a minute or two, he would float, arms forward and head like a deadman down, and only when there was none of the city's workweek grime left on him would he wade towards us, shaking like a dog and happy. The beauty was all in the charge, the brusqueness of it, the salve moistening and feathering him, turning him green, gold and white as the late twilight curled around him and brought him to us.

There was something superbly clean about that headlong running of his, that raging fire of his intensity. Speed incarnate, hardly ever straying out of the left lane on a drive to Southampton; or, on an irresistible impulse, grabbing the white nightstick out of a gendarme's holster and sprinting away with it into the Paris night. Don Regan, his protégé at Merrill Lynch and later President Reagan's Chief of Staff, wrote that he never encountered a man who did everything quite so speedily: clear a desk, pound a typewriter, whatever. Working for "Boss," as Don fondly called my father, you hopped.

A natural force, like wind, like thunder, like rain, unpredictable and therefore dangerous. To anyone who met him even casually, his presence intimidated, frightened. It took twenty years before he relented enough to call his Safeway secretary, Jeanne Hickerson, by her first name. At an early stage in his career, Bill Schreier, the current Merrill Lynch chairman, remembers receiving a "smiling ram" memo of praise. (RAM were his initials, from Robert Anderson Magowan. There was another set of stationery with a scowling ram.) When Schreier acknowledged it gratefully, Father reminded him, "There's only a few inches between a pat on the back and a kick in the ass."

The importance of my learning to live under such bombardment, wave after fatherly wave ringing in my ears, cannot be exaggerated. Other people become paralyzed, stuck in an airplane that won't take off. Or disabled by an inordinate amount of hallucinogens breaking over them, one wave of thought heavier, more terrifying than the last. I'm not, since I was steeped in that fatality at the source.

THE MAKING
OF A MILLIONAIRE —
ROBERT MAGOWAN

My father was born in 1903 in Chester, Pennsylvania on the Delaware River, the son of the local station master. The first American Magowan had emerged in 1789 in New Castle, Delaware, fresh presumably from the highland clearances—in Gaelic we are blacksmith sons, a caste attributed with the peculiar powers of those who handle fire. Ever since the family had clustered in the Delaware Gap, their marital horizons defined by the next penniless lassie off the boat from Glasgow.

Chester is a blighted milltown some twelve miles south of Philadelphia. Yet the good life could be lived there and in 1960, on my only visit, I met my sprightly ninety-four-year-old uncle, Orlando Cloud, a man well informed about the greater world who had never spent a night outside the city limits.

For my father, Chester was no Arcadia. So far as anyone knew, he had no memories of the town in which he lived until he was fifteen, none he cared to voice at any rate . Everything was sealed in the bitter grime of his poverty, qualified by him as "dire," or "abject," leaving me to infer the circumstances: the wrong side of the river where they lived? The mockery of the shop windows, too expensive for people who went out only to church? The constant penny-pinching of those days was to stay with him all his life. It made him frugal about turning off the lights and spending any more time than necessary on the telephone. He would delight in a bargain, the senior citizen card he would flash at a movie, the social security check that might barely pay for a dinner at Caravelle.

If my maternal grandfather, Charlie Merrill, was the prototype of the flamboyant Wall Street tycoon, my father was the somewhat more traditional figure, a person basically formed by the Horatio Alger stories he read as a boy. To him and his friends, he told my brother Mark, who was interviewing him for a folklore

16

assignment, "They weren't stories, but truth itself."

Not only did he absorb from them a pattern of success—of how you do it, climb that drainpipe, extricate yourself from one or another snake pit—but they also gave him his ideals: the glorification of individual effort and accomplishment; the equation of the pursuit of money with the pursuit of happiness, and of business success with spiritual grace. Likewise, the story of any American who failed to achieve in this way counted as nothing less than a tragedy. When he met Charlie Merrill, he couldn't help but see him as the epitome of everything he believed in; a man whom he would do his utmost to serve.

As a small child, Father had contracted a bad case of glandular fever. According to the medical wisdom of the time, the way to reduce his swollen neck was to make him wear a spiked collar— bleed the fever out! The little boy wore that contraption for years, never getting any better, until a Christian Science practitioner came along and made his parents throw it away. Thereafter he thrived, gleaning chunks of coal along the railroad track with his younger brother, Ned; hustling, at ten, his own ice business; doing, in short, anything to make a buck.

When he was fifteen, his father, whose health was rapidly failing, was transferred to Philadelphia. There he got his first break, a postgraduate scholarship to Kent School. From this Episcopal academy he progressed in 1922 to Harvard, then in its "Gold Coast" aura: Boston deb parties to be crashed; uncrashable black tie social clubs; the infrequently attended "great man" lecture. Kids on the make like my father and grandfather went to college less for the patina of a liberal education than for the savoir faire and social connections. Father paid for himself, his widowed mother and his brother's college tuition with one of those newfangled inventions, a typewriter.

Soon Father was banging out, not student papers, but journalism for *The Boston Globe* and *The New York Times*. By senior year he was employing five student assistants and raking in the not inconsiderable sum of a hundred dollars a week, while serving as Editor-in-Chief of *The Harvard Crimson* and manager of the Baseball Team. Two of his summer vacations were even spent not so unprofitably in Paris, with enough to spare to ship over his brother and a red Ford.

Upon graduation he took a job on *The Boston Globe*. But when he learned that the *Globe*'s star reporter was making only $15,000 (multiply by ten for today) he quit, and with the encouragement of a Harvard friend, Jack Straus—my future godfather—went to work for the biggest store in the world, the Straus-owned R. H. Macy's, for thirty dollars a week.

At those wages he kept body and soul together by snacking on the free food offered by bars and dining out at the Automat. But Father was, as Jack Straus told me, a born merchandiser. He soon became Macy's chief foreign buyer, based in his generation's mecca, Paris, for seven months of the year.

For me, it is almost inconceivable to imagine the pleasures of shopping all over Europe on someone else's oversized pocketbook. Anything that intrigued him, in a market stall or an avenue's plateglass window, was snapped up on the spot. If he thought it would sell, he had it copied, mass-produced. Back on Herald Square he made sure that, despite the boycott provoked by Hitler's unexpected coming to power, the gloves and hats he had bought in Berlin were sold. Jack Straus was convinced that Father, not he, would have headed Macy's, had Father chosen to remain. But to Father, even more intolerable than being the token W.A.S.P. in a Jewish company was having to give up his weekends and work Saturdays. When Macy's did not give him the big raise he wanted, he quit and became a rather unlikely advertising executive.

But with a personal worth now of $250,000, this thirty-two-year-old man could think of getting married. Through Johnny and Audy Baker (who later became my two other godparents), he found himself invited, while in Palm Beach in March, to a birthday dinner dance Charlie Merrill was giving at the Everglades Club for his twenty-year-old daughter, Doris, a blue-eyed petite brunette with a figure like a swan's. These feminine attractions, together with her intense aliveness and uncommon sweetness, were enough to propel his hat into her ring.

I've often wondered what my father, of such a different background, had going for him other than his irresistible self-belief, the prospective wealth he wore like a star. But to Mother this thirteen-year-older man carried the erotic fatality of The Stranger. A destiny enhanced when, as she was driving back with a girl friend from a hunt ball, their car broke down in Dunn, North Carolina. After having it towed, they were told they could be on the road again in an hour, to my Uncle Ned's thirtieth birthday party at the glamorous Casino Club in Central Park.

In the meantime? Across the street from the garage a placard advertising a fortune teller—tarot cards and palmistry—caught their eye. How amusing, they thought. But it turned into something else when the gypsy woman, looking into Mother's palm, prophesied that she was going to marry the man on whose right she would be sitting that very evening. Merely getting into New York, on the roads of the day, and finding a corsage to go with her evening dress, kept her reasonably concentrated. But when at Ned's party she found herself seated on my father's right, her wick ignited. Who was she to fight the inevitable? In six weeks they were engaged. Half a year later, on June 15, 1935, Charlie Merrill gave them a big society wedding reception on the front lawn of his Southampton house, a seated dinner for a thousand.

For all the rapidity of these events, or perhaps because of it, this rapid mutual consummation, there is much I don't know. Where did Father take her on their dates? What did he promise her besides a three-month European honeymoon and a Cartier-cut diamond? Weren't there, at the time of Ned's birthday party, more serious suitors about? If so, why did an immediate decision have to be made? What, in other words, made Mother renounce her one genuine freedom—that of choice? Or was the personal electricity, as it crackled between these two hyperactive dynamos, all sufficient?

But then this five-foot, seven-inch man was striking looking with his piercing sapphire-blue eyes that flashed sincerity even as they blazed into your inner soul; a strong, needle-fine nose; parted, medium-short black hair; a compact, slender-shouldered torso set on legs that were, like his arms, a trifle short even for one of his height. In hotels, during their honeymoon, he was frequently mistaken for that other sharp-featured fox, the Duke of Windsor. The decisive vote came from her adored father. He wanted a businessman son-in-law to help him run his empire. To Father, the prospect of becoming Charlie Merrill's right-hand man and dynastic heir must have seemed paradise itself. One can see those two men, with their not dissimilar backgrounds, conspiring while the heiress was sold, or rather transferred from one ledger to another.

Back from their honeymoon in Venice, Budapest, Paris and Berlin (where Nazi thugs pulled a Jewish friend right out of their taxi—it was 1935), my parents, with help from Charlie, took an apartment in the annex of San Francisco's Mark Hopkins hotel, while Father went to work for Safeway across the Bay in Oakland. This was Charlie's main business interest at the time.

It was there in San Francisco I was born, a Virgo under Scorpio rising, and with a moon in Libra, some three weeks early on September 4, 1936. "We almost didn't make your birth," Grandfather's second wife, Hellen, would say whenever we met, since it was only Charlie's hunch, signalled in a dream, that had brought them by rail across the country in time. Grandfather played his psychic hunches, as he had once in hastening outdoors when there was an uncanny stillness on the lawn to find his daughter in flames, too terror-stricken to scream—she had set her hair afire playing with Fourth of July sparklers. He saved her by rolling her up in a carpet. Now at the time of his favorite child's first baby—and his first grandchild—Charlie again wanted to be there, a supernova emblazoning the event.

The evening of their arrival my parents held a dinner party for them at their Mark Hopkins apartment. In the middle of it the water sack containing me burst, drenching Mother's new evening dress. Anyone else would have excused herself and left the table. But not wanting to disturb the occasion, Mother called on all her reserves to continue sitting through one course after the next. It was only Hellen who eventually noticed Mother slip away from the table, hurrying now lest I be born on a taxicab floor.

But first births take time, and it wasn't until ten the next morning that I emerged into that entrepreneurial labyrinth. "Look at that baby," Hellen cried, "all bald except for that one tuft of gray hair." And this tiny old man held up his head and everyone agreed that this Robert A., Jr., as I was named (but Robin for short, as my father was Bob), was the unmistakable heir to the old lock, stock and barrel. To assist me in making my life transit successfully between the sphinx of Leo and the narrow pyramid entrance leading into the Symphonic City of Libra, Charlie Merrill went down to his bank that very day and set me up with a trust fund.

The birth to him of a male child enormously affected my father. My grandfather remembered Father being so overcome by tears at the news that he had to step out of their waiting room onto the balcony. For the first and only time in their marriage he took to coming home for lunch, impatient to see how I had changed since breakfast. And he would resist going away with Mother to the Peninsula for the weekend for fear of missing some milestone event, like a first smile.

THE MAKING OF A ZEUS — CHARLIE MERRILL

My mother's father, Charlie Merrill, was the seminal Wall Street figure of his time; a man who may have done as much as Henry Ford to create today's middle class. The founder of Merrill Lynch and the cofounder of the Safeway supermarket chain, he is generally credited with bringing the Wall Street casino into the lives of the middle class. Charlie was also a genuine visionary. He may not have foreseen the Depression, but he did foresee the October 1929 stock market crash, and he did everything in his power to forestall it. Rarer still for a businessman of his day, he possessed a social vision, a sense of what had to be done if capitalism was to survive. Bringing Wall Street to Main Street was his formula for enlarging the base of the capitalist pyramid by giving the small investor a stake in the commercial churn; co-opting him, as it were.

To me, my grandfather's legacy was not these achievements so much as his life as I came to know it through the stories he told me about the post-Civil War rural Florida in which he had grown up. And the women he pursued—and held onto!—with every jot of the same intensity he put into his business ventures. His adventurer's life challenged me, as it did my father. But where Father saw the challenge as one of personal enrichment, I saw a legacy of paths taking me into unexplored terrains.

In 1943, when I was seven, Charlie suffered a series of near-lethal heart attacks. He remained in the hospital, after the second, for four months. For the remaining thirteen years of his life, not a day passed without severe and repeated pain. But even in that un-remitting agony a signal vitality pulsed. To a child, most elderly people that ill are distinctly scary. But the affection he entertained for me, and the relish with which in his soft-spoken drawl he clued me in to his part in my genetic inheritance, were such that I made it a point of visiting him nearly every summer day in Southampton and every spring vacation in Palm Beach where I, sometimes alone of my family, was his guest.

A number of self-made men have possessed great wealth. But few of them ever made it purr, gasp, ecstatically and convulsively. Charlie made sure he personified it in his Van Sickle tailored double-breasted suit, his wide Art Deco ties and two-toned En-glish shoes; the checkbook he always kept upstairs in his bedroom so that the pleasure, as he said mischievously, might be all the keener by being delayed.

For him, life was the paramount adventure and he was its Roi Soleil, Charles E. Money, as proud of his philanthropy as of his houses or business creations; so proud that he died with a Carnegie-like front-page splash, leaving most of his caboodle to charity. He must have figured us grandchildren well enough provided. If we needed more, we could go out like any other self-reliant American and earn it; we could build that better mouse trap.

My father liked to maintain to me that he and Charlie rose out of the same pluck-and-luck, work-and-win, American success myth. My grandfather may have been poor, but he did not hail from the same anonymous penury as my father. His family tree—Merrill derives from the French merle, "blackbird"—contained its own unusual and certainly helpful antecedents: a berth on the Mayflower in the person of John Alden; a 1644 Ipswich settler, Nathanial Merrill. His maternal grandparents, the Wilsons, oversaw a 4,500-acre cotton plantation in the Mississippi delta; a spread Charlie would buy in 1930 (unable to resist a family home with a commissary-post office in no less a place than Money, MS).

My great-great grandfather valued education enough to insist on inflicting Latin on his seventeen-year-old second wife. Something of his love of learning was passed on to his daughter Octavia, the only one of his nine children to attend college. It was there at Maryville in eastern Tennessee that Octavia met the future Doctor Merrill. After a not atypical seven-year courtship, they were married in the Doctor's home town, Green Cove Springs, Florida, in 1883.

In our family we spoke of Green Cove Springs, where Charlie was born on October 13, 1885, as if it were the sticks incarnate. But in those days Florida stopped at Saint Augustine. There was no Palm Beach, no Miami. Saint Augustine was a glamorous watering hole. Socialites descended from as far away as Europe to spend the winter months there. They would land at Jacksonville, then the East Coast's third largest port, and take the paddle-wheel steamer up the St. Johns to Green Cove. Next day they would continue on to St. Augustine.

In a well-situated resort, famed for its medicinal waters, a doctor could be forgiven for thinking there existed a clientele capable of sustaining him and his new family; all the more if he also doubled as the town pharmacist.

The reality belied these expectations. Throughout the 1890s, rural Florida remained in the grip of a prolonged, post-Civil War depression. As my grandfather recalled in an interview, "Rough going was so much a part of our existence that it was taken for granted as though it was the normal condition of life everywhere. There were few silver dollars in circulation, and fewer greenbacks, and the silver dollar looked about as big as the middle slice of a watermelon."

Of Charlie's early childhood there is one story Octavia used to tell about how, shortly after he had learned to speak, she had taken him out on the porch one evening to show him the full moon. At the sight, Charlie pointed his arm straight up and began to yell at the top of his lungs, "I want it! I want it!" When it wasn't deposited then and there in his lap, he launched into a furious tantrum.

Thereafter Octavia had him believing that anything he wanted— even the moon—could be his, if he wanted it badly enough. Over and over, as he saw her despairing over some unpayable bill, he would promise, "Don't worry, Mama, when I grow up I'll buy you rubies and diamonds." Arabian Nights stuff, but he fulfilled it to the letter. This was a man for whom dreams were reality.

This gracious, charming and charismatic man possessed a wide-mouthed smile that flashed from one ear to the other. "Merry Merrill" , his baseball teammates called him, a moniker his natural reserve allowed him to treasure. But behind the ready smile and the misty wilfulness of his gray-blue eyes, there could lie the more problematic aspect of a sultan not about to be thwarted. (In the whole of his adult life only one person ever succeeded in standing up to him—his mother Octavia.) The effect on those who got in his way, or merely happened to blunder onto the road when his chariot came blazing by, was indeed devastating. To be sure, he would do everything in his power—afterwards—to make a proper restitution, picking up his victim and dusting him off and pressing a fat wad into his hands with such heartfelt regret that a surprising number actually became lifelong friends. But for all his generosity—and Charlie never loaned, he gave—there would always remain those who could never be compensated, wives and children among them. Their views still haunt me.

To what extent my grandfather's lifelong running after the ladies was the result of a compulsive need is hard to say. In little men of his stamp, with their Zeus-sized egos, the urge to dominate can take any number of guises. But Octavia's story about his bawling for the moon may explain a drive that would never take a woman's "no" as a plausible answer. And when Charlie wanted someone, he pulled out all the stops. Knowing my grandmother, Eliza Church, even in her eighties a credible oval-faced silent film beauty, it is easy to understand how, the day after meeting her at a party at his boss's, he came breezing into the office remarking, "What a beautiful girl Eliza is! I think I'll marry her." By then he may have known about her ability to compose on the piano—waltzes with titles like "Mist on the Moon." Or that as a child she had ridden out West in her father's private railcar, a Pennsylvania Railroad executive and head of the Carnegie Institute, as well as the author, among other works, of a two-volume biography of Oliver Cromwell. That gracious, gentle, convent-educated lady repeatedly turned down the future tycoon. After a final "No," she boarded a train for far-off Florida. But Charlie was not to be denied. At every stop there was a bouquet-laden Western Union messenger waiting to greet her. The storm of flowers went on until finally at Akron, Georgia, the poor woman capitulated and agreed to take him out of his torment.

This ill-matched marriage to a woman he had known only a few weeks—she, brought up by a cruel stepmother, needed security, while he needed adventure—was, like his two subsequent marriages, to last a somewhat improbable thirteen years, the three children (my mother, her brother Charles, her half-brother Jimmy) occurring at equally precise six-year intervals. (Was there an extraterrestrial intelligence imprinting my grandfather's chaos with a more rational pattern? Knowing his poet-son Jimmy's Ouija board epic, The Changing Light at Sandover, one is tempted to speculate.)

To be sure, Charlie had his own sentimental code. "Tell a woman anything," he once advised me, "but never tell her you love her, unless you mean it." This did not deter him from marrying his third and sexiest wife, Kinta, a New Orleans belle, even though he was no longer in love. She, through an emissary, had threatened suicide; he believed her.

The marriage to Eliza and the birth of my mother soon thereafter changed Charlie's financial horizons. He had reason to believe, after churning his boss's $25,000 into a $750,000 portfolio, he could succeed on his own in Wall Street. In 1914, at the age of twenty-nine and with $8,000 in personal savings as capital, he hung out his own shingle. He knew by then that he had no hope of crashing that exclusive club and complete law unto itself that was the J. P. Morgan-run Wall Street of the time. Instead he had to find a clientele outside the elite served by Morgan and his cronies. And, as a distributor of securities, he had to find a new order of risk to underwrite.

Charlie found the combination he needed in the emerging chain store industry. Sometimes it may have even seemed, as he once claimed to a friend of mine, that he had invented them all. Nonetheless, his wholehearted backing had much to do with their ability to secure the capital they needed to finance expansion. And it was by taking his underwriting fee in the form of stock warrants that he made most of his initial fortune. "If a stock's good enough to sell," he said, "it's good enough to buy."

All the same Charlie almost went under in his first major deal, an underwriting of McCrory. For a variety of reasons the issue didn't sell, and Charlie was saved, if that's the word—it seemed certain ruination at the time—only by the outbreak of the First World War which shut down the stock exchange. That it took him another nine months to draw up a prospectus that offered his investors the various perquisites, conversion rights, and guarantees they needed shows the depths of his inexperience; how much he still had to learn about the new frontier he was opening up. (Meanwhile, without a roof over her head, Eliza took their four-month-old daughter to Columbus, Ohio, to stay with her sister.)

But the offering was a success, as was the next of Kresge six months later. With the $30,000 in additional capital from Eliza's inheritance, which he now felt free to accept, he prospered—with such dispatch that our family scrapbook contains a 1917 clipping of the newly enlisted "Boy Millionaire" in his tailored uniform. The picture doesn't show the fitted purple silk underwear underneath, that little Napoleon's way of demonstrating—to himself, at least—that he was both richer and more hedonistic than the competition.

But the military did not give him the chance to pursue the ultimate Napoleonic fantasy. Instead he found himself doing time in cooks-and-bakers school, learning the hard way the useful maxim,

"Never do a job well that you hate."

Looking for more action and hoping to be sent to France, Charlie transferred into the Air Force. "Pop," as this thirty-two-year-old was known, was top of his class in flying school. Once again he may have done too well, for he was appointed instructor and served out the rest of the war at a series of Florida bases.

To a compulsive workaholic, flying brought a freedom and a serenity he had never known. As a way of prolonging the idyll, he even volunteered for the now notorious Allied expeditionary force to Siberia. And he did a lot of stunt flying, once pulling out of a 10,000-foot tailspin only a thousand feet from the ground. When he emerged from the war, his temples were white.

After all that, shuffling money on Wall Street could seem staid. But those were the Twenties, and he was soon not only underwriting new ventures, but running them as well. Among them was Charlie Chaplin's Pathe Films, which he sold in 1926 to Joseph Kennedy, the late President's father (and the one man he genuinely loathed—for his shoddy business practices and his bad-mouthing the British when they came into the war). Charlie and the window-ledge comedian Harold Lloyd were to remain close friends, charter members of that under-five-foot-six "everyone else is a son of a bitch" club of his. Mother remembers Chaplin coming at my grandfather's insistence, when I was five and she was ill with a 104 degree fever, and playing the piano for us. But with an orange, instead of the usual thumbs and fingers, in each hand.

Charlie, in turn, plowed Kennedy's money into Safeway Stores, the West Coast-based supermarket chain my father and my brother Peter would direct.

By 1927, the stock market was looking distinctly suspect to Charlie. It wasn't merely that his customers were overbidding, often enough with money they didn't have and for which he was personally liable. It was more that the economy seemed to him little more than a house of cards. Since no one else on Wall Street shared this impression, Charlie began to wonder if he was crazy and consulted a psychoanalyst. Perhaps the new science could cast some light? This, the first such consultation in psychoanalytic annals, ended with the analyst selling out his entire portfolio. "If you're crazy, Charlie, I am too," he said comfortingly. Encouraged, Charlie took out a full-page public service advertisement in *The New York Times* warning of the coming debacle. He even journeyed to Washington to offer the retiring President Calvin Coolidge a $100,000 salary to forego the reticence of a lifetime and speak out against the rampant speculation.

Of course, hardly anyone listened to this Cassandra. All his prophesying did was make him so unpopular that "no one wanted to be near me." Nonetheless, Charlie did manage to liquidate his firm's security holdings and transfer its business to the bond house of Pierce & Cassatt (the family of the painter Mary Cassatt). He had lured most of his customers to safety when the October 1929 crash occurred.

The crash left Charlie among the few at one of the pinnacles of New York life—the tower suite of the Carlyle Hotel where he and his vivacious second wife, Hellen, a twenty-five-year-old magazine publisher whom he married in 1925, were to spend most of the next decade. For my friend, Bob Lenzner, Hellen recalled the privilege of standing naked out in the rain on their balcony overlooking Central Park ("What sexual confidence!" Bob remarked). To me, Hellen described the exhilaration of speeding through the near empty streets to a nightclub. "I know I shouldn't be saying this, but if you had the money, New York could be lots of fun."

I have no doubt that Hellen loved Charlie desperately. But she kept putting him down in front of people: at the bridge table, where she was the more experienced partner; at the dinner table, where she would interrupt him in the midst of a story, "You're telling it wrong." And she had her own notions of social position. "I can't invite your mother, Doris, to your wedding reception. What would Southampton think of me?" ("I should have divorced Hellen," Charlie in one of his Henry VIII moods later told Mother, "then and there.")

Yet for all the competitiveness they shared a lot, not least a Jacksonville background where Hellen had run a successful weekly,

The Social Silhouette. And Hellen's social adroitness must have come in handy. Charlie may have bought on his own his Southampton mini-Versailles, "The Orchard," a Stanford White designed antebellum house completed just before White's murder in 1907. But it was Hellen who helped stock its twenty-two bedrooms with the likes of Helen Hayes, Hoagy Carmichael, Gloria Swanson and George Gershwin. Hellen remembers the thrill of sitting in that vast double-ceilinged music room with its four great twisting brass columns, stained glass windows, red damask curtains and sofa, enormous white marble Milanese fireplace, and licentious Flemish tapestry, while Gershwin and Gertrude Lawrence were knocking out the future Broadway hit, "Oh, Kay!"

The new kid on the block—but with the biggest, whitest elephant in town—was not cowed by the formality of Southampton. As a joke, he had his tailor make him a pair of black shorts, cut to mid-thigh, to go with his tuxedo. When the art collector, Chester Dale, saw fit to admire two large photographs of Pompeian frescos hanging in the entrance hall, "Don't let go of those, Charlie, they're valuable," my grandfather had a second pair printed up and sent to the collector as a gift.

It did not help their marriage that Charlie was on the road whole months at a time. Much of it was out West where he was negotiating the merger of some seven chains into the new Safeway. Gus Ledbetter, his Seattle partner, told me he was in the conference room in Portland when Charlie put it together. "There were 33,000 stores and Charlie did it all, the evaluations, the exchanges of equity, in twelve hours. As a mathematical feat, I've never seen anything like it."

The travel brought its own temptations to add to the ones Charlie was forever accommodating. How was Hellen to react when he left on the top of his dresser an amorous note from his New Orleans tart, Kinta. Or when, responding to the repeated tugging of his favorite setter, Mike, she followed the dog up the stairs and into her best friend Dottie Stafford's bedroom to catch Charlie sprawled in fragrant delight, looking up sheepishly from the bed.

Meanwhile from all over the country a never-ending barrage of business solicitations poured in. Charlie avoided being head of the new Safeway—a field, he felt, outside of his competence—only because of a telegram announcing his sister's death. Two years later, in 1935, he came within a hair of buying the Brooklyn Dodgers from the Ebbets family for half a million dollars. Had he done so the Bums might still be in Flatbush rather than Los Angeles and my brother Peter might not have felt the need to save his boyhood idols, the Giants, for San Francisco.

As it was, Charlie was left with that belated expression of his vision, "The Thundering Herd," as Merrill Lynch would come to be known. For much of his life, the daily adventure had kept him sufficiently enthralled. But now in 1939, at fifty-four, he wanted more. He wanted a place in the annals of his time. That immortality was the point of those four volume biographies I always saw him reading. They were manuals on how one did it, carved out a niche and became Robert E. Lee. In the face of his bête noir, FDR, and the New Deal's perception of Wall Street as Public Enemy Number One, he wanted to make a political assertion. If the depressed economy was to be churned in Keynesian fashion into prosperity, surely professionals with something at stake could do it more effectively than the brain-trust government.

THE SERAGLIO

Merrill Lynch succeeded, but for Charlie the success did not come quite in time. Like most new businesses, the firm lost money—$309,000 in its first nine months. And at the end of 1941 it was still in the red. As his partners' life savings were at stake, Charlie drove himself harder than a man in his fifties should have. The result was a series of heart attacks.

If ever there was an overtaxed organ, it was Charlie's heart. The booze, the chain smoking, the artery-clogging Southern diet, the nonstop partying, all exacted a toll. But it was the attractions of Kinta des Mare (originally de Mario), the New Orleans beauty for whom he divorced Hellen, that blasted him into the red zone.

By the standards of Kinta's three subsequent marriages Charlie might be deemed fortunate. None of his marital successors managed to stay alive as long as two months. "That Kinta has had the worst luck," I recall Mother, in a mood of surprising forgiveness, remarking. But Kinta worked at her luck, plopping her breasts daily in a basin of ice-cold water "to preserve their freshness." While Mother and her chums were twisting tinfoil reflectors around themselves to barbecue their skins a tasty, death-defying mahogany, Kinta kept her gardenia-white skin successfully smoldering under elbow-length gloves and oversize sombreros. The effect when she swished into a drawing room—the sudden hush, the turning of heads—could not have been more distinct.

The staggering enormity of her sexual concentration was lost on me. I only saw a ridiculous, haughty, peacock-voiced Southerner whom, for some truly inexplicable reason, my grandfather had married. My enlightenment would come several decades later, at a dance we held to commemorate my father's seventy-fifth birthday. There, in a flowered silk décolleté, was the Countess di Carpegna. Kinta had it all still, an intimacy of approach, a magnetism such as I never dreamed a woman of seventy-five could possess. For the first time I understood why Proust's Swann married Odette. There are other, more imperious necessities than those of love.

It might be thought that, with Kinta disliking us children, and constantly surrounded by company as Charlie was, he might not have found time for me. But with his two great pursuits—women and making money—now denied him, he had become more than ever his stories.

I heard about all he did as a little kid to make money: buying all hundred copies of the newspaper proclaiming the destruction of the Spanish fleet in Santiago harbor and lugging them out to the fairgrounds where he sold every last one at a quarter each. Or, while working as a soda-jerk in his father's pharmacy, spiking the Coca Cola with pure grain alcohol—to everyone's delight but his old man's. Or the lucrative paper route he acquired in Jacksonville's red light district (the one no-go area where a newcomer like his father could establish a practice), where he talked about being "kindly received" (with tips? tea and cakes? I wish I'd asked) by his father's clients.

I heard too about his various athletic endeavors: how at twelve he had swum a six-mile width of the St. Johns River trailed by a pal in a rowboat armed with a paddle to fend off any alligator; or how after getting thrown out of a Florida military academy for concussing a passing master with a water bomb dropped out of a fourth floor dorm window, he had landed a scholarship to Worcester Academy, a quarterback to be hurled over the line in short yardage situations.

With his small strike zone he was an effective hit-them-where-they-ain't leadoff hitter. But any chance of a professional career as a shortstop ended when the kid who was his enemy broke his throwing arm while demonstrating an over-the-shoulder ju-jitsu throw. But the bad arm did not keep him from playing a shallow centerfield for an undefeated 27-0 Shaw Mississippi, semipro team. The betting was so heavy, I remember Charlie telling me the last time I saw him, that after a 9-2 away win over a Pelham reinforced by several pro minor leaguers, they found the whole male population waiting for them, bricks in hand, by the one bridge out of town. At the end of the season his teammates chipped in with a railroad ticket to New York and the clerking job on Wall Street, obtained through the good offices of a Smith College student to whom he had become engaged the previous summer while playing semipro ball in Maine. "I must say," he told me, "I felt like a damn fool going to New York knowing only one person, but with that ticket of theirs in hand there wasn't much I could do."

His life wasn't lived to make wonderful yarns, but in those last declining years it certainly seemed so. To a man whose life hung suspended by the slenderest of threads, each day survived could seem a miracle. As could the distance between his own rural childhood and what he had achieved. That's perhaps where I, his oldest grandchild, fit in. I provided a magic reference point, someone with whom he could share the wonder of his boyhood, and of what it was like growing up in that remote other world of the post-Civil War South.

Of that South of his, I knew only "Merrill's Landing." It was the only remaining property in Palm Beach whose grounds ran from Lake Worth to the ocean. After razing the old house, he had built a new one, along with a series of guest houses where children like us, down for the spring vacation, could raise all the hell we wanted. Across the county road, by the ocean, lay a two-room cabana that Mother would eventually transform into a pink, peak-roofed, Bermuda style house. The ocean waves splashed through a restraining coral reef and there, in shoulder-high water, I paddled about, eye out for the entrapped shark. Or the bright red coral snake sheltering under a garbage can. Or the alligator found on two occasions in the sulphur spring-fed swimming pool. They may have been revenants from the pack that, as late as the war, frequented the surrounding swamp. I remember peering down at them from a little bridge, just as I remember the boathouse with its yacht on which Grandfather used to take us deep sea fishing and on jaunts up the Loxahatchie into the Everglades.

When the swamp was drained after the war for property development, Grandfather elected to turn his portion into a romantic pond. There were snowy egrets stalking about, and the odd snap of mullet breaking the water, as well as a number of giant tarpon that had swum up the sewer from the lake in search of shrimp and gotten too paunchy to leave. An entrance driveway wound around the pond before reaching the main grounds with their red clay tennis court, ornamental citrus trees and thick, prickly grass. Because of the sulphur, the swimming pool was an impenetrable white, smelling of rotten eggs. But when I viewed it at night, with a glittering white channel running down to it from its source under the live oak outside the dining room, it seemed—and was—a singular privilege; as if I were far away from everything, with only the star people nearby.

A BATH IN
HIS RIVER OF GOLD

For most of this time Charlie was too ill to do anything about Kinta. But now in 1952, at the end of another thirteen-year cycle, he did not want to die in the arms of someone he loathed. Kinta's final mistake was to complain about Leroy Johnson, the Negro valet he had inherited from his partner Eddy Lynch. Family myth has it that Leroy had been General Pershing's chauffeur in World War I. Or was it that he had married the daughter of General Pershing's chauffeur? But for the difference in skin color, Charlie and Leroy might have seemed twins. Leroy shared not only his boss's suits, but his appetite for women. Often Charlie had to come up with the wherewithal to get Leroy's current flame out of town when the wife appeared. When they traveled together first class on the Saturnia to Italy in 1950, Charlie introduced him to one and all as Mr. Ali of Pakistan, a diplomat traveling incognito, so he could enjoy the pleasure of Leroy's dinner table conversation. So when Kinta delivered her ultimatum, "Either you fire that rascal or I'll divorce you," Grandfather replied, "Leroy may be a rascal, but I can't get along without him and I can get along without you."

That, like most divorces, turned out to be a far from simple proposition. Lest anyone think of him as a New York property holder, he donated The Orchard to his alma mater Amherst as an economics institute where the best minds of the day could exchange ideas, and he sold the Beach House to my parents.

At sixty-seven, there now came a seemingly miraculous final blooming. Feeling he had nothing to lose, and not anticipating the era of multiple bypass operations, pacemakers and open-heart surgery in the offing, he consulted his friend, Samuel Levine of the Harvard Medical School. He had heard about the easement of pain that dosages of radioactive iodine had brought about; could he offer himself to medical science as a human guinea pig? Ever the optimist, he was convinced some good could come out of the technology that had led to Hiroshima and Nagasaki.

The transforming effect of Doctor Levine's radioactive cocktail was like an episode from The Amazing Hulk. Visiting him in his lead-protected room at Peter Bent Brigham, where even the wallpipes were sheathed in lead, I remember Grandfather pointing in awe to the two-inch increase in his neck size. But, along with the fuller neck came a return of sexual potency.

One need not have seen "Volpone" to conjure up the galaxy of ladies that now orbited around him: the candidates for anything, everything; a place to the right or left of his chair; a bath in his river of gold. If an attractive woman was available, he pursued her. And he was more than willing to consider marriage in return. My parents, seeing only harpies out for his money, did all they could to deter him, provoking, in one instance—it's the starting point of my uncle Jimmy's novel, *The Seraglio*—Lillian Coe's slashing of the Brockhurst portrait of Mother wearing a Chinese brocade bed jacket which she had given Charlie. (The police had detected signs of entry in the boarded-up Beach House. But it was Mother, to her horror, who discovered the stabbed portrait, the first of a row stacked in a closet. She felt the power of the gesture and, despite herself, burst into tears.)

Not that any inheritance was at stake. But a widow would have been entitled to a portion of Charlie's estate, greatly skewering the Merrill Lynch partnership and any possible family control of the empire.

Three divorces—a large number at the time—may leave a certain residue of scarred familial tissue. In our family, Charlie may have loomed as a financial emperor, an all-knowing prophet and philanthropic saint. One thing he wasn't was an Oriental pasha. And any ascribing of a sexual motivation to anyone was likewise taboo. We five sons, collisions of sperm and ovum, were never kids, but putative adults, sprung like Athena from the dynastic godhead.

In this respect I find striking my father's effort to neuter Charlie's commissioned biography so as not to cast him "in an unfavorable light to [his] darling grandchildren." It was as if Father was fully aware that this double-walled family labyrinth he had designed, with its one generation of business achievement flowing seamlessly

The Brockhurst portrait of Mother

into the next, contained an inherent flaw. And to elude him we had only to spot that one chink of sexual light.

My grandfather refused to be caught up in Father's trompe l'oeil. "You can imagine," he wrote his ex-wife Hellen, "to what extent I would ask any Author to 'soft pedal' some of my weaknesses and foibles which have become dearer to me as the capacity to repeat them becomes less and less."

If Father did not succeed in bowdlerizing Charlie's biography, he did in blinkering me. It wasn't until I read *The Seraglio* that I realized how much of what was taking place under my sixteen-year-old nose I had misperceived. To me, Guitou Knoup, "Xenia," was merely a well-turned out Roumanian sculptress who had come to Southampton to do a bust of my grandfather. (After she finished, Charlie commissioned a head of my brother Peter just to keep her about.)

In reality, Guitou was a Parisian bonbon whom Jimmy had brought back from his three years abroad—in the same spirit that an earlier generation might have returned with a marble Venus, or an Adam-designed rococo salon. And the lengths Charlie would go to produce an amatory effect were impressive. Turn, as Jimmy once did, your apartment over to him for an assignation and you might find yourself endowed with a lifetime supply of percale sheets.

His sexual eagerness remained to the very end. I spent the last afternoon before returning to college in the great drawing room of the Beach House waiting with him for his dear love of those final years, Lady Constance Saint, who had flown in from Barbados to discuss the financing of a beach cottage. Two days later he would pass into the coma from which he would die, the victim of a liver malfunction brought on by his radium cocktail. But that afternoon one would never have suspected that the sword, poised over him so long, was about to descend, so buoyed was he by her antici-pated arrival.

To pass the time, I told him some of what I had gleaned from the manuscript of *The Seraglio*, due to be published that winter. A portrait, I hazarded, even its sitter might relish—after all, how many septuagenarians get to play Zeus? Encouraged, Charlie told me how he and his partner, Eddy Lynch, in their early bachelor days in New York used to cruise the nightclubs. Too poor to date, they would return to their rooms after work, set their alarms, and then rise at midnight to shave and don tuxedos. At that hour, he said, the well wined and dined ladies were more ready to appreciate the attentions of two young men who liked to dance. Every now and then, while her date was off in the gents, he managed to walk off with a young woman.

In full stride now, he told about how, as a twelve-year-old, in imitation of Huck Finn, he had lit out for the fabled North. "I got as far as Waycross, Georgia, seventy-five miles away, before they found me. When my Dad finally arrived, all he said was, 'I'm glad, Son, you didn't get any further.'"

"Did he punish you when he got you back home?" I asked.

"Having me back was enough—especially when I promised never to run away again. But," he went on, nodding reflectively, "he did whip me once after catching me like a damn fool smoking in a hayloft. Worse than the pain was not being able to go swimming for weeks afterwards. I loved my Dad so much I couldn't bear having anyone see the welts he made."

The reminiscences were cut short when his chauffeur returned from the Westhampton railroad station without Lady Saint. "How long did you stay?" my grandfather asked, clearly alarmed.

"Long enough to know she wasn't there. Maybe she missed the train?"

By now it was six o'clock and I was due home for a farewell supper with my parents. Yet, like any amorous man, Charlie did not want me to leave before I had met this woman from Barbados who had cast such a glow over his last years. I don't recall the remainder of our conversation, only the deepening gloom in which we sat. Finally, a half hour later, the Lady herself swept in, out of sorts from a ride in a hired taxi and grimly determined on a bath. Grandfather presented me as a friend of his and Jimmy's—one who could stay only a few minutes more. But no cocktail was going to deter her from her sulk.

As I was saying good-bye, Charlie told me he loved me as if I were his own son. Little suspecting it would be the last I'd ever see of him, I went home for my farewell meal with my parents. In the next two months this twenty-year-old received two letters from Lady Saint: of condolence, but also of felt remorse for our missed acquaintance; a woman not afraid of reaching out. That was one trait she and Charlie shared. Both knew that a moment comes but once.

BARON SAFEWAY

From before the age of five I have only vague memories: a room's feminine clothing, white lace reflected in a mirror on a wall. My mother's room? My nurse's from which I waddle forth to my ablutions, this water I feel running over me, this formal baby's dress I must put on for some reason. I want so much to be good, to please these people who shower me with attentions. Yet I also feel repelled by them. Why do they insist on treating me like a doll?

Focusing, I see my mother, the lady of those early memories, holding me grass-high in the wind at her knees' white-laced edge. In contrast to the males of my family, she represents another, softer way of being. It may be for that reason I have always resisted her. What doesn't declare itself, doesn't push, is to me suspect. Precisely because behind all the caring, the love, the tenderness, there must exist a motivation of which I was part. But what part, a puppet looking with rapt gaze upon its creator? Yes, that would sum up not only Mother, but so many prospective Ariadnes. All the same, I feel lucky. The life that has befallen me is so much better than what as a child I felt sentenced to, penned as I was in my preoccupations, my lessons, my duties, wooden staring eyes, round clumsy hands.

Penned—the various playpens where I spent so many formative hours? The verb may seem opaque, but then you were not this two-year-old in his terrier-like harness traveling from San Francisco to New York. With me in one train compartment were Mother, my newborn brother Merrill Lynch, and my father's mother Estelle; in a second compartment, all our luggage. Estelle had come out especially from New York so she could mind me. It was the summer of 1938 and we were returning to New York.

My parents led a charmed life during their three years in San Francisco. They always spoke with a lingering nostalgia of the beauty and warmth of the city; of the variety of friends they pulled in, of different ages, from different walks of life.

But my father had his own timetable. To an ambitious thirty-five-year-old man, it was frustrating to be serving as the personal assistant to a stupid, stuck-up chairman, Ling Warren (a Jacksonville crony of Hellen's), who had no intention of stepping aside and would, in fact, hang on for another twenty years. So now, after the birth of my brother, Father returned to New York to work for Charlie Merrill and perhaps persuade him to start up a business in which he could figure more prominently.

Father sat in on the discussions with the various merger candidates that would result in the new Merrill Lynch. And his merchandising success was acknowledged in his post as Head of Sales. But just as the firm was approaching solvency, World War II came. To some extent his decision to enlist represented a personal sacrifice. At thirty-nine he was, for the moment, draft exempt. But he was also intensely patriotic, glad to buy his cars from Detroit and pay the full share of his income tax. For him, the strength of America was the chance it gave a man to better himself. He was willing to pay and fight for the continuance of the opportunity.

I was six at the time, but I clearly remember Father, as he drove into town in our red-leather-seated Buick convertible, telling me of his decision to join the Navy—the gentlemen's service—as an Air Intelligence cadet.

"It's not been an easy decision. But after weighing the various pros and cons, of what I owe you and Merrill and Mommy and what I owe the country, I've decided to enlist. I want you to know I'm not deserting you. There are a lot of people who can't afford to volunteer. We're fortunately well enough off so I can. If we're going to win this war everyone has to pitch in. But I promise I'm not going to do anything foolish and get myself killed."

What did I feel—tears? That would come later, watching him bid me good-bye after a leave. Rather, pride. How I wished I was old enough to be out there too in the South Pacific. The war was fought far away across the seas. But it was always with us, in our rationing cards, our victory garden, the drills we schoolchildren carried out and the shades we had to keep drawn at night in the country. I learned to read by following the advancing Allied campaign in *The New York Times*, noting the pincerlike arrows of a tank attack, the star-like spread of the Solomons, Gilberts and Marshall Islands. And I know exactly where I was when Japan's surrender was announced—among the deliriously honking cars of the white tiled East River tunnel; that evening, standing in Times Square among the celebrating hordes, I remember feeling this was it—imperial center stage. America, once so peripheral, had arrived.

For Father, the war was the epitome of everything heroic. Danger, adventure, and people—pilots young enough to be his sons, Americans from all walks of life—were present to him as they would never be again. And he took it all in, from the coral atolls to the boisterous shore leaves on Hawaii. His diary and his letters all reflected the awe and excitement he felt at being part of such a vast and necessary male enterprise.

But two years on a carrier was war enough, and Charlie's serious heart attack, in April, 1944, brought Father home before the dreaded final assault on Japan.

I was glad to have him home. I needed my father and felt close to him: the distinct acrid taste of his cheeks; the lacerated neck that defied anything short of an electric razor; the antediluvian nightshirt in which he slept, always on his back, hands crossed onto his shoulders, feet even on the coldest nights sticking out of the covers. Ferocious as he could be (especially mornings, clamped over his *New York Times*, unable to utter a greeting), he nonetheless took the well-being of a child to heart, sacrificing much to be with me, at a picnic, on a tennis court, or huddled among the droves of a ballpark. Such companionship gave the feeling of a man who truly cared, who saw my being as an extension of his, his boyhood, his aspirations.

Later, his involvement would seem all too proprietary. Like many another who had pulled himself up from nowhere, he regarded his children as the testing ground of his success; to the extent we were approved, so was he. For him, the social conventions—the right club, the best restaurant table, the number one Roman or London tailor—defined achievement. And his boredom at the fatuousness of the business life was defied by a rapid-fire execution that left most bystanders gasping, if not plum terrified.

Father typed all his letters, just as he answered, often to a caller's distinct shock, his own phone. He rarely brought home a file or a manila envelope, and no financial discussion ever blighted the cocktail hour. For Father, successful management was not, as it had been for my grandfather, so much a matter of planning as an acting job: of appearing to hold the right cards and the right men to go with them; team logistics, only it was crucial that the team members should regard themselves as separate individuals competing for a pat on the back and a raise.

Father had, as Don Regan said, "boss" written all over him. He knew how to lead men. What he lacked was a sense of the complexity of the arena into which he was leading them, the interdependency between a business and the surrounding society. It was that vision of the symphonic whole that Charlie possessed, an orchestra always capable of taking on new members, pieces and roles. Whereas for Father, there was always the permanently demarcated, labor-management, racial-sexual battle lines. My father was a good man, my grandfather once said to me, for marshalling the troops and driving them from one campaign post to the next. But he was clearly not someone to whom you entrusted the reins of state. And it wasn't until the year before Charlie died that he finally turned over Safeway to Father.

Father's instincts were basically sound. In Southampton he would never set up a game, or arrange a luncheon date, without checking first with his own boss, Charlie. "Well, pops," he'd say when he saw him Saturday morning, "what's the schedule?" But his instincts failed him when they encountered a person or a milieu that did not share his aspirations, his compelling necessities.

Investing in the stock market is, of course, gambling. To make a decision fast enough, Charlie was fond of saying, you have to trust your instincts. But you can narrow the margin for error by seeking outside advice. It was here the two diverged. Where Charlie was forever commissioning market research reports, Father could not see throwing away good money on an item that did not show up on the bottom line. "If those economists know so much about how money works, why haven't they made themselves a bundle?" he'd ask self-righteously. His dealings were not so much policies as alliances, man with man against a common emergency.

Yet from what I could tell, the notion of achievement he held up to me was itself little more than a fantastic practical joke. Out there was the American social ladder and the supposition that, by climbing it, rung by rung, you might eventually reach the top—that roof with the society orchestra and the tables and the city-wide view. The bad joke, of course, was that each guest, as he arrived, hauled up his ladder after him. And once up, he found himself in the midst of another black tie stag party, since how were ladies encumbered by skirts expected to manage? Asked the secret of his success, Father invariably replied, "Decisiveness. I decided to marry the boss's daughter," in effect acknowledging that all his exhortations to start at the bottom and work your way up were little more than ploys.

Rising from peanuts to pearls, Father made clear, was less a matter of talent than of how you sold yourself—or, as he used to say, what ass you were prepared to lick. His great admirer, Ricardo Sicre, went so far as to maintain, "I've never made a business deal with a man whom I hadn't first met with my hand around a cock-tail glass."

Father's own emergence was sufficiently astonishing that he could never imagine an alternative to that straight, vigorous, up-ward climb. He could do it and, when his father died, he had to, there was his mother and brother Ned to support. As an American, was he ashamed of the crack in the middle-class floor through which his mother had fallen? I ask because he never discussed those hard times and any intrusion of curiosity found him reeling in an amnesiac blank. The lack of a relatable childhood, of an ado-lescence as far as one could tell, made him unlike any man I knew. Others were never so driven, and so concealing. This muffled per-son, one felt, had never experienced a sustained moment of unam-biguous pleasure. Nor would he have wanted to. It would have smacked of decadence, a mockery of his consciously assumed self-creation. A complex man and yet one curiously forgiving, boy-ishly spontaneous and, when the chips were down, deeply loving.

Scottish, too, in these contradictions.

When he came home from the Navy to find his job usurped and Charlie too sick to stand up for him, he came very close to chucking Merrill Lynch and going out on his own. Mother did a lot to instill the patience, the fortitude, the situation required. Trusting her, he stuck it out and, by 1949, he was finally back in his old job as the number two in the firm, presiding over the expansion of Merrill Lynch. He was now, for the first time in his life, an achieved man. "The only real fun in business," he once admitted to me, his prospective underling, "is running your own show."

But to Father smallness was less than beautiful. Offered by Charlie the choice of running Merrill Lynch, the "world's greatest money-making machine," as I remember him calling it, or Safeway, he chose Safeway and its 170,000 employees. With those numbers there was more he could accomplish. And any success would be his own, not something Charlie had set in motion.

One might see success as a confirmation of the inner man. For Father, I think, it offered a good deal more, a chance to retailor himself. It would not do for those Californians who were seeing this forty-five-year-old man for the first time to think that he had only now arrived. Instead he had to make it look as if he had always been an achieved man. Out went the pink and raspberry shirts, the vibrant houndstooth jackets, the startling, daringly synchronized, celebratory neckties. He whose art form had been his dashing clothes, the arch peacock of our family motto, now unveiled himself as Mister Conservative: dull, single-color tie, blue or pinstriped blue suit, a midnight blue that did not quite match his lovely, piercing sapphire eyes.

THE IDEALIST

For an adolescent consumed in his own physical changes, Father's refashioning of himself could not have been more bewildering. There was the image I held of the father I loved. And there was this new man who looked the same, but who wasn't. All the more when the new man was insisting on my changing as well to corroborate him in his new image. Here I was trying to reach out, grow, make something of the extraordinary opportunities that had befallen me. And here instead was a man insisting on my seeing myself as someone smaller, a rich kid, a suit-wearing English fop. It could make for some conflict.

The public arena now found Father serenely posed on his business pinnacle: the recipient of some four honorary knighthoods, two honorary doctorates, his picture gracing the covers of Fortune, Business Week and Forbes. But it was as if in his own heart he knew he was clinging only by the whites of his nails and an ill-considered gesture on any of our parts could send him reeling back to the anonymity from whence he had come. He who used to take me to dine on a restaurant's straw floor and hobnob with whomever had now become the single entity of his money, the accumulating pile he regarded as his true legacy.

On that eminence of envy, of distrust, like a fire-breathing dragon he sat, unable to deal with anyone who did not share the picture of unlimited power he projected. I remember him deep in his cups at his sixty-fourth birthday dinner telling us, "I'm more powerful than President Johnson." And, unlike the president, he had no intention of abdicating, having instituted mandatory retirement at sixty-five for everyone but himself at Safeway.

There was only one criterion now—money. Rather than reason with us, we were bribed, sent scurrying like lackeys down one or another silver-baited tunnel. Merrill was paid not to smoke and, until the end of his life, Father actually believed that the solemn exchange of banknotes had cured him of his addiction. But to us in our coddled luxury what were a couple of grand? Devils of various sorts might seduce me, but not one wagging a dollar bill.

Rather it was a different sharing I craved, of his past with my present. Only his past had become so entangled in the particularity of his successful rise that I was left surrounded by threats or sullen disappointment. The older I got, the more I was reduced to the short hair, the shirt and tie at dinner, that alone satisfied him. As if a son were an item on a balance sheet, a pawn waiting to be moved. But could I wait, didn't I too have to create my own luck?

His forte was his superlative energy, his intense caring. But he couldn't step outside of himself to equip me for a different world of alternatives and its chosen roles. His teaching was all by rote, "Take me, for example, watch how I do it." And we would watch, cocktails in hand, aghast, as right there on the library rug he set about trying to teach six-year-old Mark, who suffered from a periodic potassium deficiency, how to sprint, as if any such inability amounted to familial treason.

At other times the intensity seemed all too compulsive, "Do this, son, or I'll throw a fit." No doubt, the threats kept the office slaves hopping. But among beings who weren't seeking a promotion it could draw a blank. Father was forever seeing issues in hysterical either-ors, imminent as the face of a cliff. And any attempt to suggest a measure of equivocation found him pressing the panic button, the high blood pressure-hypertension that had killed his parents. Then we'd be sorry to have his world class Earning Power taken from us—how on our own would we manage? We'd explain that, much as we loved him, we couldn't be constantly galvanizing ourselves on some phony errand just because he had caught us curled up with a book. In effect, he so little believed in the family edifice, except as an expression of his will, that when one of us diminutive pylons collapsed he was thrown into a panic, as if his own achievement were about to come crashing down then and there .

The confession of Charlie's he passed on, of his never knowing whether a woman loved him for himself or his swag—as if there wasn't a fairly copious middle ground—held absolutely for Father. In his presence we sons existed only in our financial aspect, our stock market investments, our home's resale value. It made for some lonely final years—for all of us.

What kept his inner man from calcifying was his innocence, the faculty he had of admitting surprise, and even mistakes; unable to recall the next morning over whom his fiery kettle had just erupted. His doghouse did not hold permanent residents.

Yet that could leave the rest of us passive spectators, condemned to watch a bleak performance on an outsized field. Corporation heads, members of the institutional oligarchy, floated up the stairs into our library. Father greeted them, handed them their cocktails and sped them on. Were the worthy of sufficient stature, he might even throw open the portals of our living room. I remember a splendid dance, given on two days' notice on the parquet floor of that magically stripped room for the visiting Nizam of Baroda, reputedly the richest man in the world.

On a country ramble nothing so tickled him as the spectacle of acre upon acre given over to the same absurd soybeans or sunflowers. That was the kind of mercantile gamble he could applaud, whereas complexity rightly bothered him. His response was to grab hold of a pair of scissors, or a power mower, and level it.

One of my brothers had in his college rooms, under the obligatory Mao poster of a rice field with hoeing peasants, a blown-up photo of Father at his farewell Caterpillar board meeting. Picture an outsized green baize table with tiny directors seated around it. In front of each stood a toy illustrating some facet of that earth-moving concern. Father's was a forest-clearing bulldozer.

An electrical short circuit might catch him fanatically wringing his hands. But it could also be an excuse to call in a specialist and take pride in the multiplicity of talent city life afforded. He believed there was not a problem mankind could not solve, if we all set our minds to it. And it was the prospect of an ever-increasing prosperity he looked forward to: a Wall Street with more and more players gathered at the tables; or perhaps the stakes raised higher for those able to ante up, undeterred by a grim Uncle Sam peering over their shoulders.

For Father, it was his very freedom to carry on, Tamurlaine style, that was at stake in the grapeworker-organized boycott against Safeway; one which would last, off and on, some fifteen years, and make Safeway, next to the Bank of America, the Left's most hated company. Cesar Chavez, the charismatic saint of the Left, had singled out Safeway because it was the biggest supermarket chain. Crack it, he probably reasoned, and he'd crack them all. But he hadn't reckoned on my father, who was not about to let himself be trampled by a bunch of itinerant grapepickers. What would be next, Father asked, Polish hams, Cuban cigars? And why should Safeway be intimidated when the union's battle was with the growers? Yet there was more than principle at stake. Father was holding the anti-union line for a host of others, among them the nation's largest private agricultural business, the Boswell Company, of which he was a proud director. The struggle between the two men, my father and Chavez, who personally liked each other, became increasingly bitter. There was even a big march up to Mother's Pacific Heights home, without anyone in Chavez's office having bothered to inquire whether she was in residence. She wasn't.

The loyalties could cut the other way, too. I remember all of us being perplexed when old Ernest Gallo, by no means a personal friend, showed up in a black suit at Father's funeral. On a bitterly cold Saturday, a week before Christmas, one would think he had better things to do than drive all the way up from his Modesto winery. He certainly wasn't collecting brownie points. Not only that, he contributed $10,000 in Father's name to the Children's Hospital Heart Fund. Because of the stand Father had taken twenty years earlier—had it meant all that? Yes, probably, and there Mr. Gallo was in the back row, silently, on his knees, doing his best to render it back.

To his family, Father was always projecting himself as a man of his word, as if all I had to do was stand up to him for his river to shine gold. But it was hard facing down a Proteus who could never be held to any one utterance. For only by promising, and then denying he had promised, could a son be kept on his invisible tether. Father's offers of support were not all quicksand. But I never knew to what new whim I was supposed to trim my sails. (Blind filial obedience carries only so far!) His favorite ploy was to coax me to the edge of an abyss, "Here's some cash, go hang yourself!" If I blew it all, he had the last laugh. If I didn't, I was a mistrustful coward.

Yet he must have found it lonely to be sitting behind *The Wall Street Journal* when there was a houseful of us sons with whom he could be sharing his fascination with the daily mood swings, the gyrations of those stock exchange all-stars of his. "At what price should I trade Winn-Dixie? With what should I replace it?" One evening, when he had us all assembled, he announced the "deal of the century. I want each of you to pick ten stocks to invest in. At the end of the year, I will turn over to you whatever profit you've made."

For some reason we older brothers desisted. Maybe we didn't relish the vision of a league, each with our own Big Board team competing against the others and eventually Father himself. Or it may be that writing some corporate names on a scrap of paper required more energy than we could summon. But Stephen, the youngest, was gullible. He did a little research and picked his ten stocks. Twelve months later he had lucked out on every one of them.

"You promised, I picked them—now can I have my money?" Stephen asked Father, who hadn't bought the stocks, yet wasn't about to admit that Stephen's profit was all on paper.

In a bid for time—perhaps Stephen would forget—Father promised him the money "when you reach your majority."

Stephen understood. A fourteen-year-old is still a minor. But he remembered, and when he turned twenty-one he asked Father to deliver on what he believed to be rightfully his. "I've reached my majority. Now can I have the profit you promised on those ten stocks I picked?"

But Father was not about to turn over $200,000 on what he hadn't bought, much less pay the gift tax Uncle Sam required. Instead he decided to stonewall Stephen. "Your majority is when I decide it."

Gullible to the end, Stephen persisted in believing Father would make good on his promise. He had reached the age of thirty when Father decided that the time had come to expunge this so-called promise of his from the family record. "It's all your imagination that I'd hand over the profit from your stocks. I never said any such thing."

All the same, Father still wanted to appear generous to Stephen. One evening, a year or so after Stephen had graduated from Yale, he offered to buy him a new car as a delayed graduation present. By now Stephen was aware that the money for it would not come from Father, but from his own trust fund. Thinking carefully, Stephen replied that, living in New York, and with such means as he had, a car was something he could ill afford, what with insurance, garage fees, and general upkeep. "Why not instead," he countered, "buy me a bicycle? I could really use one in Southampton."

Father wholeheartedly embraced Stephen's proposal. "But I want you to shop around," he said, "and buy yourself the best possible. Remember, I'm paying."

Stephen took Father at his word and canvassed the two local bike shops. When they didn't have what he needed, he had himself driven to Easthampton, forty minutes away. There he bought a ten-speed, state-of-the-art machine and pedaled it the whole dangerous way home. That evening with considerable pride he showed it to Father. "A beauty, isn't it? Thank you very much."

Father gave it his once over. Then, pausing a moment reflectively, he asked Stephen how much he paid for it.

"A hundred and seventy-five," Stephen replied.

"You paid too much," Father declared, and, peeling off a hundred dollar bill from his wallet, he handed it to Stephen.

So much for the offer of a car.

I SANG
IN MY CHAINS

Early on Father used to teach me tennis, from a basket at the Beach House court patiently doling out the balls I'd be implored to hit. But as I reached adolescence, the field for my instruction now shifted to an arena more appropriate for his new dynastic ambitions, the family dinner table.

The pressure from him became more intense as I got older. In his eyes I could only be this pint-sized Robert A., Jr. Any signs of rebellion I evinced were apt to be misread and laid at the feet of some interfering genie, a teacher, a maternal uncle. Whenever I sat down to dinner—out of lingering affection always on his right— he would set out to demolish my friends.

"I don't want you hanging around with a bunch of kikes and fairies," he'd say, referring to the local art crowd that had taken me up.

"How about that kike godfather of mine, Jack Straus?" I'd retort. "Your Jewish friends aren't kikes, but mine are?"

For a moment, maybe, I'd have this shape-changing Proteus clutched in my grasp. But just as I was about to wrest an agreement from him, he would turn and lash out at a "pinko" history prof of mine. No doubt, the slurs gave him a way of taking on an adversary. Like a tribal chieftain he would set out behind them, one tawdry banner after another proudly fluttering in the wind.

My former sister-in-law, Jill, remembers Father visiting them in Houston where Peter was running the local Safeway operation. Jill was herself Jewish and, during their courtship, Father had tried hard to keep Peter from marrying her. But with time, he had grown fond of her and their two daughters, and now that she was carrying a third he wanted to make amends. It was late in the dinner and Father was in his cups waxing sentimental about his family—the one he had married into.

The Merrills, he was explaining, had a formidable pedigree, they were even on The Mayflower. As for the Magowans, he said, throwing up his hands, who knows where they came from, there were hardly any records. "Maybe," he said, turning to Jill as if the thought had struck him then and there, "they were Jews—how else could I have been so acquisitive?"

For the wretchedly poor, as Father was in his formative years, anti-Semitism often makes a convenient scapegoat for the capitalist oppressor they don't dare acknowledge. But it was hard for me then to understand how a person of his intelligence could believe such inanities. And I wasn't about to let him ram them down my throat. My study of history pointed to another reading of the social struggle. But any citing of precedents was so much fuel to the now raging fire. "Who's going to pay for this new society of yours?" he bellowed from a seat away. "Tell me how," he added, changing tack with a demonic swiftness, "you intend to pay for yourself, let alone support me, as all sons should, in my old age?"

Those hysterical, screaming Sunday night meals often saw Mother, within minutes of sitting down to the cold borscht soup, reeling upstairs with a migraine. But there was no way of discussing anything with Father without his attacking me personally. As with tennis, his forensic tactic was to get me so riled with a bad call I would forget myself and make an adolescent exaggeration. Then from a seat away the master of the self-fulfilling prophecy would pounce, delighted to show me the dolt I remained, for all my high-toned schooling.

"Just look around you!" Father would say.

"At what?" I asked, bewildered.

"At all the no-goodniks, the scroungers, the pinkos your New Deal is supporting. Do you think they'd want to live in Russia?"

"I don't know," I ventured, "but some might find it appealing." I was about to enumerate some of the more positive features of the Soviet system: the shared purchases between friends, the way in a restaurant one sits down at a table with strangers, when I was zapped again.

"Do you think I'm giving you the best possible education so you can become a goddamn intellectual? Shirt sleeves to shirt sleeves in three generations! Well, I don't intend to let that happen in my family."

"Education?" I snorted, horns lowered, unable to abandon what I saw as my values.

"Well, a college degree," Father retorted, backing away. "It's the same thing in the end."

"If words are only things to twist." Oh, in that family, to be allowed to crack a joke!

And there was Mother jumping in with a superior authority. "Don't be rude now to your father. Remember the fourth commandment."

What was I to do, except scathingly reject their thought control. "The two of you would make a fine pair of Commissars. I'm just supposed to toe your party line?"

But Mother, distant at the other end of the table, had heard enough. "I think you should leave the table."

And the court jester, with a slight bow, would slide back his chair, knowing this was by no means the end of it.

Next morning there I was, summoned into her bedroom to hear once again how I had ruined Father's farewell supper.

"I wish you'd see there's a time and place for everything and it's not the family dinner table." That was Mother at her conciliatory best. The peacemaker. Harmony at any price. Fine for her who had the bedroom in which to legislate, but what other occasion but the dinner table did I have to let them know who I was? Or was it merely dutiful nods they required, clean fingernails, combed hair?

"But Father says such weird stuff," I said, deciding to meet her head on. "The world wasn't created by money alone," I added, punctuating the remark with as direct a look at her in her pink houserobe as I could muster.

"Perhaps not," Mother replied, pausing until my eyes had shifted away from her and onto the upholstery, the china bowls and lamps, and the rest of a considerable moneyed creation. She continued, "But whatever your opinions, your father is entitled to your respect. What's more, you're staying grounded until you apologize to him."

"For what?" I asked indignantly. "I haven't done anything wrong. You yourself admit I'm right."

"Still, you must apologize and, until you do, you are not going anywhere."

Wonderfully two-faced, yet her conduct fit perfectly into a marriage in which the dynastic emphasis was assumed from the start and the fundamental sores were never allowed to surface. To keep the vital tension going, and their own liberty of action, my parents had instituted a policy whereby one or another of us children, selected it would seem almost at random, would be sentenced to the doghouse. That way each had the other to blame. "He's your son!" And the son, for his part, found himself caught in the crossfire.

THE DYNASTIC VESSEL

My parents may not have known whose son I was, but I did—Father's. To say I was obsessed with him hardly begins to describe the depth of my involvement. Even at college he was all I could talk about. Yet my mother, Doris, was in many ways more remarkable, and to this day I know a small army of fans for whom she represents the highest possible of human courts. As one hears over and over, she is that genuine article, a lady.

Yet for all her love and unflagging concern for me and my entire family, and for all her efforts to treat me with a generosity that to this day takes my breath away, ours has been a somewhat murky relationship. Father was someone I think I understood. He was a bull and he charged. Mother was considerably more complex, and to this day, I find myself being surprised and indeed astonished by the quality of an insight, the directness of her compassion.

The most important man in Mother's life was Charlie Merrill. Since his death, she once confided, not a day had passed when she hadn't thought of him. But for all their mutual respect and closeness—she was his favorite child—it could not have been easy being the daughter of someone so powerful and so mercurial. Charlie's was a thrall that, at a moment's whim, he could withdraw, as he had in divorcing my grandmother Eliza in 1926 when Doris was twelve.

The divorce had come on the heels of one of the key events of Mother's girlhood, her Roman Catholic first communion. It had taken place while Charlie was away on business in Chicago. On learning about it he flew into a jealous rage; not that it had happened, he told Eliza, but that it had happened behind his back. On and on he blazed until Eliza, a timid woman—it was exactly why she had scheduled it while he was out of town—pronounced the words whose consequences she had clearly not thought out, "I want a divorce. I can't stand these horrible rages of yours."

Granted. Mother remembers the two of them at the dinner table barely an hour later, Charlie still shaking and Eliza looking "absolutely awful, as if her life had come to an end. Which," Mother went on, after a reflective pause, "in truth it had." As she spoke, I saw the lonely penthouse from which my grandmother hardly ever emerged in the remaining fifty years.

Charlie Merrill did not spend his lifetime courting an array of luscious women without also seeking to turn his daughter into one—a sparkling diadem at the center of his seraglio and his financial empire. It was a control all the more insidious in that he was so good at it. He knew exactly what fabrics, colors and styles looked best on her and bought her most stunning outfits himself. But that wasn't all. Before sending her off to school, or letting her go off to a party (never in anything but the family sedan, and always called for by both his chauffeur and a maid—this at a time when no one else was being chaperoned), he used to inspect her personally. If so much as a wrinkle was found, she would be sent back upstairs to change.

Her father was soft-spoken. But as her brother Charles remarked, he had no need to raise his voice "to cut you into a thousand pieces." His admonishments were all the more humiliating in that they were nearly always imparted over the dinner table before the assembled multitude. Fail to eat whatever lurked on your plate and you were banished to your room then and there, plate in hand. "The amount of spinach I've flushed down the toilet would astonish Popeye," her brother Jimmy once lamented.

The fear of displeasing a monster of such obvious power meant my mother was always playing a role. She had it in her to be the Miss It he desired: pretty, popular, successful, and a good girl. But at the key moment her nerves invariably failed her and the pretense of being Charlie's Doris showed its insecure face. She took bad pictures not because her nose was slightly too large or her bottom teeth overcrowded, but because she had too much at stake. Blessed with an excellent spatial sense, able without measuring to say exactly how many rolls of wallpaper you needed, there was no reason she should draw a blank at geometry, much less fail senior algebra two years in a row. But the crowning blow was delivered by her father. "Don't worry, Doris. I feel confident your future husband is not going to want to see your report card when he proposes matrimony." Words of consolation, maybe. But, for the poor girl, one can see the book of possibilities slamming shut. She wasn't going to make it to college. She wasn't going to pursue a career. And she was going to get married. To whom, it might be asked, a man of whose choice?

Mother grew up disadvantaged by a society that did not encourage women to pursue a professional career. Medicine fascinated her and, if born a man, she probably would have been a doctor like her grandfather. "You're going to be locked up for practicing without a license," Father once remarked, recognizing the quality of her obsession. But my grandfather did not approve of women who "knew how to dissect earthworms." After graduating from Spence

School, he wanted her to study in Europe where she would be exposed to languages, art and a different culture. He wanted his princess to be "finished."

At seventeen there she was, removed from the attentions of a young man who drove a beautiful fire-red Bugatti and dispatched to a Florentine finishing school. A change that would provide far and away the happiest schooling she ever knew. It was followed by a year working for the Junior League and studying silver connoisseurship at the Metropolitan Museum.

She knew what lay in store, a coming out party for several thousand at The Orchard, marquee tents covering the front lawn. Another might have shrunk at the invidiousness of the dollar princess tag. It was, after all, 1932, the nadir of the Depression. But to Mother, her debut meant precisely that—a new chrysalis—and it never occurred to her to question her society's values, its excesses of wealth and heartlessness, its unremitting pursuit of trivia at the expense of valuable feeling. School had been reasonably satisfying, especially in the group of devoted life-long friends she acquired. But in trying to earn her teachers' approval her own human yearnings were short-circuited.

Did Mother have doubts about her marriage—its financial, social and sexual inequalities? She must have suspected she was not the unique prize for which her suitors were bidding. Was her choice of Father a fatalistic one? Romantic? Compassionate? Or was it her way of skirting an auction for a man who somehow must have seemed her safest bet. Too frequently, we are willing to escape the trammels of freedom. By marrying the man she married, she became, not so unwillingly perhaps, Father's and Charlie's pawn. Yet there must have been a compensation in knowing herself to be the object of an ongoing duel between those jealous lovers. Was it her way of keeping the two of them at bay while reserving a future liberty of action?

Doubts about her marriage there may have been, but I never heard them voiced. In marrying, Mother had scrupulously chosen, "Until death do us part." Since Father was capable at any moment of throwing up his hands and breaking with everything—us children included—it was up to Mother to be the "good sport" who

55

kept our brittle show on the road. It was no wonder she emphasized the surface values of family harmony, courtesy, agreement at whatever price, as well as correct clothing, speech and deportment.

But for all her tugging at her skirt and the occasional nervousness of her conversation—silences were not tolerated—the results were stunningly effective. Parisian evening gowns, soft as sherbet, floated down the stairs with an effect all the more telling in that they remained more a sign of social distinction than anything sexy. Her tanned skin gleamed, her graceful shoulders hung bare. By now, at thirty, the square-cut "angel" hairdo of her early photographs (never pictured smiling and thereby all the more soulful, a woman with a secret mystery) had grown into a hip-length chestnut mane which she wore coiled in a chignon. The more relaxed she became, the more the soft milky blue of her deepset eyes added to the picture of intense aliveness she conveyed. One of those pert, small-chinned women who sparkle in a hat.

Not for her, long tête-à-têtes on some corner sofa. Instead she felt a need to combat a wife's presumed decorative role with volunteer work: ace fund-raiser; board member of several national foundations; dame of the order of Saint John of the Cross. She was a doer, summoning meetings, notifying commissioners, changing zoning laws. The war had given her volunteerism a patriotic glamour. When it was over our various family consulates—thirteen houses at one point—took up much of the slack in her schedule.

The scale of her activities, viewed through the foreground of her almost daily migraines, could give rise to genuine perplexity. "Why are you running yourself into the ground?" her sister-in-law Mary once asked.

Surprised by Mary's concern, Mother thought a moment before replying, "I'm afraid, I suppose, of being bored."

"But when was the last time you actually were bored?"

Mother thought again, scratching her head, "I don't remember."

"You could," Mary suggested dryly, "give it a try."

But slowing down and readjusting her personal clock wasn't Mother. Life had stacked her deck with valuable cards, but moral courage wasn't one of them. Without it, she kept getting stung.

The Gershwin song "I've got you under my skin" received an utterly new gloss as her flesh erupted in horribly painful hives, rashes that stung like "a thousand jellyfish." Her "quacks," as the man under her skin called them, did what they could. But they could only treat the symptoms, not the tension brought on by the impossible perfection required of her every transaction, her every remark, her every golf swing. There were a number of activities she knew she enjoyed such as tennis, painting and playing the piano. But she wouldn't take up anything in which she couldn't excel. For her, as much as for Father, life was competition. And part of winning was bluffing, never being a bad sport about her migraines, never admitting to being less than right.

Our family motto reads, "Qui patitur vincit" (she who suffers triumphs). By those standards Mother deserved an alp of her own, innocent of novocaine, toughing it out in a dentist's chair. No migraine was going to keep her show from going on.

Her migraines dated back to her parents' divorce. They became more frequent when, during the war, the canvas-roofed Buick convertible she was driving, with all of us in it, skidded on some black ice and rolled some three hundred and fifty feet down an embankment. (I remember the man in the car behind us, whose daughter was between my brothers in the back seat, running down and with his bare hands tearing the roof apart and pulling us out, one by one. Does my back's reversed lower lumbar curve stem from this accident?)

More serious even than the migraines were her allergic reactions. A single dish of scallops consumed at Proust's old stand-by, La Pérouse, was enough to keep her from ever tolerating seafood again. On another occasion, the ripeness of the odors as she threw open the doors of a barn in the Sacramento Valley caused such a fit of sneezing she ruptured her first back disk. More recently, a hospital I sent her to found her allergic to some 241 different substances. They had never encountered such hypersensitivity and were adamant in not letting her pay for her two-week stay. Hers was, they told her, a rare learning experience.

In a newspaper column not long ago, Mother came upon the question, "Which would you rather have—health or wealth?" After a spate of bad fortune—a broken hip, a third spinal operation—she was sufficiently troubled as to run downstairs and consult the maid. The maid, a sensible soul, replied, "I've never had any wealth to speak of, but you're nothing without your health." Mother was less than convinced. On another occasion, I remember the "little dynamo," as a magazine article fondly summarized her, coming in gleefully holding a caption, "Rest is rust." But what else was her lividly red skin?

For the sake of family harmony before my father, she saw it as her role to surrender. Then, from beneath, she chipped away by adding her civilizing touches. Unable to sleep in the wee hours of the morning, she'd come downstairs and start rearranging the furniture. These were not minor pieces either, but sofas and even the piano. With a large and willing household at her beck and call, she knew she was being foolish. But for her it was the one way she could present Father, when he woke up, with a fait accompli.

To others the demands of running so many houses could seem a problem. "Doesn't it bother you not knowing in which house you're spending Christmas?" a friend once asked.

Mother understood her concern perfectly. "But I have boxes of Christmas ornaments in all my houses." And a room, I should add, just for wrapping presents. This woman was highly organized.

Occasionally, one hears of some autocrat going to great lengths to perfect a certain house feature. But it was Mother who, upon purchasing her present Southampton home, filled in the swimming pool. Then she built another of exactly the same size, but turned in the opposite direction, fifty feet away, where it would not spoil the romantic view.

Even more characteristic was what Mother did to her Pacific Heights house. She had viewed well over a hundred before settling on her elegant palazzo, with its Italianate loggia and breathtaking views of the Bay, fronting on the top of Octavia (that steep winding roadway known from so many horror films, with the unattended baby in the baby carriage about to rattle down it). She had been in her new house a while when she noticed that it lacked what was for her a necessity—a cozy nook where she could lunch with a friend. So she acquired the house immediately below her on the hill and had it razed. That allowed her to tack on the ten feet she needed for a breakfast nook off the dining room. My father could not believe it.

BLUE STOCKING DISTRICT BEGINNINGS

During my childhood Mother's monument was our Mott Schmidt-designed, limestone-fronted townhouse on East 69th in the so-called Blue Stocking district. A five-floor house, though no more than thirty feet wide, it was set back from the sidewalk behind a black iron fence. Mounting a small series of steps between black Doric columns, one entered a striking diamond-patterned black-and-white marble hall whose elegant arches struck the architect's neo-Georgian note.

Here there were choices of an oakwood elevator or a deep balustraded staircase, its semicircular rings soaring towards our fourth floor nursery. Or one could go on down the hall into the dining room with its murals of "The Orchard" and view of the garden. The garden, with the sixty annual inches of soot peppering it, was more a visual attraction than a place to sit out in, though we did freeze it over for skating. On the other side of the entrance hall, with its own "delivery" door, lay the servants' domain: the pantry, our children's dining room and the kitchen, from which steps led to the cellar. There we had our model trains and not quite six foot high basketball court and Father his wine closet.

Ascending the main stairway, one gained the second-floor receiving rooms: a library whose baroque carved panelling had been brought from an English country house. It was decorated with hunting prints and austere Queen Anne furniture, including the little Chippendale chair Mother had creweled for me during the war, full of animals, birds, flowers and trees shining out from a warm yellow background. It was here guests collected in the evening for cocktails to hear me proudly recite the major league batting averages, while my brother Merrill entertained on the piano in the long, lemon-yellow drawing room across the hall. There, for bridge and after-dinner coffee, guests might convene before the Brockhurst portrait of Mother in a blue-gowned, sapphire-ringed formality. At the garden end, two ceiling-high display cabinets with their Dorothy Doughty birds mocked my bird-watching. Here and there Regency furniture, always paired, denoted a showy taste within which Magowan peacocks might happily blaze. Those muted peacocks were us in our blazers, ties and cufflinks as we escorted visitors through that impeccable neo-London. Did it succeed, or was it stiff and pompous?

Our fourth floor retreat, above my parents on the third, below the servants on the fifth, belonged to a different order, dark, gloomy, intensely claustrophobic. Perfect for the night wolves that, slithering like fishes down the chimney, ran round and round the precariously poised island of my bed. Perfect, too, for the burglar apprehended in the depths of the playroom closet who allowed himself, very meekly, to be taken by the elbow by the maid into the elevator and shoved out the front door.

In our playroom I had my Uncle Jimmy's enormous world stamp book, the maps from Volume XXVI of *The Britannica* I used to trace for hours on end (as if by committing their outlines to memory I might possess something of the labyrinthine life, the courtyards, the forests, the antediluvian reptiles), as well as the cupboards crammed with those legions of stolidly parading tin soldiers and the clumsy building blocks to which I would be directed whenever Mother's planning left me with an unstructured hour. But did her planning fail? No, she was good at providing opportunities, as she called them: riding lessons on big, frightening, steel-mouthed horses at Aylward's across Central Park; skating sessions at Rockefeller Center; dancing lessons at the ballroom of the Pierre. When lessons flagged, there was the orthodontist to rectify my rabbity overbite, the eye doctor so I wouldn't see everything double in each store window.

In another family a clock may have represented merely an heirloom by a wall, a jewel on the wrist. In a business family like ours, it was nothing less than Mammon himself, and we were always amazed that others—doctors notoriously—did not share our respect for the ticking word. And word is exactly what it was. If somehow I wasn't there on that dot, everyone would start fidgeting, wondering whether I had had an accident, calling the police even, "It just isn't like him." Even as a small child I seemed to be always in a rush, hearing the appointment clock ticking bomb-like as I hung on a strap in some fuming bus or ran, dodging in and out of the stalled traffic (miscalculating now and then, like the time when jaywalking in mid-block I forgot about the lanes of traffic hurtling the other way and landed, shaken but miraculously unhurt, on some terrified man's hood).

Growing up in the inner city it was impossible to savor the adrenaline rush provided by the hurrying, heads down, pavement-oriented throngs, the delicious prospect of danger lurking behind every garbage can, every fire escape, the Mondrian boogie-woogie of pulsating lights and energies. For the child, the city was the tunnel. You were conveyed into Manhattan by one or another such subterranean passage and, even once emerged, a consciousness remained, formed by all that kept you tip-toeing about, afraid and small at the bottom of all the rectangular life.

But then New York may not be the kind of city one encourages a child to explore. For my parents, the great merit of St. Bernard's, the excellent, mainly English-mastered school we attended, was the way it kept us until 4:45 p.m., doing sports and the whole of our homework. From there, on the fringe of Harlem, we were bussed home by way of remote Gracie Square and the tough white kids waiting on their brownstone stoops, pea-shooters and all their saliva poised for the chance of an open window. A reminder of how, even within the confines of our "blue stocking" district, there lay another milieu of burnt, gutted tenement buildings, of kids roaming in packs through the park, armed with clubs of pig iron and razor-sharp umbrellas, while we schoolmates huddled in a circle, protecting a precious leather football.

If we escaped that time thanks to the intervention of a random police car (what did the police say? Why didn't the gang return when the car disappeared?), there was the day when, in too much of a hurry to change out of my riding clothes, I tried walking from the Squadron A Armory on Park Avenue to the bus a block away. That, even I knew, was foolish, and two gamins my own age spotted me and at knife point pushed me into a basement alley. There they proceeded to relieve me of the $2.25 squirreled away in various pockets.

When, still shaking a few minutes later, I told my father about the incident, he was appalled—a son who had submitted to a mere knife. "They wouldn't have done that to me at your age!"

Yet the need for vigilance could also raise a question or two. For all the elegance of our surroundings, it was plain that we existed within such circumscribed boundaries that I could not help but wonder whether the variety of activity our set indulged in might also be illusory. Did free people really live behind drawn chains and multi-bolted doors, afraid even to acknowledge one another in the elevator?

In our fourth floor quarters life too was awfully close, four brothers, eight years apart, kennelled two to a room. But fortunately we had a young, warm, wonderfully spirited peasant nurse, Eileen, and her fellow household servants to insulate us.

To a couple unable even to pry open the lid of a can, servants were a necessity. The only item Mother cooked was toast. Whereas Father's talents did not go much beyond boiling water for spaghetti. And what held for the kitchen applied equally well to the nursery. Conceiving and giving birth to a dynastic heir was one thing; taking care of him was something better left to a trained professional. One hired the best possible—a couple of years off the boat from Europe—and let her get on with it, the feeding, the burping, the changing and washing of diapers. Then at the designated hour, dressed for those maternal kisses, those popping flash bulbs, Nurse brought him in, that living doll. Mother still remembers the panic she felt on Nurse's day off when she had to cope for the first time. What if she broke me?

In my grandfather's houses the help were colored, as they were then called. That's who this Southerner felt comfortable with. In ours, they were Irish. Cook was something of a curmudgeon, reluctant to serve us rationed victuals in the quantity on which Eileen insisted. But for the more visible roles, Mother liked having young nymphs about, and our Gaelic-speaking maids with their intense white skin and mischievous blue eyes could not have fit the bill more voluptuously. To a child, such beauty was not particularly unsettling. They were my friends, smuggling me off to mass and teaching me the jig steps they danced at the Tuxedo Ballroom in Yorktown. Most people's servants come and go, but Mother ensured that ours stayed until it was time for them to marry their inevitable policeman.

Besides the staff of four, there were the part-timers who appeared to wash Mother's long hair, do the laundry, or merely pay her bills. Of these the person who most impressed me was the big, ruggedly handsome Neapolitan janitor, Mario, who took care of our block. In our pre-Lego, mechanically helpless family, electric trains, or virtually any toy, could only be something I'd break, snapping like putty the first time I took it in my hands. Mario fixed them, assembled them, glued them back together. And he was always bringing our family presents of food picked up from a delicatessen in East Harlem: sausages, panettone, black olives in their own brine. And on occasion, he would have his little Swiss shrew of a wife cook us a mouth-watering spaghetti. So far as the pleasures of the table went, it was clear that Mario on his humble salary made out a lot better than we did.

But if anyone stitched me together and put me on my two feet, it was Eileen. I was a physical mess, at six, when she came to us. Along with unsightly, rabbity teeth, weird eyes and a perpetual sniffle—my tonsils hadn't yet been extracted—I had a pronounced stutter, the result in all likelihood of being switched to a righty by her Swiss predecessor, Soeur Ami.

The enforced switch took all too well. There is hardly anything I do that is not right-handed. But it left a missing person I kept trying to revive. Batting left-handed, playing tennis ambidextrously, choosing always the left side of an ice rink, a soccer field, were all unsuccessful ways of trying to reconnect with that awkward, sweet-faced, moody lefty.

Looking back at those pre-school years, I think I must have been very frightened. Frightened by stern Soeur Ami whom I loathed (yet whom I remember mourning the afternoon Eileen arrived—she had been, after all, my proxy mother). And frightened also by my peers. My body, with the corrective eyeglasses Father soon had me discarding—glasses, this Christian Scientist believed, weakened the eye muscles—felt so vulnerable, my first instinct was to run away. Wrong, Eileen felt, don't run away, fight! And hardly was she with us a month than, in her battling Irish way, learned surely from her seven brothers, she had me down on the floor, wrestling and tussling with her. Of the many later school fights I somehow or other got into, I don't think I ever won a single one. But the fact that I had stood my ground, waving my fists about, somehow counted. Many classmates may have had their reasons for wanting my blood—the singular tension I exuded, for one. But no one pommelled me about who didn't thereafter accept me as his friend.

For most of their childhood, Eileen's principal charges, Peter and Stephen, six and eight years younger than me, were each other's best friend. But Merrill and I did not get on. As the older brother, I believed that age carried its privileges. This "Me Too" would have none of it. And he insisted on having his meager powers acknowledged. To him, little Stephen, all of three, was a new kind of dormouse. He didn't dip him in a pot of tea, but he was forever salting him away in an obscure drawer, or dangling him by his little heels over our fourth floor bannister.

But when Merrill started to take piano lessons (he could identify any ten notes you struck, or play back a melody he had just heard at a concert), I insisted on learning to play too, even though I was tone deaf. We were intensely competitive because our parents wanted to encourage, if not provoke, their two little terriers squabbling for their crumbs. A cruel competition erupted and endured between two brothers born almost two years apart.

But to our parents we were two chips off the old dynastic block, to be poured into matching sailor suits and marched down to Merrill Lynch where we inspected the ticker tape and, in tribute to Father, away in the Navy, sang "Anchors Aweigh." Or for the mid-winter school Pierrot show, because of our extraordinary resemblance, made to act out the Stevenson poem:

The author and brother Merrill at Cooper's Neck, South Hampton.

> I have a little shadow
> That goes in and out with me;
> But what can be the use of him
> Is more than I can see.

The trouble with Merrill, as with me, was the inflexibility of our one permitted role. We had our short pants, our blazers, our closet-full of suits, and we were expected to be well turned out wherever we went, training for some best-dressed male award. In our forest of conformity we could not, like trees, seek out our separate light. In time, with greater brawn, Merrill would turn out to be the better athlete. And his were the sharper male edges, as he gloriously demonstrated by banging his then ten-year-old head, night after night, against our obnoxious new governess's wall until she finally caved in and quit.

In those early days, Merrill's hopes lay in trying to provoke me into smacking him so he could tattle and exact some sympathy from our parents. Still, in their book what counted was performance—grades, teams—and their system of rewards usually ran my way. Like many another older brother, I got to go places and do things. And I was talked to. After a meal Merrill had alone with Father at Pavillon, I remember him saying as he lay weeping in his bed, "You know he talked to me. For the first time in my life he actually talked to me." Merrill was sixteen at the time.

SOUTHAMPTON

New York is where I lived and went to school nine months of the year. But Southampton, a fashionable resort on the south fork of Long Island, is where the life I made for myself began. In the city I was one more kid training to be an adult. In Southampton I could live each day as it came. To see a friend, all I had to do was hop on my bicycle. And we could play anywhere, out in the wind and along the waves of what was then one of America's whitest beaches. And the barns and potato fields and horse riding stables brought me into an older rural life.

But it was the presence of so much surrounding water that stamped my dreaming. With less than four miles between the ocean and Peconic Bay, Southampton was a virtual island, a maze of ponds and brackwater creeks. Wherever I swam, I paddled, I sailed, I encountered a mirror that, try as I might, I could never penetrate. For a small child, water is never neutral, and I never knew when any one of the creatures it teemed with—the snapping turtle the size of a coffee table, the swans that could break a man's back, the shark lurking out at a sand bar, the Nazi U-boat reported fifteen miles down the coast at Amagansett—might rise from underneath and spirit me away. And worse than the water were the winds whipping it up. Did anything in the world pack a wallop like a big hurricane?

But it was more than the mists and the water that made Southampton a must on a socialite's calendar. Arriving there from the dwarf pine barrens of eastern Long Island, the first sight that caught the eye were the barriers of green: the tall elm and maple-lined lanes, First Neck, Cooper's Neck, Captain's Neck. And, most Southampton of all, the privet hedges. "Big Hedges" is the name a friend once gave to the village. Nowhere else have I encountered hedges so high, so defying.

Behind the hedges, buried usually at the end of a gravel driveway, lay the houses. The structures might vary from the low-ceilinged cottages put up as long ago as 1640 by the first English settlers to the block-long mansions that dominated the beach. But all, big and little, shared the same white and green-shuttered look. A look to hide behind. I never thought of them as having contents, only windows: views out over gardens and lawns; the vivid green of a cattail-fringed marsh; the cobalt blue of a late summer pond.

In the old world, the oligarchy barricaded themselves behind iron gates, moats, and high stone walls. In the new, we defended ourselves with space—terrifying vacancies of lawn. Against it the intruder, the child with his birding glasses, the visitor in his sedan advancing up the gravel driveway with the roar of an incoming wave, couldn't help but feel conspicuous. On what business was one challenging the right manifested everywhere—in the raised glance of a gardener, in the yelping of labradors and the barrage of "No Trespassing" signs—of a family to its own privacy? At 1990s prices of $100,000 an acre, one perhaps understands.

The big estates hailed from a time when a mercantile prince's house was a self-sufficient island in the midst of nowhere. Charlie Merrill's pile, "The Orchard," was of this order. To my begoggled eyes it had just about everything: an old-fashioned icehouse; extensive chicken and turkey coops; a pair of cows whose main function, it seemed, was to keep our two families supplied in home-made ice-cream; four pigs; a great kennel of yelping flame-colored setters, the progeny of Mike, whose full-length portrait adorned the entrance hall. From behind the house, classic columns led the eye into a three-sectioned Italian garden, flanked with wisteria-hung pergolas and ornamented with Roman goddesses and copper fountains bubbling from within a labyrinth of formal boxwood. Until I came upon the Alhambra in my twenties, I had never seen a garden more paradisiacal.

But it was the lawn off the lateral wing's card room that stunned visitors. In a society that worshipped lawns—not going anywhere, just extending between you and the others—this was the greenest vacancy going. Broad as a stadium, the lawn ran the entire length of the sixteen-acre property before succumbing to a row of maples and a containing hedge. The problem, of course, was what to do with it, and with a smile, Grandfather would encourage sugges-tions—a driving or archery range? Eventually, his third wife Kinta installed, in line with the card room, a croquet course. Against their manicured grass, and the immensity of the lawn, the white hoops stood out like some wondrously distant sailboat regatta.

The one activity The Orchard lacked was swimming; a deficiency that Charlie more than repaired when he bought from his partner Eddy Lynch's estate a second sixteen-acre property, the "Beach House."

The Beach House's great feature was a brick-and-flower enclosed swimming pool with its thumbnail-sized tiles of a rich sapphire blue. At the deep end towered a high copper slide. Poised there, trembling with vertigo, we children would launch off to land on a rubber mat and carom halfway down the pool. On the sides were sunken pool lights that made the night swimmers look absolutely enormous, miniature whales sporting about. All this pink-orange, sapphire blue tableau needed to suggest uncommon splendor was the droll sepia countenance of Charlie's tuxedoed valet, Leroy, advancing around the pool with a silver tray of daiquiris in cham-pagne goblets. The potions might circulate once more, and, suit-ably relaxed, the company would adjourn to one of the two aw-ninged porches for a sit-down lunch.

Behind the pool lay Father's shrine, a hedge-shielded clay ten-nis court. It was here he instructed me, although the Meadow Club lay across the pond from our house. But its courts were grass and Father preferred the privacy and considered bounce of the Beach House surface.

The inside of the one-storey house was articulated around a raised, roof-high living room. With its false beam supports it had something of the grandeur of a medieval hall. Nearby lay a Spanish-tiled bar lined with cedar wood cabinets and decorated with New Yorker cartoons: a waiter in a phone booth, its counter covered by a white linen tablecloth full of scribbled jottings, saying, "Hello, Merrill Lynch?"; or the Peter Arno woman in a pompadour, looking up, cocktail glass in hand, at the short, balding man bearing down on her, "Merrill Lynch, Pierce, Fenner & Carruthers?"

To the casual visitor, houses like my grandfather's two could seem the last word in beauty. But beauty of such opulence is rarely pure, and to me it all seems part of the nonstop charade our family lived.

In a working-class family a man sells his labor, indenturing himself for so many hours a day. But once the whistle stops he is free to lead something that can be called a life. In a mercantile prince's family, the pretense never stops. You are at it twenty-four hours a day. Even when the children go to school, they are doing their part not to let the family down. Everyone is constantly playing the role of appearing successful and credit-worthy. Some, of course, do it better than others. They become the company chairmen.

But behind the household name may lurk little more than a man and his word. For a few that was enough. They took in the sincere blue eyes, the handmade togs and firm handshake and staked that twenty-six-year-old Charlie Merrill to the two-month loan he needed. But usually bankers require more: guarantees, hostages. That's where a firstborn son comes in. You must seem to be their hostage.

In a capitalist economy the notion of permanence—"you're going to be dealing with me and my brood until the end of time"— can never be more than a sham. Among all the debts, the divorcing wives, the competing children, there is much that can and will go wrong. But as Minos of Crete discovered long ago, you could create much of the needed illusion, of green acres and acres of banknotes rolling away to the near horizon, by the device of a showpiece house.

Somewhere, in the midst of all that mercantile display, lay the sacred labyrinth where Minos' son and heir-apparent, the minotaur, spent his days and nights. Over the centuries, conjectures have varied as to the nature of the prison-sanctum-dance floor. Many have pictured it underground, composed of a maze of paths, intersecting and spreading out like fans, or twisting in upon themselves like a ball of twine. But not all prisons are walled and no less than André Gide—the wealthiest French writer of his day—maintained that, so far as appearances went, the labyrinth did not differ from the rest of the palace grounds. What kept the monster from wandering off and scaring the visitors was an invisible network of carefully selected smells, tactile sensations and sounds. He was drugged, Gide claimed, by the beauty, or more accurately, the beauties of his surroundings.

The essential, for those overseeing him, was that the filial monster should look happy. Or, if that was asking a bit much, wondrously idle. To the visiting grandee, the appearance that the young man liked it there, even revelled in his gilded confinement, constituted the one proof necessary that the family business was that living miracle, a sound investment.

To this end, the minotaur—a master of pleasure—was encouraged to take up a variety of pursuits, one more costly, more time-consuming than the last: court tennis, skiing, polo, falconry, grouse shooting, sailboat racing, motorcar racing. The very number made it all the more unlikely he would ever excel. Rather a certain proficiency was expected—the perfect weekend guest.

By the time he came of age, the minotaur may have grasped that the promised life was a sham and that he was effectively immured. Wherever he turned, he came up against that wall—money—the scads needed to maintain him in his accustomed finery, hobbies, houses, divorces. To be sure, there was a generous allowance, a harbinger of what might one day be his, outright. It would be "infra-dig" to have the poor beast forced into a freak's career, exhibiting himself before a paying public. But no capital was actually forthcoming. It was to be controlled, in his "best interests," by experts in the matter, meaning the lackeys in service to the grand potentate.

When the time came to seek gainful employment, the wizard made it a point to remind the minotaur that his talents were such that there was probably only one outfit willing to pay the inordinate wage his style of life required—the family firm. "But it's the same old labyrinth," the son and heir protested.

Still, all the power lay on the father's side, including the access to the money tap. With no alternative—"Why don't you go to work for your old man?" the feedback from one employment agency after the next—it was inevitable the minotaur should capitulate. Not that the wizard ever expected his son to succeed him. He merely wanted him tethered to a desk, a bureau, where he could be pointed out as the upcoming generation. Not only would it keep the lad out of harm's way, eight hours a day, five days a week, but the princely wage could be read as a sign of corporate solvency, a sum only the most prosperous of firms could afford. There, for as long as the wizard directed the corporate helm, the minotaur would remain. He could not have been more effectively imprisoned.

But the labyrinth has many corridors and, now and then, despite the legion of monitoring personnel, the carefully vetted learning establishments, a minotaur might rebel. As he wandered about in what to everyone else seemed enchantment, he found himself questioning his own part in the ongoing charade.

***

In the middle of nowhere there was reason enough for a dinosaur-sized estate. As transportation improved and land values soared, the burden of providing labyrinths for us minotaurs shifted to a new institution, the club. The more elaborate the club life, the more exclusive the resort. The ability to afford it all—golf, polo, tennis, bridge, yachting—became as good an indication as any of a mogul's status.

No one understood this quite as well as Father. In our cost-conscious family, where there was never a light bulb knowingly left ablaze, everyone was always after Father to cut back on his memberships. Did he really need a hundred, since he only set foot in a few of them from one year to the next? But Father felt about clubs the way Imelda Marcos felt about shoes. And my refusal to join—at his expense—a Harvard social club flabbergasted him. For what else but the right friends was I attending that august university?

During my childhood Southampton looked, for five days of the week, like a rural village. There were few people about other than mothers, nannies, gardeners, servants, and the usual rut of labradors and setters. In my age bracket that left some eight of us males scratching around, wondering what to do. And as far as organized activities went, there wasn't all that much. The ponds, the marshes, the mists, drove us in on ourselves while making us almost frantic to be somewhere else, in a larger life full of teams and pennant races such as we read about in the sports pages. Many afternoons of a long summer, all we did was sit around a radio's play-by-play ballgame, imagining us as them.

But after five days of quiet, the Friday "Cannonball" train would arrive, and all those superstars of the Business Pages would troop in with their weekend guests, bringing their inevitable excitement.

It was for this that all week long we had been mowing lawns, practicing forehands and backhands and all the rest of it. For the next forty-eight hours an intricate and maybe even newsworthy life sprang up, since who went where and what they wore in those days concerned seemingly everyone: from the lucky participants themselves, to the shops and fashion emporia they patronized, and even finally the man or woman in the street, poring over the gossip columns to deduce what they could of the glitterati's shifting alliances.

After renting for two summers, Mother bought in 1941 the house on Cooper's Neck Lane in which we would live until I was twenty-one.

Deferentially, she called it "Little Orchard." But only in respect to my grandfather's pile could a twelve-bedroom house with eight acres of surprisingly varied grounds have been called little.

Our house stood so surrounded in hedges, stands of tall cryptomeria and overarching, maple-lined driveways you were not struck by how big it was; only perhaps by the three-floor height of its peaked roof, visible from The Beach Club, a half mile away. Each outside door seemed to open onto a different lawn, another thickness of turf.

I knew those textures because, from the age of six, I worked an hour a day in the garden. And I could not go anywhere until I had put in my hour's work. For Father, it was a way of imprinting his work ethic: just because a boy was born with certain advantages, he should not allow himself to become lazy. At first, the work consisted of weeding and deadheading the flowers, raking the gravel driveway, and picking vegetables, flowers, and berries in the big "victory" garden we maintained during the war years. By the time I was nine I had graduated to the power-mower, making the grasses plume all around me as I bent and pulled and figure-eighted towards an ever-diminishing sward. I was proud of the beauty of the place and wanted it to be perfect for Father's Friday night inspection. For me, those words of praise were the high point of my week.

Among my friends, each of our grounds had its function, and ours suited the games of hide-and-seek tag that we played.

Our home base was down by the lake, home to a family of swans and a number of birds, as well as the now vanished muskrats and a legion of snapping turtles. With the quicksand and the voracious turtles, it was not a great place to swim. But I had a rowboat, "The Cowpens" (after Father's aircraft carrier), in which I explored among the cattails and fished for perch out by the stakes in mid-lake, the remains of a bridge demolished in the 1938 hurricane. Now and then when my stable of turtles needed replenishing—we sold them for races at birthday parties—I might venture past the stakes into the swans' half of the lake. But warily. Even if I succeeded in wrenching out an oar, what protection did it offer against a creature of that wingspread bearing down at forty miles an hour?

Our property did not end at the lake, for out in the middle we children had our own little island. For an exploring five-year-old, the island was quite scary, wondering at each step if you were going to disappear into a quagmire and never be heard from again. But at the end of our first summer, Mother had the island's shrubbery bulldozed and a plank bridge with guard rails erected so we could wheel our bicycles to the Meadow Club on the other side in more safety than the dune road allowed. With the bridge came a log cabin straight out of the F. A. O. Schwartz toy store on 57th Street. We shared it with a nest of hornets who never attacked us as we sat directly underneath, playing dice baseball.

On the island we had our own vegetable garden which, with our nurse Eileen's considerable help, we turned over ourselves, spade by painful spade, using for fertilizer the droppings of the swans, who were nesting that year at the other tip of the island. We grew strawberries, carrots and various beans to add potash to the soil as well as potatoes in honor of Eileen. By then I was reading Douglas Fairchild's *The World Was My Garden* and Louis Bromfield's *Malabar Farm*. The dream of an organic, self-sustaining farm remained more Eileen's than mine. But the island gave me a refuge from which I could imagine a world of my own that fulfilled me and made sense.

We played hide-and-seek in two teams. Those guarding home base down by the lake counted to a hundred. By the time they opened their eyes, I was likely to be on the far side of the house, by one of the two gravel driveways. The idea, as in guerrilla warfare, was to lure my pursuers as far as possible from home base. Then, while they were chasing some will-o'-the-wisp from one hedge hole to the next, the rest of us would infiltrate through the shrubbery until, at a signal, we all converged on an undermanned home base.

Of the two driveways I preferred the service one, as I had only to dart through a hedge to be in the Rose Garden. There I could melt into the dense cryptomeria that flanked its two sides, crawling my way further and further in until everything around me was utterly black. Around me feet would rustle, voices would call, but I would lie there gaining back my breath until I was strong enough to rise, feeling my way by one or another tunnel back into the running light and down, by one of the five fingers of lawn, to home base.

More obsessive was the hide-and-seek I played with birds. I had first become aware of them at the age of seven when Mother placed a chart of the twenty most common on our bedroom wall. Another child, I suppose, might have closed his eyes and allowed them to fade into the surrounding wallpaper. I couldn't, and before long I was completely fixated. The radiator would squeak and I'd rush out, convinced some new wonder had alighted.

At first I birded on our grounds. But there was little variety other than the usual garden birds and I soon found myself, Alice-like, crawling through a hole in the hedge into a disused eight-acre lot. The lot was infested with brambles and crawling ticks, interspersed with a dead stump here or there or a small clump of maples. But to a small child it seemed a magic mirror, a wilderness where anything from anywhere might alight. I never knew what I would stumble upon next.

To identify creatures so small, so elusive, you usually need binoculars. But my parents must have felt that expensive prisms were not to be entrusted to a child. Their chromosomes had resulted in two oddly calibrated eyes: the right slightly farsighted and the left so myopic it had no way of telling a bird was about. Squinting with my good eye, I would do my best to assemble the elements of the flitting mosaic—rump, wing patch, eyering, lore, mandible— into an identifiable pattern. Then, with my reading eye, I would pore through the folio-sized *Birds of America* I had retrieved from my grandfather's library, comparing the vivid colors I remembered with the plates Audubon had made a century earlier from dead plumages.

As I pressed forward in my wet sneakers and short pants, I felt my shadow sticking, my breath become a hushed, mouth-open pointing—a silhouette, size of a nugget, gleaming in a far crown. Without binoculars how was I to identify it while, all but invisible, the bird twittered and called? How but by imagining I had become the bird, as I flitted from leaf to light to song-lit perch. I saw, no, I was the ripple on the lake where a pied-billed grebe dove and surfaced, stretching me to silk again.

Plunged long enough in that watery silk, I was off to the next bush of waiting cardinal flame. "Nowhere to go, but up!" I'd exult, flat on my back against a root as I scanned the treetops for a vireo eyestripe.

What could my quarry have experienced as this great crashing child-oaf blundered about? Hard to persuade them I was not an oversized cat, or a new form of bulldozer? But as their pursuer I sensed my own intrusion, that I had no business disturbing their efforts to feed. This sense reduced me to the thinnest quiet as I crept along—a dime in a vase of wind. Only one aspect counted— color. Above, color shifted, color sang. Color may even have had me crying out in submission, "In my next life let me be you, little gem, just stay put until I've named you." Was that the dream that feathered me, as if by craning my neck a single degree more I'd no longer be this robin-named human, but a new bit of ore bent on a bough, a moment in a landscape that was itself a flicker in the ineffable scale?

For an incandescent moment I strained, squinting my good eye as I made with everything I was, everything I yearned to be, that one undying pledge of identification.

The birds were lightning rods to a quickened destiny. Attached to one bird, one word, I was attached to all that came with it— pond, meadow, sky, forest; an entire lexicon of possibility.

COMING OF AGE ON THE CONTINENT

The great divide of my childhood occurred in 1949, as I was going on thirteen, when Mother took us to Italy for the summer. Before going away I honestly believed there was no place better for a child, or more beautiful than Southampton. Its skies were me, its ocean waves, me, its hundreds of grasses, me. There was no differentiation. By the time I returned, briefly, thirteen months later, something else had altered the equation. In Europe an un-suspected door had been flung open and I had stepped by a magic causeway from a country island into a vast treasure chest of his-tory; of century piled upon century, one maze after another of stairs, squares, arches, all leading back, back; a world of differ-ence and arrival.

The chameleon in me felt challenged by the foreign distinctions. Could I make myself into a peasant, a fisherman, a café waiter? I studied how they went about it, the hands fluttering earnestly as they talked, the almost gliding walk, as if one was the ripple of a line thrown forward. To that end I fitted myself out with phrase books, irregular verb manuals, as if the ability to talk, to advance on the ladder of the language, would allow me to penetrate to the heart of their reality.

In the cities they took me to, Florence, Rome, Venice, I was free to ramble wherever I liked. And I, that snooty, hyper-alert New York child, sticking out so uncomfortably in a subway, a park, was now someone invisible, a tourist. With the lightest of baggage— no longer an "I," but a "one"—I proceeded from one street, one square, to the next, never knowing what new marvel I would stumble on. After being cramped in a single foreground running an errand, making an appointment, here was space, and like a bird released, I flew, singing away.

The further I flew, the more at home I felt. Gone was all the incessant twisting and untwisting of a necktie, my hands flailing in every unlikely direction as I spoke. I was not lost, I told myself; rather I was starting anew, in a different place maybe, a different culture, but one that allowed me to remain that same open-mouthed child on tiptoes, startled by a flash of wings, a squeak high in the branches, craning my neck towards a name newly alit. On the threshold of puberty here I was suddenly awoken in the greenest of possible forests.

Like everything Mother undertook, our summer abroad was meticulously prepared. She wanted it a success and, by success, she envisioned nothing less than the complete and utter seduction she had known at seventeen studying in Florence. The previous November she had sailed by herself all the way to Genoa, for the sole purpose of procuring a suitable villa. That turned out to be the first three floors of the Contessa di Robillant's lemon-colored palace, rising from a rock over the sea in Rapallo. Leaving the staffing to a

Mother

friend, she returned to New York to prepare for the great removal.

By June, the last props were in place and we sailed off: Mother, the four of us brothers, a tutor, and our thirteen steamer trunks; one trunk alone bulged with pink toilet paper. To transport our gear, we brought a behemoth De Soto station wagon. It aroused virtual awe, if not downright worship, wherever we appeared.

Nothing in my experience had prepared me for the sensuous bombardment of Italy: the gray-green, olive-filled heights; the steep, terraced contrasts of hills and sea; the rich, creamy blues of the sky; the sherbet-like houses, peppermint pink, raspberry, apricot; to say nothing of the beauty, the well-being the people themselves exuded.

The effect might have been less had Mother not been so present, pointing, exclaiming. As it was, I was soon grievously smitten.

Why I couldn't hold two such hardly rival resorts as Southampton and Rapallo in my heart—as Mother herself had—I don't know. Immaturity probably has something to do with it. And Rapallo in 1949 was still the Rapallo that had enchanted Pound, Yeats and Beerbohm, not to mention Mussolini, whose gutted palace overlooked the adjoining cove. We swam right off the villa's rock, climbing to a projecting pinnacle and from there, over the hissing brine and the spines of the clinging sea-urchins, plunging in head-first. For sport there was tennis, with high bouncing balls and ballboys to chase them, on the Casino's red clay courts. Across the bay at Santa Margherita we kept a sailboat, now and then anchoring it off our rock. Two villages further was Portofino, with its red and green fishermen's boats and tiny horseshoe-shaped jewel of a harbor. From there we would climb up and up a several hundred step staircase cut in the rock to an unbelievable restaurant with views stopped only by the opposing headland.

With Mother as guide we traveled to Florence, a city I came to know in a way I had never known New York. And when in August Father arrived, our expeditions extended: to Rome for the fittings with his two tailors; to the stone tapestry that is Venice. And everywhere, buoyed by a dollar that would never be again so high, we shopped: silk ties, silk dress shirts, calfbound books for me, brocade fabrics, antique gilt chairs, marble tables, and of course the suitcases to cart it all home.

Not all our treasures reached home. There was, famously, Father's custom-made white gabardine suit. He had collected it from his tailor in Rome and was wearing it for the first time in Orvieto a day later when he made the mistake of sitting next to me at a trattoria. A particularly expressive flash of my hand and a glass of red wine spilled, ruining the suit in a way he was never to forget, much less forgive. To him, the spill was tantamount to a bloodstain. The minotaur had gored him. Whenever afterwards we sat down together, he knew and I knew the fate we were tempting. What we didn't know was that in Italy a spilled glass carries magical properties. "Si porta fortuna," as our waiter remarked, a consoling smile on his face as he quickly laid out a new tablecloth and steered Father, salt shaker in hand, to the gents. As even Father ruefully acknowledged, from that moment on he was a fulfilled man, number two and heir apparent at Merrill Lynch or Safeway, as he wished. The summer in Italy was for him, indeed for all of us, the high water mark in our life as a family.

Our Italian summer, unrepeated miracle as it proved—and Mother always regretted not having taken the opportunity to add a Tuscan villa to her string—had come into being as a solution to the problem posed by my graduating from eighth grade at St. Bernard's at the age of twelve; not too young to attend Phillips Exeter Academy which had accepted me, but too young, Father felt, to stand a chance of earning a varsity letter. Realizing how important for a boy's self-esteem making a team was, he decided to "redshirt" me for a year by sending me to Le Rosey, a Swiss international school located in Rolle on the Lake of Geneva (and for the winter term in Gstaad in the Bernese Alps). There I could make a start at acquiring the French that had always eluded him. And the school, with its winter classes that broke up for skating and skiing at eleven, its princeling cast of a hundred boys drawn from some twenty-seven nationalities and ranging in age from eight to eighteen, sounded as if it might stretch me in some of the right directions.

But there was such a thing, Mother felt, as being overstretched. A boy who had never been away from home could hardly be expected to land all by himself in Geneva and make his own way around the lake to Rolle and his new school. If I had to be accompanied, why not smooth the transition and make the logistics easier for everyone by renting an Italian villa for the summer?

It was ingenuous logic, and perfectly compatible with the "Let's move the swimming pool" side of Mother's character. And, after the rest of the family had departed, she showed me great kindness by personally taking me by train to Lausanne and, after an overnight stay at the Beau Rivage, depositing me at Le Rosey.

For Mother, the thought of not seeing me for another six months was wrenching; far worse than the flood of tears with which she had launched me on my first school bus. In the barroom of the Beau Rivage that evening, some Belgian fellow parents took one look at her, propped on her bar stool, and insisted on a very stiff, dry martini. That once, she later confided, it had really helped.

Of anywhere on the globe, Switzerland, with its seven hundred-year history of neutrality, would seem one of the safer countries to leave a child. But in 1949, at the height of the Cold War, it could feel far away. I remember Father issuing instructions as to how, should the Soviets invade, I was to strike out for the Pyrenees. (To the end of his life Father was convinced that war with the Soviets was inevitable. When my brother Mark asked why he remained on the naval PX stores board, a chore he clearly despised, Father replied, "I want to have some influence so that when the war breaks out you and your brothers can be officers in the Navy.")

Earlier in the summer in an effort to spare me the hazing he himself had undergone, Father had taken me aside to try to explain what sexual intercourse involved. I, who thought babies were things created under a cabbage leaf, could not have been more dumbfounded. If Father put sex on an impossibly remote pedestal—something a man did only when he wanted a baby out of the woman he loved—I, at least, had been forewarned.

Their misgivings were well founded. For the first weeks I was acutely homesick. To my utter astonishment I even missed brother Merrill. In an effort to get news of any sort, I unleashed a flood of letters to my godparents, the family servants, a gardener's wife, anybody.

It did not help that my Italian roommate took an exception to something about me —the different suit I donned each day?—and began popping away at me with his BB gun. I coped with that easily enough by burying myself under the covers. But when he began threatening me with a belt I appealed for a transfer. That landed me in a room with three fellow Americans. Not what I had come for, but hard to avoid in a school dominated by our then imperial dollar. More sexually mature than I, they spent much of their free time secluded in their respective closets, trying to bring their erections to seminal fruition.

It may have been the beauty of the Italian maids, or the nearness of Geneva with its prostitutes, or the hothouse atmosphere generated by a school of princes (the Shah of Iran was an alumnus; I roomed with Amin Aga Khan whose current stepmother was no less than Rita Hayworth), but the student body exuded a randiness unlike anything I've encountered. I learned never to stoop over a faucet, a soccer machine, without first cupping a hand to my exposed parts. And I moved with a karate-like readiness lest a paw reach out and, with a chortle of triumph, claim a symbolic prisoner.

On the academic side the teaching was hit or miss. Often a master was more memorable for his toupee, or for the aplomb with which he plucked me out of my chair by the ears and transported me thus to the blackboard, than for any wisdom he imparted. The curriculum ran on the continental model, a dozen or so courses a term. But this could include such useful oddities as a yearlong history of the French revolution and its Napoleonic aftermath. And the best teacher I ever encountered, Signor Mastelli of the pulled ears, effectively combined intimidation and his own stingy marking system, "Good work! You've earned 3.8" (out of a possible 10), to such effect I was eventually competing with the native speakers. It might well have been worth staying just for his Dante.

STRANGER IN A STRANGE SOUTHAMPTON

In going to Europe I had crossed one kind of threshold. When I came back for the first time thirteen months later, I saw that my friends had undergone a rather more serious transformation. They still gathered every afternoon at the Meadow Club. Only now it was not on the tennis courts, but with their girl friends in a plush sitting room adjoining the bar, among overstuffed couches, ashtrays and Coke bottles. In the evening, the scene transferred to a dune and became a "party," a word pronounced with sacrosanct intonation, as if it would not do to arrive there on a bicycle and without a date. But for me the reality of girls had not yet replaced the fantasy.

I had barely settled in when I found on my doorstep a delegation of all my old playmates come to welcome me home. They told me about the summer of mat-riding I had missed, the sand bar that extended out from the Beach Club barrels for a couple of hundred yards, giving rides almost like those on Hawaiian postcards. On calm days, they could see, looming beneath them, the weird farm implements of the previous century.

A kind gesture, and one that impressed Father. But would they have come if they had not sensed how alienated I felt? Yet I think that, even alone, I might still have been welcomed among the blankets and cigarettes of a dune, if I could have only found a way of playing down the impact of the Europe I had experienced. Perhaps I could have said, "You can't put such things into words." Or an emphatic, "I don't want to talk about it. I'm here now."

Of course my old friends would ask, "What's it like over there, tell us!" But as I rattled on about the soft creamy blue of the Mediterranean sky, about the big lunches and the people and the narrow, cobbled, Vespa-noisy streets, I could see their eyes clouding over. They just didn't want to know. Being thirteen and fitting in was difficult enough without my dragging in my own extraneous surreality. Yet it was exactly those comparisons of place, of style, of attitude that I wasn't willing to renounce. They were the one stalk of difference I had on which to grow.

All the same it might be wondered what, in a year at Le Rosey, I had learned. Certainly not the French for which I had been sent. Even before coming home, I had persuaded my parents of my need for a second year. Those two, along with the traveling and the people we met on the month-long vacation breaks, rather disoriented me.

Among the disorientations were the sensationally divorced and now newly married Ingrid Bergman and Roberto Rossellini. We had been taken to their house by some producer friends of Mother's. I was too young to appreciate the rarity of Ingrid's beauty. But I did get on with the director of "Open City," and I still remember Roberto's story of how he filmed it, walking, camera in hand, among the retreating German tanks. The next night, they invited me back—by myself! Was it a way of giving my parents a romantic night out on a Tiberian dance floor? Probably. But for a gangly, acne-pitted fourteen-year-old, dinner with them came as a gift.

One year abroad was easy enough to discount, but not a second, and one chosen. Where before my dreams were exclusively American—to have seen, say, all six hundred of our native birds—now I found myself straddling a bewildering divide. Would I ever wake from the foreign enchantment? Or was that earlier existence, of our riding the waves and playing baseball and doing everything together a dream and their life with their new girlfriends the reality? If so, what had brought about these changed circumstances? Was it I who had brought it on by taking too big a bite of the foreign apple? Or my pals who, in maturing more quickly, now found me hopelessly juvenile. Either way, the verdict registered. And there I was, failed, expelled, in a word, finished.

Compounding my bewilderment were the changes Southampton was itself now undergoing. Up to then the life had been relatively low-key. The cars were those you didn't mind seeing rust away in the salt air. The big houses were strictly for summer occupancy, and the dress style was informal—sweaters with holes, baggy slacks, sensible shoes.

Now after twenty lean years came the 1949-51 stock market boom. There was no way, as Father said, not to make money. But some made more than the others. What brave new world were they to conquer? Why not try Southampton, and here they were, muscling in on the clubs and on our minotaur life. And they came in hordes. Where I had my eight coevals, my younger brothers commonly attended parties of forty to fifty.

For all our efforts to barricade ourselves behind a new, minimal, five-acre zoning, village life changed. Out went the potato fields, the duck farms, the riding stable, and up went the houses. Most of the development took place on the village periphery, in the Shinnecock hills and the North Sea. But it affected us too. I could see it in Father. When the next-door lot where I birded came on the market, he bought it "to preserve our privacy." He could have left it the thorn-riddled, tick-infested, bird-rich wilderness it was. But that wasn't Father. He had been bitten by the English bug of "lawn," Capability Brown's rolling immensities, and wanted a sward of his own stretching away into the ocean mists.

By the following summer everything had been bulldozed. In its place, to celebrate a fifteen year "wood" anniversary, there stood my grandfather's gift of a long, formal, maple-bordered driveway. Where before our house, shielded by towering trees, had come as a surprise, now it loomed up at you head-on in all its twelve-bedroom pomp.

To accommodate the added lawn, our grounds changed as well. The future knight wanted the five separate fingers of lawn that reached from the house down to the lake fused into a single green palm. Mower in hand like a battering ram, we sons did our best to comply, over and over again hauling it back and blasting forward until the last vestige of shrub had been ground up.

A green vista may thrive in England's ideal gardening clime. At a quarter mile from the sea, all that sprouts is crabgrass. Where before there was a mystery of shrubbery separated by secret lawns, a book with no end of pages to flip through, now there was only the great eye of the sun on the reflecting lake, staring in at our vacancy.

After buying the Beach House from my grandfather a couple of years later, my parents decided to sell our Cooper's Neck house. They saw no point in maintaining two estates, and the Beach House had the two essentials, swimming pool and tennis court, on a highly prominent position on the beach. "But you are selling my childhood," brother Stephen, all of eleven, lamented. But we older siblings understood. The childhood we had birded and romped in had already vanished. And there is no putting back what you yourself have destroyed.

What applied to us, our failure of character as it were, held in a different way for Southampton. To a visitor from the city, the village, with its ever-changing play of water and sky, its shingled houses picking out the seaside light, may still have looked pastoral, the very embodiment of the good life. But it wasn't pastoral because it remained so exclusive. And exclusivity brings its own range of demands, a buzz of nervous expectation that none of us ever succeeded in stilling. It made us adolescents restless, unable to countenance being alone another minute. It sent wives in their bright pastel outfits scurrying into town, where they might meet outside the post office and confer. If nothing was going on, hopefully their eagerness would create it, a party, a foursome of golf or bridge. Ours was a society in which conspicuous activity had to be maintained from morning to night.

The energy fueling the frenetic activity was money, money, money. By the end of a weekend I'd be hearing it in my sleep, dripping off the tongue, a little wave rolling over and over. Everything, the lawn you were standing on, the instant trees that framed it, the children and the wives, was measurable and, among us natives, an assessor's eye sharply appraised the going values.

THE MINIATURE MASTURBATOR

In my isolation I became like an animal in rut. The adolescent shore loomed, and as I hurtled down toward it, a pillow now instead of a mat wedged between my legs, I felt a future identity hardening under me. Who was I? A spoke on what advancing wheel? A hand tunneling a hole from under the hill of what new infatuation?

In my need, the pillow between my legs became hope itself decked out in all the allurements of female nubility. As the invoked goddesses grew and extended themselves—no body too vast, no body too skeletal—I became aware of something all my own: an imagination; one wondrously at my disposal.

With the onset of adolescence I had been moved out of a room shared with Merrill to a former guest room on the third floor. The room could not have been more impersonal. A pair of Audubon prints, of birds I would never see, above the bed; a small white desk lit only by the ceiling's sixty-watt bulb; and, gained by way of a barely waist-high door, the long, hot, uninsulated attic. A floor below, in the other wing of the house, was my adored mother, then in the full ripeness of her beauty. How I wanted her, all the way down there, to hear my loudly creaking, throbbing bedposts and come succor me in my male loneliness. If I was to receive a transforming initiation, why couldn't it come from that subtly responsive dancer's body, with its roseate musk-scented skin, its great coil of chestnut hair and deeply chasmed breasts?

Mother was not the only sexual object in my world. But she was the major one, acclaimed as the exemplar of all the female virtues by no less than Father. In my arms on the dance floor, or alone among the inflating lights of the Beach House swimming pool, I saw her as wanting, and even needing, to attract me.

But despite the heady mixture of prudery and enticement on both our sides, the barrier would not yield. The bond between us had already broken down—when I first stopped kissing her good night at age eight? Was there, I ask myself now, no other way for trust to have been restored? Yet from my own ogling, pinhole sized viewpoint at the time, I earnestly believed that we both might have benefitted from a sustained incest thus consciously chosen. But it wasn't to be and instead we drifted off into a mutual apprehension, a sundering, until recently, of all but the most formal ties.

Surrounded in my family by males as I was, and going to a succession of all-male schools, women could not help but seem a distinct species, with different goals, habits, ways of being, talking, and communicating. Yet not only did they attract me more than men, but I admired them to a degree where much of my later life was spent in trying to acquire the otherness they represented; to be, insofar as they could make me, complete.

But at that stage I was reduced to narcissism: to knowing them in myself, through myself. One way was to pore through Mother's dressing room drawers in search of her magic accoutrements: chignons of hair; douche bags; nylon stockings; lace panties; girdles; waist-held garter belts; variously lifted, cupped bras; and, best of all, the gorgeous couturier-designed transparent negligees. Then, a pair of tennis balls in the bra and head all wrapped in an androgynous towel, I would stand in her mirror-walled bathroom contemplating a new female self, unspeakably sweet, predisposed to care for me and no one but me till the end of my days. In bed later, that mirrored imitation became Venus of a thousand shapes as I straddled the bed pillow, imploring it to do no more than gently canter, while I prolonged as best I could the ecstasy, all that loveliness rustling with my name. A hand towel completed the essential equipage, of use in those last convulsions when rider changed into survivor.

But there was an earlier time when, as a boy of ten, I felt very suspicious of girls and their ways. I wanted to be a man and I felt that it was with boys, and boys alone, I should associate.

My bias was so pronounced that Mother decided to enroll me in dancing school. "Girls, yuck," I remember saying when informed of her decision, "Only sissies like girls."

But over my protests I was packed into blazer and tie and bundled off to the ballroom of the Pierre Hotel. And of all my city activities, dancing school is the one I still think about. It wasn't just the girls in their blouses and flaring skirts, this flesh within an inch or two of me that I held. Or the absurd crush I lavished on the few girls my size, a sparkling-eyed, jet-black ringleted Natasha. For hours, one weekend after the next, I planted myself outside her

Park Avenue apartment in the hope I might catch her emerging without her governess, declare my passion and spirit her away to an atoll all our own.

The dancing lessons brought a new unsuspected way of moving, of being with. Not that I was particularly adept at the steps, this box that—arms extended and raised, I had to convert to a roundness and fluency. As if the quick-quick-slow of the fox trot were a wave and there on its crest, firmly held, right hand in the middle of her back, were a couple gliding ever so slightly ahead of the next looming beat. I didn't have to ask where that most throbbing of pulses was coming from when there was the wind itself of the music filling the sails of our arms, our two revolving bodies. As I turned, so did the rhythm's beat turn me. Backwards, forwards. In, out.

The steps, so restricting at first, conferred a freedom within which all illusions were permitted. Even that of flight itself, a double-winged soaring. For a moment, maybe, held, sustained in the rhythmed water, a female consciousness took me over. I understood what stepping backwards permitted—the gaining of a new leverage from which to sail out past all the surrounding congestion. Imagine the primitive who, having lived all his life exclusively on one plane—going forwards—discovers that going backwards offers a comparable deliciousness; as does swaying between the two, neither of you knowing what will happen next, but nonetheless balanced, supremely with each other, ready.

The intimacy I knew on the dance floor was not one I could translate into my teenage life. I was at the acme of my sexual powers, exuding semen at a rate that would never come again, in such encyclopedic volumes. But between the opulent promiscuity of my fantasies and the meagerness of my reality lay a considerable divide. A minotaur might be greeted with open arms at a cotillion—especially a minotaur who could waltz. But he might not be whom you wanted mauling you in a movie theater. Add the requirements of petting, the female cliff of straps, buttons and hooks which had to be faultlessly escaladed, and one might understand how I spent the better part of two summers sprawled in the dunes beside one future fashion Woman of the Year without ever embracing her; for fear of shattering the experienced image she allowed me to think I was projecting.

In a Southampton where even the grass was money, a would-be man could wish to reverse the Midas touch. Couldn't I reach out and, by breaking the sexual chasm, restore the disorderly wilderness? That was always my burning question as, for hours at a time, in my new Italian walk and a fixed smile on my face, I glided round and round the Beach Club: past the swimming pool's cleavages, up onto the guzzling, tippling, half-naked terraces and down onto the baking, body-by-body outlined, strapless sand. It was all there, the most paradisiacal of feasts spread out before this one lone male, and for some reason it was unavailable. Why? Why? Why?

In the circumstances it does not seem odd that my frustration should be vented on a village that had so misled me. Anywhere else on the globe, I knew, there would be a maid servant, some older woman or a specialized prostitute willing enough to exploit my voluminous urges. And it wasn't a desert I was living in. If Southampton was famous for anything—other than the amount of sheer wealth packed into it—it was the sexiness of its women. Pick up a fashion mag, a newspaper's society page, and there they all were, that voluptuous figure, those million dollar legs, moving faultlessly from one diamond ring, one divorce, to the next.

To come of age in a village where everything involved money, bought at one auction and unloaded at the next, was deception enough. But to find that the promise which kept an adolescence inflamed—that initiatory boat with the seven gorgeous maidens— was never going to arrive, could throw into the air a minotaur's whole raison d'etre. For what had I spent my youth preparing if no adventure, no volupté, was ever going to alight my way? And it didn't help to be told that the great things in life are not those that come at the lowering of a horn, the pawing of a pair of hooves; that sex is not merely an act, but two people; or rather, an emotional fusing of act and person. For my part, I could not help but feel that something was monstrously wrong.

ACADEMIC PURGATORY

My three years at Phillips Exeter could almost have gone by in a whistle, a blast of wind off the New Hampshire coast. It may have been the shock of reentry to American life that was still affecting me, or my continued immaturity, but from the moment I arrived I felt lost. But what could I do when it was I, as Father kept reminding me, who had chosen the place. To an ambitious twelve-year-old seeking an education, the number one ranked prep school could seem the right arena. As did its size. Big. Like Father, that's how I wanted my competition. And Exeter was competitive. With seven applicants for each place, a boy crammed to stay in. And you competed with the lucky seven hundred and fifty to be a wheel around whom the school life revolved.

It should be remarked that schools of Exeter's sort don't acquire their endowments by educating free spirits. Rather they are putting you through their version of teenage hell, "Hic venite pueri ut viri sitis." (You come here, kid, to be turned into a man.)

As for the kind of man, one need only note the three debating societies (four, if you include the school Senate) to see a less than open cast of mind: lawyers, judges, politicians, a trail extending from Daniel Webster down to the present-day likes of Al Gore, Supreme Court candidate Dick Arnold, Senators Tim Wirth and my doubles partner, Jay Rockefeller. We were all of us cynics, determined to avoid the embarrassment of being surprised or, worse, astonished. It got some ninety of us into nearby Harvard. But at what cost, it might be asked, to our development, our sense of others' styles and complexity?

For myself, I was so put off by this oversized world I had stumbled into that all I did, for the first year and a half, was play bridge in the dingy dormcellar buttroom. I'm not sure what drew me. I certainly didn't smoke and my concentration never lasted beyond a single 200-point rubber. Yet there I was, all 5'2" and 100 pounds of me, hanging out among the white buck shoes, khaki trousers and swept back "duck" haircuts. "How are they hanging?" one scholarship ringer invariably greeted me. A not impossible koan. But nothing I came up with, "A bit down on the left," or whatever, sufficed. I was too dimwitted to fling back the "Up your ass!" he evidently required.

For my parents, bridge offered a social diversion. They could compete with their guests without having to extend their conversational powers. For me, it made little sense. But in a high-pressure school it could somehow seem important to waste what little time I had. At least I wasn't being a grind. And I may have needed a hands-on pastime that filled the hours the way my endless map-tracing had as a child.

Then, in the winter of my upper middle year, my English grade plummeted: C-, D+, D, on successive papers. Not being a grind was one thing; but letting down Team Magowan and flunking out was another matter. In some anxiety I called on my teacher, Darcy Curwen, a tall, ruddy complexioned Englishman with a shock of white hair whom we all regarded as the reincarnation of his often quoted Dr. Johnson.

At Exeter, we rarely saw our teachers outside the classroom, or the playing field. Recognizing this, Curwen tried to put me at ease. "I'm glad you've come by. You're not somebody I've had a chance to talk to. What brings you?"

"My grades," I blurted out. "I've always enjoyed English, and I don't understand why I'm faring so badly."

After hearing me out, Curwen asked, "What have you been reading on your own?"

I looked up at him, somewhat startled, recalling a time not all that long ago when I hardly went anywhere without a book glued to me. *Freddy the Pig, Mysterious Island, La Chartreuse de Parme, The Count of Monte Cristo*. There was even a moment when, under the spell of *Northwest Passage*, my nurse Eileen suggested that I might have in me a historical novelist. But at Exeter, the only literature I cracked were my roommate's Mickey Spillanes. Enough Mickey Spillane and your brain turns to jello. I didn't tell Curwen about Mickey Spillane, I just replied, "I used to read a lot—every free moment I had—but I guess I've gotten out of touch."

"Why don't you try this?" Curwen offered, taking from his shelf a copy of *Barchester Towers*. An alien world, but I read it compulsively and, when I finished, I asked Curwen for another book. That turned out to be Matthew Arnold's verse novel, *Sohrab and Rustum*, of which I don't recall a scene. But my truancy was cured and, by the year end, I was doing well enough to be allowed two senior tutorials, in classic political theory and French.

With only two courses to attend, and rooming in an old shingle house at the edge of the campus—the original setting for Maxwell Anderson's play, *Tea and Sympathy*—senior year was bearable enough. Other than read and write my weekly tutorial reports, there was little I had to do, no image I had to maintain. I had a tall gawky Hungarian roommate, Blaise Pasztory, a person of remarkable sanity with whom I would room for four of the next five years. (He had left Budapest with his mother, an art historian, on the last train in 1949.) The other members of our house, most of them friendly, oversized football jocks, coped well enough with the mascot I must have been for them.

Knowles titled a popular novel about Exeter, *A Separate Peace*. A boy can, in his own way, opt out. In the course of those three years I had discovered something about myself—who I wasn't: a newspaperman like my father; a leader of organizations like my mother; a wheel. I just didn't have their social instincts. It remained to be seen what I could do. But I knew one thing—I wasn't a lawyer.

Harvard may have been, as a friend remarked, "A prison, too, but without the walls." But it seemed, after Exeter, freedom itself. I could audit any course, attend or not attend a class, the choice was mine. And the courses, for all the midnight oil burned on their behalf, comprised a minuscule part of what I was taking in. Harvard was, above all, a community, and it was the foreign films at the Casablanca, the up to twenty plays that were being performed on any given Saturday, the taverns, galleries and specialized bookstores, that opened the vistas to the future that awaited me.

There were also, for the first time in my school life, girls. Compared with the desert of Southampton, Radcliffe was everything a randy young man could want, a meadow bedizened with flowers of every possible hue and shape, one seemingly prettier, more intelligent than the last. By the end of the first week I had fallen in love with almost the entire freshman class. I memorized their year-book photos, and, despite the competition, I dated as many as I possibly could.

At most colleges it is the subject, the field of concentration, that counts and the student learns to advance gingerly, from one stepping stone to the next. At Harvard it was the professor who counted, not the canvas he deigned to draw upon. From the globe's far quarters our wise men had been procured, solely, we were told, for our instruction. Some departments were reputed to be crammed full of them, lectern upon lectern of beaming, gesticulating twentieth century sages. They were the ones we majored in. Other less starworthy departments, even if offering a French that had meant everything, we shunned.

It was the professors' reputations we were checking out, enrolling in a major almost regretfully, because it so circumscribed the banquet. There was, first of all, the course catalogue's two hundred-page menu to be drooled over. Then, after much conferring, we chose the semester's four course repast. The more arcane the courses, the better. What interest could I possibly have in the bureaucratic ins and outs of the Soviet nomenklatura? Or in post-Kantian German philosophic idealism, of which I grasped not a concept, but somehow emerged with a parrot's "A."

Our wise men were, above all, performers. We came to watch their expertise glowing through them, paunchy white-maned Perry Miller nothing less than Moby Dick personified. If the whale intrigued, we followed him, from one mouthful of plankton, one great briny sea, to the next—until we had unmasked the inflated nature of his reputation. We were, after all, a generation formed on *The Catcher in the Rye*. What better place than Harvard to catch professorial phonies?

Yet all such concerns about courses, condiments, flavors, paled before the ever more imminent prospect of a career. Each day that carried me closer to graduation increased the panic I felt, surrounded, like Tarzan in the pit, by the crouching snakes in their business suits on the one side and the Southampton desert on the other.

My grandfather's sons, my uncles Charles and Jimmy, had shown little inclination for the family business. But they were only fifteen and nine, respectively, when my father took them off the hook by marrying their older sister.

What placated my grandfather could not satisfy the man who had married the boss's daughter. From the day I was born it was assumed I would not only go into, but eventually head Merrill Lynch. I sometimes think I was conceived with no other end in mind. While still a small child, Father was propping me next to him at dinner, initiating me in the great restaurants, and, above all, teaching me his beloved tennis and, through it, what business itself—WINNING—was about.

I'm not sure how well I absorbed his earnestly imparted lore. But by now, Father had seen enough to know I could fulfill most of the essential social expectations. I could handle my liquor, don a tuxedo and play, after a fashion, most of the exclusive sports. And I was reasonably bright. Not that he had forsaken his dream of a dynasty, of the realms five sons working in tandem might conquer. But such a succession, he knew, had to be taken one son at a time. If he succeeded in coaxing me into my invisible cage, my brothers presumably would follow.

But the promise I showed made my parents all the more anxious, as if all that they had built and sacrificed for hung on my decision. The family business, they pointed out, did not have to be the bottomless pit of my adolescent fears. To be sure, before being given any position of trust, I would have to prove myself before all those eyes gauging the aplomb, the studied nonchalance, with which I approached my career fences. But, if I could stick it out, a substantial world awaited my beckoning. Didn't I want, Mother asked, to be a philanthropist and go out and make a bundle so that, like Charlie, I could bequeath it to charity?

The hitch, of course, lay in sticking it out. For every achieving Tartuffe, there must be thousands who, for one reason or another, have disappeared along the wayside. The failure may be one of character; an inability to sustain the required hypocrisy, day after day from one club, one cocktail, to the next, all the way to the boardroom or the governor's mansion.

But the failure may say something about the nature of money. Money, alas, is value and values don't exist apart from people. For the scions of the rich it can make for an enviable luxury and a distinct uneasiness, since money in those quantities is a highly toxic substance which keeps poisoning those who touch it. In a society of image, what you resemble you become, because others treat your appearance as your creation.

To have accepted the birthright I would have had to feel that, like a queen bee, I was someone unique. My mother may have felt some such pride. I couldn't. The elite are seldom the enlightened.

All the same I think I could have become the businessman I was brought up to be. But it would have had to be for another outfit than Father's. Working for him, there would always be that fox barking out his commands. And I had better be prepared to drop everything and go off in search of that golfball belted into the shrubbery, those "stolen" cufflinks.

The rub lay in Father's refusal to accept what my life, let alone life itself, might be about. Instead, one asserted one's penis in the dynastic vessel, and sons, satraps of the prospective empire, issued forth. Ideally, there should have been not a mere five, but a whole royal guard of us sons mounted on our stallions. Then, when the occasion demanded (having, of course, earned our stripes), we could be sent off to quell that labor riot, to fix that congressman.

Brought up as I was, I could not help but be aware of my obligations, the need to make something of the genetic material bestowed on me. What I objected to was Father's notion of me as his clone and dynastic chattel. Instead, I wanted his respect. And there was, I knew, only one way to earn it—by so shredding my advantages that I started out on my path equally naked. "I don't care what you do with your life," I remember him challenging me, "so long as you make as big a success of it as your grandfather and I have."

By "success," I realize now, this monomaniac meant money, scads of it burning green for a lifetime. But imbued as I was with their two trajectories, I understood a different measure based on where you started and ended up. Never mind that so far I had done nothing to suggest I was something other than a dwarf. Perhaps I hadn't applied myself hard enough? From now on, I told myself, I would think GIANT. And I would go out and find me some larger than life mentors, male and female. Who knows what might rub off?

But there is no changing what you are. A dwarf is a dwarf, just as a leopard is a leopard. You can't win so long as you are playing on another's terms. So what if you slay that dragon, or return with the golden fleece, the king is still not going to turn over to you his kingdom. You have to know you are a king yourself and beat your birthright out of him. No giant has ever lived by another's prescription.

To my entering freshman class, my career dilemma was far from unique. And the gloom, not to say the fear, at what awaited our "silent" generation in that post-McCarthy era conditioned our choices. Asked on their registration forms what they wanted to be, an amazing seventy percent of my freshman class responded "doctor." Feet planted thus firmly on the ground—do something socially useful and well-paying, why not?—the best and brightest went out to try to survive Chem 20. Others, for much the same reasons, found themselves choosing a professorial cubbyhole.

At Harvard there has always been a considerable legacy of public service. But in those gray-suited times any such access seemed reserved for generals and businessmen. So, we enrolled in courses like Perry Miller's "Introduction to American Literature," which traced our exclusion back to its post-Civil War roots in Henry James and, more poignantly, Henry Adams. As Susan Sontag remarked, it was the plight of educated Americans to find themselves held by an elastic band of irony. Only by stretching it thin could we maintain a place in a culture that had made us such strangers. What marked our professors—the Schlesingers, the McGeorge Bundys, that soon-to-be Kennedy White House—and in turn marked us as a generation was the despair we felt about our having any public impact. That's why, when the Sixties' counterculture exploded, so many of us rushed in. It was our first chance to make a difference.

Of a different concern was the new imperial mission thrust on us Americans, creatures of incident, by the Allied victory in World War II. The globe was then divided into two dark or livid zones: we, the so-called free world, and they, the Communists. The political battleground was Europe, the military one, Korea. We did not foresee that this empire of ours was about to vanish, victim of the same eleven-year cycle as any business. Instead, many of us viewed corporate capitalism (the Safeways and Merrill Lynches) as the at-home empire which had to be infiltrated and controlled before the better-dead-than-red folk of my father's ilk blew us all sky-high.

That a solution could involve casting myself as a writer would have seemed highly unlikely to anyone who had encountered me during that first freshman year. My essay writing, with its convoluted periods and tortured syntax, struck my social science section-man as positively Germanic—"worse than Carlyle" was his comment. He went on, on the front of the same paper, to note "a tendency to pontificate to the point of error; a persistent habit of making too much of too little, and too little of too much." After several more such remarks, he concluded, "Don't succumb to the temptation to rest on bright insights alone (and the way they sound). Nobody has ever become a scholar that way. If I can help you in this respect, let me know."

His strictures struck so to the marrow I had no hesitation in taking him up on his offer. What at the bottom of my pit did I have to lose? A good bit, as it turned out. I had failed to reckon on the dating to which I was now subjected: the Chinese restaurant; the celebrated horse steak at The Faculty Club; the evening of contract bridge at another venue. In the course of this Faustian education I was even made to lie in bed with him, albeit fully clothed. Something about my body language, perhaps the way my hands fluttered as I talked, must have struck him as innately gay and he wanted to be the first to coax it out. But in my family situation, with the Wall Street entombment closing in on me, how was I to reject out of hand a Mephistopheles who was holding out the empowerment I needed?

At the year end he provided a suggested summer reading list. Among the items was Stanley Edgar Hyman's study of the New Criticism, *The Armed Vision*. There I found a chapter on William Epson's ambiguities. With that single revelation poetry opened. Puns, like sex, popped up everywhere, the more outrageous, the better. As a reader I no longer pondered sentences, but words in their new prismatic contours.

That fall I enrolled in a close-reading course. I still remember the shock of the first assignment, a Hopkins sonnet, "God's Grandeur." To me, as I first scanned it, it looked as if Hopkins had let fly with a stick of dynamite. But as I put together the fragments of alliteration, assonance and rhyme, a jigsaw puzzle emerged of what Hopkins was depicting. Language was gesture; gesture, language.

A second exercise, and a third on the metaphor of the wheel in *King Lear*, helped build up confidence. We were next asked to trace a strand of tidal imagery through *The Portrait of the Artist as a Young Man*. I found Joyce's summons to write irresistible. After briefly fulfilling the assignment, I used the remaining pages to give birth to the mat-rider inside of me. Though my knuckles were properly rapped, "This is NOT a creative writing class!" something had broken free. I had crossed the boundary between reading and writing.

MARCIA

That autumn I crossed another line. At a get-together for new history and lit majors, I met Marcia Reithauser, the woman who was to become my wife. The previous year we had shared a large lecture class. Often enough I would find myself walking across the quadrangle behind this big-hipped, swift-striding, long-legged heron of a woman, wondering who she was. I thought of her then as a Scandinavian, a luscious, almond-skinned blonde with a striking face set off by high, savage cheekbones that bore down on one and blazed like the full moon.

Introduced to her, I was all the more intrigued when she called herself a Roumanian. I did not grasp that she had merely spent the first two years of her life in Bucharest, the daughter of an MIT-trained engineer who would move back to the States at the beginning of the war. Not to draw a blank, I started telling her about that Roumanian bonbon of my Uncle Jimmy's, the sculptor Guitou Knoup.

Why Marcia paid any heed to this malarky beats me. Perhaps she did because even then she harbored her own painterly ambitions. Or because her exotic birth, reinforced by the furnishings her parents had brought back from their seven years in Roumania, had been the one flame sustaining her in the monotony of Summit, New Jersey.

Though we chatted that evening at some length, it was a month before I summoned the gumption to call her. Just after she slid into my Chevy wearing a red and yellow Mexican blouse, I, attempting to appear casual, sidescraped a parked car. As we started assessing the damage, the barriers dropped, and we found ourselves talking sincerely, intimately. The Europe that had everyone rolling their eyes was for her too a desired world. Hearing about Charlie Merrill and my Uncle Jimmy and the family novel he was writing, she seemed, to say the least, intrigued.

By the end of the evening I was in love, with an emotion different from anything I had ever known. Nothing in my experience had prepared me for the fierce blue directness of her eyes, the frecklings of her wit; for the way each remark burrowed in, something I had to repeat whether any roommate wanted to hear it or not. She was no mere mortal.

Marcia was a younger sister. Her older sister, coddled and protected as she had insisted on, had bloomed into Miss Suburban New Jersey. Marcia became the wildness she could not be, never happier than on some wind-blasted bluff, some Brontean moor. "My stormy petrel," her self-taught, Greek-reading mother called her, fondly throwing up her hands.

For Marcia, New Jersey was the equivalent of my Southampton. Except there was no ambiguity about the deadly smugness she had fled. The joy with which she found herself at Radcliffe could not have been more palpable. The wit of a shop window, the perceptions and bearing of a lecturer, the friends who shared her sense of possibility, all that burst from her, street by street, as we talked.

Marcia knew how to do things: cook, keep up a house, cut out, without so much as bothering to measure, an actress's costume; with a speed that took one's breath away—unless one happened to spot the uncertainty lingering under it. If, in a first rush, a water-color or a poem ignited, fine. If not, she put it aside and forgot it. To behold such self-conviction and see so little coming of it could be frustrating. But it made for a companion genuinely apprecia-tive of any opening I offered. Best of all, she was loyal. Embattled as I was, I needed an ally I could trust.

For the next several weeks Marcia was all I could think about and any time she granted I regarded as so much manna. For a while this attitude generated its own success. Marcia had never known a man to invite her out without naming the occasion and the time. This I refused to do. I didn't need to go anywhere, I just needed to see her. Before long I had so succeeded with this approach that I was mo-nopolizing her, prevailing over my rival paramours and her own studies. For what coursework can compete with a young woman's self-discovery, that flower-like body which would remain unknown but for another's mouth and fingers, his bee-like intuitions.

But there came a time when the classless post-Christmas "read-ing" period, that had allowed us to be with one another, came to an end, and we each withdrew to repair as best we could the two months' neglect. In this I was the more fortunate, as my exams fell late. But while I was cramming, Marcia found herself free to re-sume dating her other suitors.

I did not take to this any too well. My first meltdown occurred during a performance of Don Giovanni at the Boston Opera. Could it have been the green dingyness of the second balcony in which I was stranded? Or the way I identified with the rake—everything a grandson of Charlie Merrill could aspire to? But the picture of Marcia regaling herself with a determined rival, on top of the fe-male havoc that was befalling the Don on stage, had my nerves so jangling that I was up and gone long before the Stone Guest had made his final appearance.

A few days later I followed a friend's advice and took some dexedrine so that I could stay up the night before an exam. I had no particular desire to enter a cerebral fast lane. All I wanted was to reread Scumpeter's *Capitalism, Socialism and Democracy*. Scumpeter's apologia for Charlie Merrill's kind of entrepreneurial money-churning had done much to salve my conscience when I had encountered it, two years earlier, in my Exeter tutorial. Now, as I reread Scumpeter, his whole argument seemed indefensibly reactionary.

Then again, dexedrine may not suit a metabolism of my hummingbird order, one that needs to be slowed rather than stimulated. I remember next morning taking the exam in a pounding mental din that resembled an air-raid shelter during a major bombardment. When it was over, I walked on eggs, as it were, back to my room, seated myself at my desk, and proceeded to take down the automatic dictation of "The Wanton Current," the prose poem that convinced me I was a writer. Then I repaired to my bed, to wake some hours later in a pool of bodily sweat.

But my flipping out was perhaps no more mysterious than that of the next overly possessive man. Nor does it seem odd that any nervous disorder I might have had vanished when classes resumed and Marcia began favoring me once again with her undivided attention.

Marcia's kissing career had begun at fifteen when a steward on a cruise boat had told her she was beautiful and, reaching out, had taken in his hand her upturned face. "Please," she had exclaimed, beside herself with delight, "do that again." For hours afterwards she found herself traipsing about in a giddy daze. But in the pre-pill era, getting pregnant was frightening; especially to one who regarded her virginity as her sole dowry and wanted it bestowed on the man she would marry.

It may be wondered what Marcia saw in so callow a youth. I don't see how I could have figured in her eyes as more than a curiosity, the sort of "find" one might turn up on a hunting trip or a dig. To be sure, I had my patrician connections, a hint of prospective wealth I could not entirely disguise. And it must have pleased her to be charged with that head down, all-embracing minotaur intensity, while she stood feet firmly planted in the date arena, twirling her little red cape. Yet there was no telling what, as a man, I might amount to. I was merely another animal out there, and I assumed she was one too. That was, as she once remarked, the basis of our attraction, two sniffing dogs who had found one another.

Then it may be the anomaly of a person so unformed, hailing from my background, which appealed. To a suburban girl any animality could have an attraction. Even so, a wild animal remains a wild animal and, much as she might want to domesticate it, what finally could she do but release it to its native haunts?

Unlike most of her classmates, Marcia did not want the independence of a career, but the security of a marital situation. To that one end she had been raised. Whereas for me, just beginning my adult life, marriage could only be damming of the waters. Europe; my family; myself; that was my world. For Marcia, all those rivers finished in the delta of marriage. For me, the sea of women, island upon island stretching into the mists, was what I had been denied as a youth and therefore craved.

UNCLE JIMMY

"The Wanton Current," the piece that was to sweep me, while still at Harvard, into a writer's life was there in the wings, shuddering, about to burst. But what would cause it to burst forth? For the revelation I have only one person to thank or blame—my uncle,

Jimmy and Charlie Merrill, Merrill's Landing, Palm Beach, 1933

James Merrill. Sometimes I think he created me out of nothing—the Southampton vacuity, the dreams darting like dragonflies at my boy's feet.

Jimmy was Mother's twelve-year younger half-brother and Hellen's only child. In our family album there is a photograph of him, all of eleven, dressed in his Knickerbocker Grays uniform and holding me in my baby dress. Mother reports that he seemed to know instinctively just how to play with this almost two-year-old; something hardly surprising to one who had seen him with a dog or a cat, or for that matter any of my own children.

But a few months later Charlie plunged into their close and, I think, deeply sexual union the sword of divorce; a loss from which neither Hellen nor Jimmy ever recovered. (When his mother, Jimmy told me, learned of Charlie's intent, she had offered to retire into the background for as long as a year—whatever it took for his fires to cool. With great sadness Charlie turned her down. He could not bear, he said, to be with Kinta and suffer the guilt.)

But in the divorce proceedings self-regard took over, and the two provided the tabloids with a field day. When Hellen named two correspondents—Kinta and Dottie Stafford—Charlie trotted out a preposterous five. When he sought a quick Reno divorce, she socked him with an injunction. Not to be outdone, Charlie made Jimmy a pawn in a custodial battle with his "unfit mother." He even produced his own spy in the person of Mother's old nurse, Emma Brown, whom he had planted as a housekeeper in Jimmy and Hellen's tiny house on big, wide 57th Street.

The divorce, the product as it was of a willfulness so irrational, was the biggest event in Jimmy's life (as it had been in Mother's). And it broke him in two. At St. Bernard's his grades plunged to a row of F's, and, instead of going off to Lawrenceville, he had to repeat the year. In consolation he began to stuff himself. By the time he was sixteen he was a two-hundred-pound little whale. Jimmy took charge soon thereafter, but the damage was done. I remember him at thirty with his Tiresias-like breasts and the way his high-slung fleshy hips hung out over the bone.

I did not know Jimmy in his fat period. All I remember is the college kid walking with a borrowed lady's racket onto the tennis court at Merrill's Landing. Or, in our city library, defending Walt Whitman, "Prose poetry is so much more difficult to write than verse." But as a child I inherited his pictured, folio-sized, world stampbook. And one day, while rummaging about The Orchard playroom, I came upon his old butterfly net and his jars of mounting and paralyzing equipment. If I have been in some other existence a bird, Jimmy was just as definitely an insect.

Jimmy may not have known until he was twenty-two and offered a job teaching at Bard College that he was going to do anything but work at Merrill Lynch, but it is hard to conceive of a more thoroughgoing literary apprenticeship. Charlie brought out Jim's "Book" as a surprise sixteenth birthday present. One glance at the book, with its array of verse forms, its faultlessly rhymed translation of Baudelaire, and it's apparent that here was a poet born to sing in his chains. And one intent on doing a rare American thing—growing. By the time Jimmy embarked on his first novel, *The Seraglio*, he had read Henry James's *The Ambassadors* six times. One winter abroad was spent devouring all of Dickens, another Balzac. He kept a full diary. And what he was aiming at was clear—someone bigger than a mere poet. A Cocteau, an Oscar Wilde.

The consistency of Jimmy's progress with its summa degree, prizes and awards was such that, when he decided on a writing career, his father did not throw up his hands and bark out a thousand threats. Disappointed he may have been, but what counted was his son's welfare. Instead Charlie fired off missives to the editor of *Poetry*, to President Cole of Amherst and three of Jimmy's teachers there, asking what they thought of his son's succeeding in such a difficult career. Their responses were positive, and from then on he supported Jimmy unstintingly.

What Charlie privately felt is unknown, but Jimmy remembered watching a polo match with his father at Delray Beach, a sport new to both of them. It must not have been the most thrilling of matches for, at one point, Charlie put his arm around Jimmy and confided, "I'd rather have a poet as my son than a third-rate polo player."

My own acquaintance with Jimmy really began in 1950 when I was beginning my second year at Le Rosey. Jimmy had recently gone abroad for an indefinite stay, determined to make himself into A Different Person; a feat more easily accomplished where the Merrill name did not evoke stampeding bulls and Wall Street dollar signs. Jimmy happened to be in nearby Geneva one Saturday, attending the dying Dutch poet Hans von Lodeizen, when he found himself strapped for cash. Whom could he touch up for a quick loan? Why this nephew, around the lake at Rolle! For a fourteen-year-old to be projected into the role of family banker could not have been more delicious, and I remember racing off, heart in mouth, to withdraw my emergency traveler's checks (the ones that were to get me across the Pyrenees if the Russians attacked) from the school vault. On Jimmy's firm handshake the most charmed of friendships began.

Jimmy was living in Rome later that fall when I received permission to fly down to meet my grandfather who had arrived there from Naples the previous week. While there he was expecting an audience with the Pope. An opportunity, Charlie told me, to check out Father's tailors by commissioning for his audience a double-breasted white suit—worn with a gold tie-clip in the form of a dollar bill.

As a special treat my first night, Jimmy and Charlie took me to dinner at Alfredo's. Charlie was in the midst of a story as we were all tucking into the renowned fettucine—served with a solid gold fork and spoon by no less than the proprietor—when, suddenly turning scarlet, he dropped his head and coughed up his dental bridge into his plate. Was I witnessing the start of a heart attack? Reacting quickly, Jimmy paid the bill and in a taxi whisked us back to the Excelsior.

Hours later I was still shaken by what I had witnessed. "Is Grandpa going to live?" Jimmy remembered my asking as we sat in his room some hours later, dining off a tray on wheels.

"It's nothing serious, his doctor said, just an angina attack brought on by the traveling he's been doing. All he needs is some rest."

"How did you know how to react?" I asked, wanting to be prepared in case I was alone with my grandfather during a similar attack.

"I don't want you to think it's eerie," Jimmy said, rising to fetch a black binder. "But I have with me a novel I started a little while ago which opens with the very scene we just witnessed. Only the restaurant in my novel is in Manhattan. You might want to read it. But be careful, it's my only copy."

I still remember the pride with which I bore it away—a real manuscript! Of its five chapters, however, I only recall a scene describing an "Orfeo," with the black-tie opera crowd in their gilt boxes mirrored on the stage as Hell, which Jimmy was to salvage for *The Seraglio*.

As a writer Jimmy found himself early. But growing up in that little Versailles with the Man with the Golden Touch as his father could not have been easy. The unreality comes across in the title of his novel, *The Seraglio*, an Italian word for a Turkish harem. That's a measure of how alienated he felt.

The Seraglio may be too overwhelmed by the example of Henry James to be a good novel. But if any novel ever changed a life, that one did. Our family life, so driven, so illegible, was suddenly transparent. Anything everything, I now knew, could be memorialized. You just had to be a Jimmy.

At the hub of the novel is the vast wealth embodied by the divorced and sexually restored septuagenarian, Benjamin Tanning. Who will land the prize? Briskly, Jimmy lines up the concerned parties: on one side the ex-wives and candidate wives; on the other the business types led by my caricature of a father, Larry Buchanan.

As the novel opens, we learn of the stabbing of Mother's portrait. There are a number of likely suspects, but Jimmy's stand-in, Francis, opts for Mother's barely teen-age daughter, Lily: a way of underlining at whose expense the maneuvering is taking place; we, the nephews and nieces, to whom *The Seraglio* is dedicated. Will Francis somehow rescue us? Or will the novel's last scene, in which the grown-ups merrily consume the chocolate children ornamenting my brother Mark's first birthday cake, demonstrate that this is indeed a society that eats its children?

Before Francis can save us, however, he has to save himself from what his money, he thinks, has done to him. With this in mind he descends, as he did in real life, on my father to see if he can renounce his fortune. But Father turns Francis down, pointing out the unbreakable nature of his trust. That leaves Francis determined to do the next best thing—castrate himself. A marvelous stroke, not least because it looks as if he has attempted suicide. But it does reduce the remainder of the novel to a series of pageant-like scenes, in which Jimmy learns to negotiate his way in a new gay life.

I was not in *The Seraglio*. Freudian casting required an invented daughter to be blamed for the stabbing of Mother's portrait. But as a concerned spectator I could have my use.

How the scales dropped from my eyes as, one completed chapter after the next, I watched the imbroglio of my sixteenth summer unfold. For my parents sex was taboo. We children were not created out of animal need, but dynastic heirs sprung fully formed, or deformed, from Charlie's godhead. It was precisely this myth that *The Seraglio* sought to explode. For Jimmy, the curse of his growing up had been his father's uncontainable sexuality. And it would go on haunting him, he knew, so long as its inherited compulsions remained unidentified. In this a nephew could be helpful. We were both convinced that our understanding of our sexual imperative (read, of course, backwards, from our two vantages on the gay/straight divide) held the key to our development.

The motor of sexual need may not have drummed quite as loudly in Jimmy's breast as in Charlie's. But from the age of nineteen, a sexual subtext coated his every action—from the inflections of his speech to the hip-waggling shuffle with which he glided about. Jimmy could see beyond the dazzling surfaces of gay life, but barely, such was his absorption in the breaking out of a new sexuality in which he found himself delightedly participating. And what to others could seem a ghetto was for Jimmy a source of intense pride. Nor was he alone in this view. For much of the present century the artistic vanguard has been preeminently homosexual. They carried the flag for the rest of us. And the brio with which they pursued the adventure of identity, out at the cutting edge, made them our heroes.

As our friendship grew, Jimmy and David's house in the coastal village of Stonington became my refuge. For some, Jimmy's furnishings, on the upper floors of a converted clubhouse overlooking the harbor, could seem antisocial. "There's not a comfortable place to sit in the whole apartment," my mother once complained.

But if there wasn't much to sink into, there was plenty to marvel at. The walls of his tin-domed dining room were a lobster pink, the furniture lavender. Wherever I turned, from the street window with its clear pane surrounded by panes of orange, blue and red, to the prisms fastened to the casements, firing their rainbows over the dining table, to the scores of curios, totems, jewelled Buddhas, scrolls and folding screens, the little stones that on closer inspection turned out to be plants, everything reflected Jimmy, personae he would liberate in one or another poem. The visual oxygen his rooms gave off was such that I would come away feeling a new lightness, a new possibility. I floated. Nothing, it seemed, would ever bring me down.

The speaking surfaces formed the backdrop to Jimmy's conversation. Not that extracting it from someone as shy as he was then was easy. That's where his companion David Jackson's social talents, always wanting to know when I, or Marcia and I, would be returning, served him so well. While David poured and entertained—and I've known no funnier storyteller—Jimmy withdrew to that other lab of his, the kitchen. There, as colors simmered and sauteed, a conversation came into being of how a vocation might appear, seen from a decade further along the genetic turnpike.

For conversation to prosper you have to maintain a semblance of dialogue. My first lessons were spent in learning to talk to those raised eyebrows that steered, questioning, confirming, as I lurched along. What I said counted, to be sure. But equally important were the comparisons I employed to illustrate and expand what I was saying. "Give an example," Jimmy would interrupt, and, drawing in a breath—ah, the lure of revision!—I would reconstruct what I had said in view of a specific image, the more original the better.

Soon I was talking not in sentences, but images, the cadence slowed sufficiently so I could alter the image if I could see it was going to draw a querying eyebrow. Add, for emphasis, a certain verbal underlining, a recourse to the marvelously plastic pronominal "one" (to deflect any need for mere sincerity—if you can't speculate, why talk?), and there were the makings of a scene in a cameo theater. It was that theatrical quality and the prismatic cadences of his voice, dropping into a sibylline tone as a metrical line flashed, that made Jimmy the best conversationalist since Oscar Wilde. I can still quote him at will, on virtually anything.

Because Jimmy seemed to know who we each were in our secret self, it was, as Richard Howard once confided, to him we turned when we needed advice on his real specialty—the art of living. On our behalf he was always trying out the latest fad: a vitamin program; a meditation technique; a mouthwash or toothpaste; a pyramid box in which to revive spent razor blades. Or trying to get me to switch from revising with scissors and Scotch tape to a laptop—how he wished he had had one while rewriting the last book of *Sandover*.

His own presence was remarkably unified. I don't think anyone meeting him for more than a few minutes doubted before whom he stood. If he did, there was his Volkswagen license plate proclaiming it, POET. Nature was not only to be dug in, or looked at, it was also to be worn. I remember once, strolling in Kew, his remarking of a Chinese birch, "Wouldn't you die to have a shirt of that green bark!" His own taste in color ran to the hot end of the spectrum: Uncle Zinnia gliding along in his Birkenstock sandals, apricot shirt and pink pants, with that look that never left him of a precocious youth.

Jimmy loved writing. "If you don't enjoy it," I remember him remarking the last Christmas we spent together, his voice rising with incredulity, "why do it?" And the joy he took in it must have made him feel that it could be for me, too, a solution. As he put it, "Anyone who can talk, can write after a fashion."

It was not as if the wish hadn't crossed my nineteen-year-old mind. I remember the previous summer thinking, as I walked everywhere with Ellison's *Invisible Man*, what I would give to write something as compelling. But other than a satire at eleven, imagining a Wallace presidential victory, I'd never written anything I liked. What was I to cut my teeth on—poetry? "But I don't like poetry," I remember telling Jimmy when he brought it up one day that fall.

"I didn't either," Jimmy replied, taking a leaf from Marianne Moore, "before I began to write it. But verse does allow one to work on a smaller scale than prose. One is not compelled to know as much. It's not so much a whole milieu one is bringing into being as the world of an obsession, a desire. Anyway, whatever you write, I promise I'll read."

With Jimmy encouraging me, and my need to find an escape from Father's threatened incarceration, the chance of a breakthrough must have been fairly good. All I needed was a catalyst. It was this the dexedrine provided in the middle of my second year at Harvard.

THE WANTON CURRENT

I was nineteen, I had been cramming for exams and hadn't been to bed in forty hours, and I was worried about losing Marcia to a rival. I had just regained my room after taking a final exam when I found myself writing:

> A naked mariner pitches on the bobbling pillow, then rolls over, awake. With eyes see-sawing he raises up supple beings, summoning them forth from eider depths to share the vulgar lot. An iceberg discloses itself. Maidenlike it floats, proof to the wanton current that thrashes about its submerged parts. Slowly then, the iceberg begins to melt— compelled, like the mariner, to contemplate a dissolution.

In the midst of this masturbatory celebration appear voices, parental:

> "Where are Tino's pajamas?"
> "In the wash, dear. I hope he won't catch a cold."
> "The boy can't go to bed like that. It's indecent. What if Boopsy should come?"
> At the sound of the proper name an eyelid quivers. The Contessa. As it quivers, a summer afternoon unfolds, the

afternoon she first heaves in sight, broad as a barge, breasts tossing in the direction of the drowsing mariner.

A bourgeois member responds, beckoning. The Contessa vacillates, swaying like a door waiting for its hinges to slip, or rust away. Then she swings alongside and, after a decent interval, ties up.

The yellow tide advances, swelling in ever-widening stains across the pillow's wrinkled surface.

This expiation which had popped out of nowhere, or almost nowhere—there is a touch or two of Firbank—utterly took me over. During the next weeks, like a child with a picture puzzle, I must have rewritten the first paragraph a hundred times. Just to learn what it was that had befallen me. But I also had to try to expand on it, borrowing the stuff about mat-riding from my Joyce paper and inventing a scene between the child and the provocative mother set in something like the sands of the Southampton Beach Club. The climax occurs, later the same evening, when the two arrive for a formal dance at the same club:

They descend at midnight at The Club where the party is still bubbling on. The mariner leaves her, propped at the bar, and begins to circle the flooded dance floor, wading past the paddling couples to where a woman in pink organdy stands smiling, her face done up in flames. The mariner holds her taut as he can and they dance, throbbing through the crowd like two shadows come together to make light. Then she is at his arm, tugging. "Tino, have you forgotten all you ever learned in dancing school? This is a waltz. Now count after me: ah-one, two, three; ah-one, two, three."

Walter cuts in.

And the mariner falls in with a conga line swishing toward the latrines where the men all stand, four deep, waiting their turn in the rain.

When at last the mariner comes out, he hears his name being called and, turning round, catches sight of his pink mamina surrounded by the twelve extra men of the ball. He pushes his way through the ring and demands the dance, making her spin in tighter and tighter circles until she can stand it no longer and topples over in a dead faint.

Kneeling over her with a damp rag, the mariner gently washes her face. Coming to, she starts to curse. She curses long and loud and she is still cursing when the waiters lead her outside.

When he wakes several hours later, it's with his head jammed in the toilet.

That morning the mariner floated out with the tide.

The mother is someone very much like the ghost of a Noh play. In making her reveal herself as she dances, the child mariner has succeeded in exorcising her. Yet "The Wanton Current" remains, as my teacher, John Hawkes, pointed out when I showed it to him a year later, incomplete. If the Contessa is the father's mistress, who is the father (a mere disembodied voice in the story)? That I had no way of entering that chunk of equally forbidden territory has, I believe, much to do with my subsequent inability to write fiction. I was too panic driven to be able to plot out a story, let alone work from a general outline. Instead I would have to make do with whatever the involuntary current hurled up on my banks.

But for me "The Wanton Current" was a revelation. It was as if everything I had been up to that moment had been magically re-figured. Where before all I could see was a dark imprisoning family pit, there was this glimmer of a path climbing to light and possible freedom. Blind to everything but my new compelling necessity, I put my head down and paddled. I was, indeed I had to be, that naked mariner.

To that drumbeat my student life now marched. There was so much about aesthetics, prosody, poetry, I had to learn and learn quickly. And most of it I had to do on my own. It was perhaps too much to expect a history-driven university like Harvard to offer the crash course in the moderns that I needed. (It was not a traditional poet like Jimmy I wanted to be, but a modern one with a capital P.) But if courses did not offer what I needed, there was the periodical room, where I pored over the little mags. And I combed the

Widener stacks for iceberg poems, John Simon's prose poetry dissertation, anything that might propel "The Wanton Current." I even enrolled in John Hawkes's beginning writing course in the naive belief it might give me time to polish my eight hundred word gem.

Poetry has always been, as the Berkeley anthropologist Bruce Berlin once admitted to me, a way of "fucking up language." Like others, the poet is trying to get away with expressing something— the otherwise forbidden—only in his case he is doing it word by word and even letter by letter. It may not even matter how one goes about it, as long as one goes far enough. "It's not the precious," I remember Jimmy insisting, "but the semi-precious one has to resist."

Parachuting as I did into poetry of a sort, it behooved me to locate a central core. Image, metaphor, any New Critic would have insisted. But images come outfitted in quite a number of diction or sound choices and the "force that through the green fuse drives the flower" struck me as patently rhythmical. A poet differed from others in that he "heard" experience and it was the auditory memory that unleashed the containing words. It was a magician of sound I wanted to be, "through the green fuse" driving my flower.

A somewhat constricted point of view. "Do you write sonnets?" Jimmy's Amherst thesis advisor, Reuben Brower, innocently asked when I handed him some free verse experiments. Brower went on, "I don't see how anyone can call himself a poet if he doesn't tackle the sonnet form. How else can one grow without a form that allows one to correct one's mistakes by repeating oneself?"

But if any writing teacher had insisted on my composing a sonnet, I'd probably have chucked the course then and there. It was not the sonnet's ticking box that fascinated me, but something more akin to what as a child I had known out on my mat waiting, endlessly waiting, for a wave terrifying enough to ride. To me, space was freedom: to become the female sea, the fathering blades of the waves, whatever survival required. That may be why I responded to Freud's image of the mind as an iceberg. If nine-tenths lay beneath the conscious surface, wasn't more to be gained by diving down and exploring the uncharted depths?

The question, for both of us, was fundamental. The unconscious, Jimmy pointed out, exists to throw its lights onto the waking surface and it's there, and there only, we apprehend them. Appearances, viewed correctly, are reality.

"What about history?" I argued, "doesn't that make us what we are?"

"Not history," Jimmy replied, "but one's history." To him poetry was self-expression, an act of conscious subjugation. Whereas for me, it was the unknown self that the words gave rise to, the hope of transforming myself, that drove me. And what held for words, held also for places, people. As Rimbaud put it, "I is another."

Jimmy understood everything that was to be known about time, music, meters. (Before thinking of himself as a poet, he had wanted to be a composer, and the novelist Frederick Buechner, his roommate at Lawrenceville, remembers him rolling his trousers up over his knees so he could better resemble the child Mozart). But space rather eluded him, and he thought it eluded me too. "Try to find some other word," as if this were a crutch one could overuse. His way out in his poetry was to reduce it: a prism or jewel viewed under a loupe; a blank distanced by a fire-screen, a crocheted curtain. You were aware of the intervening pattern, not of anything on the other side.

In his house the colored panes let in light, they did not refract a view. For that you went to the roof. His office was a reconverted closet. Wasn't the point, he said, not to look out, but inwards? Even his outdoor scenes were versions of that same Inner Room, like the subterranean Blue Grotto. When struck with an impasse in his writing, he repaired not to the sandbox of a garden or a bicycle, but to his piano and the dream of other voices—Handel's, Mozart's—running their particular fingers over the far corners of his skin, one hand guiding the other.

Yet Jimmy's commitment to me never swayed. Whenever in my verbal dives I came up helplessly foundering, he was there, lifeline in hand. With other's revisions I've often felt that something precious had been stolen; the poem, however improved, was no longer mine. Whereas Jimmy's suggestions fortified. Even when they didn't resolve the immediate dilemma, they pointed to issues, of wording, of viewpoint, I'd be facing some months down the road. One distich, a koan of everything I thought I aspired to, once read:

> The green dream of things
> Springing into the force of shadows.

"Why not through the force of shadows?" Jimmy suggested.

"That's not what I mean!" I objected, aghast.

"Yes it is, only 'through' makes them see it."

The advice registered all the more in that Jimmy seemed always to know exactly where I stood in my projected self-transformation. While I set a tempo, Jimmy did his best to make sure that I rounded my cape, reached my next port; that my boundaries were, in short, respected. Yet I was firmly guided. "You can't go to a deb party!" I remember him exclaiming when I produced an invitation, sorely tempted. "You've made a choice and you've got to stick to it. You're a writer, not a socialite." If I didn't in this case agree—what better arena did I command than that social dance floor?—his line of reasoning was clear. To feel committed, I had to make sacrifices.

There was no friend I loved more. I don't know what scruple kept me from moving where I could visit him every day; or, as almost happened one night in Stonington, of overcoming my squeamishness or whatever barrier it was—are sexual boundaries that innate?—and discovering what that most tender of arms had to offer.

All the same I knew moments of rebellion. For the apprentice, the master incarnates the truth. But it is his truth, that of the work he is intent on bringing forth; a truth that resonates all the more powerfully in that, for the apprentice, the man and the writer are one and the same. For it was not so much a lesson in craft I was receiving, as one in readying myself, for the moment of vision that might befall me.

The danger arose in that the Jimmy I was taking in remained a foreign antibody. That's why, time and again, I have struggled to reduce a larger-than-life presence to the mere flame I needed.

For Jimmy any such weaning carried a ring of desertion. In his battle to change the world he needed every ally he could muster. I didn't mind taking up an outrider's flanking role to his advancing gay phalanx. I did mind being jerked about on a puppet's string. But most of the time my strands were so consummately woven I hardly knew I was his. The exclusivity of a priestly art-circle never attracted me. But what about the mandarin tone I affected? Wherever I turned, I was enmeshed.

CALIBAN AND THE TEMPESTUOUS ARTISTS

If the making of art, as Jimmy proclaimed, requires a distinct adaptation, it behooved me to meet those living it. Of all the works he owned, he was most proud of an enormous Water Mill landscape by Larry Rivers: cows, grass and clouds rendered with the freshness of an ex-jazz musician from the Bronx discovering the countryside for the first time.

Jimmy then longed to write the way Larry painted: the same big format, the same bravura mixture of outrageous self-revelation and historical parody, the same speed of hand and colloquial exuberance. And he insisted that I meet him. "Larry lives right behind Southampton High School. I know he'd welcome seeing you."

I happened to be in Southampton in the dead of March for a legal matter when I decided, late one afternoon, to call on Larry.

"You must be Jimmy's nephew," Larry remarked, fixing me with a falcon-eyed scrutiny as he opened the door. "There's a definite resemblance." When I admitted as much, he invited me in, introduced me to his family and made me stay for dinner. By the end of the evening we were friends. Larry's became a second home where I could drop in any time. And the house became a passport to a circle of poets: Frank O'Hara, Kenneth Koch, John Ashbery and Jimmy Schuyler (who inclined more to the other Southampton painter, Fairfield Porter). For conversation there were the duo-pianists, Bobby Fizdale and Arthur Gold, who I saw every day at the beach and who brought me into a milieu of composers: Samuel

Barber, Vittorio Rieti, Alexei Haieff. For all of us painting was the preeminent twentieth century art form. In Larry we had a standard bearer with no qualms about letting his life be the basis of what astonished and elated.

Larry could not conceive of doing art except in commercial terms, as a way of making a living. The factory aspect of getting himself "up to the wall" every morning he genuinely loathed. It was only his pride, "If Rauschenberg can do it, so can I," or the pressure of a show, that got Larry painting. I had hoped the $32,000 he had won on Charles Van Doren's fixed quiz show would allow him to paint for himself. But that was not, as Larry explained, the reality of America. "To do pure art I'd have to move abroad. An American artist has no choice but to fight back."

I failed to understand that for Larry, as for Father, the point of competing lay in finding out how far up the ladder he could climb. Enough was never enough, there was always a rung more. That may be why he was always asking about Father, wanting to meet him at our house. "It's the zoogoer in me," Larry explained. The curiosity wasn't returned. Father always singled out Larry as that "kike friend of yours."

It was the instantaneous quality of Larry's art that impressed. In this connection I remember his remarking of Tennessee Williams' "The Night of the Iguana," "Once you step out of the theater, it's hard to remember what you've seen. But in there it's electrifying, just as great jazz is." It was that jazz-like theatricality Larry brought to his big shocking paintings, thinning out the pigment until it was so transparent that the preliminary drawing, the charcoal marks and erasures, became as much a part of what I was seeing as the half-complete image itself.

My horizons expanded the next summer when I met Jimmy's close friend and Larry's dealer, John Myers, a former editor of the surrealist little mag, *View*. John had taken a house in Southampton despite being unable to drive. But Southampton was not Venice and I found myself pressed into service as the chauffeur of that "tracker of the marvelous." A number of John's Tibor de Nagy gallery summered nearby. With John's social appetite, the scene extended into a veritable pantheon of the art royalty of New York who, for reasons obscure, had suddenly blown onto my native isle.

I must say I enjoyed playing Caliban to their shipwrecked Tempest crew. That I now despised Southampton did not keep me from taking them to the best beaches, showing them where to obtain oysters and lobsters, and having Leroy serve them daiquiris at the Beach House pool. As for the drunken Trinculos, they too were to be found, helplessly prostrate at dawn in the back seat of my Bel Air, doing their best to vomit gracefully into the ashtray.

The dereliction owed much to the deceased genius loci, Jackson Pollock. If he could drink, dance and generally spatter his way into immortal oblivion, why couldn't they? Like Pollock, their focus was the Whitmanian self. A painter was his gestures, his private Morse of colored dots and dashes. And courage was everything. This celebration of one's instinctual self couldn't have been more Fifties. But the painters brought to the daily adventure a revolutionary fervor, as if it were life itself that, with each stroke, they were changing. And it was clear how fulfilling they found their instantaneous medium. "You don't paint—why you must!" At party after party that's what I heard, urged with such warmth, such insistence. For this interloper the parties may have provided a welcome escape from the Southampton life. But for Larry and Fairfield, they were something more than a social scene. In a much needed sense they were family, an expression of bohemian solidarity.

FATHER DROPS THE SHOE

If my parents were upset by the art crowd I was frequenting in Southampton, they were even more upset by the letters I was writing from Harvard in which I attempted to share with them the thoughts, the emotions, the whole exam-time turmoil that had unleashed the little flood of "The Wanton Current."

"What have we said or done," Father wrote back, "to merit such treatment?" After explaining the shock with which the two of them had read my letters, he proceeded to drum home the social verities as he saw them. "The very basis of a collective society," he wrote, "is conformity. This applies to manners as well as morals and it includes deportment . . . I have little interest in the intellectual world, or in people who claim to be intellectuals. I hope, personally, that none of your brothers will ever want to take a course in modern poetry." Some six pages later he concluded, "I think it is very nice to get such good marks at Harvard, but I can tell you this Robin: I'd rather they be C's and D's and have you healthy and cheerful in the examination room than to 'lose control of my voice, and part of my body . . . perspiring madly, face half-drunk' etc.—your quotes. I'd like to see the expression on your face if somebody were to read to you those last two morbid letters ten years from now! I hope you'll resume communication with us—in simple English—soon."

If the truth lines were now permanently shut, I could have my reasons for feeding them their pablum. The previous summer Father had found me a job in Merrill Lynch's research department, drawing graphs for a chartist researching the turns in a stock's buying volume: the moments of frenzy; the swarming sharks. Now I wanted to see something of the America I had been studying, but had never experienced. Could Father tailor me a job at Safeway to this end?

A rub of the fingers and presto I had a market research job evaluating store sites in a variety of places: Astoria, Oregon, where, entranced by an article in the Sunday paper as I drove, I careened into a parked station wagon; tawdry Venice Beach where, swimming without a board, or fins, I almost drowned trying to dive the placid rollers. In Oklahoma City I stood at the bar with a pile of salt on the back of my hand, talking to a succession of wastrels undone by Los Angeles and that pair of blue eyes. Everywhere as I drove my quarter sections, the rainbow-bright wives stood waiting in the lights of a front lawn, a hose in hand.

My reconciliation with Father failed to survive our first weekend in Seattle. From then on, I traveled on my own. But by the end of summer I had become sufficiently absorbed that I was dreaming about Safeway most nights. But to any suggestion of mine—to hire, say, women executives—I now knew there would be Father's "over my dead body!" There was no way I could win.

Among the remarks given at my leaving my two-month Safeway career, I remember my desk-mate's "I hope you get to do what you want." That he couldn't name the activity—writing—shows how doubtful it must have looked.

Back at Harvard in the autumn I became, at Jimmy's insistence, a psychiatrist's patient. He had become alarmed, he wrote his brother Charles, by my haggard looks and the two bouts of nervous disorder that preceded "The Wanton Current." Yet it was not what I was doing to myself that troubled him, but what I might be inadvertently inflicting on Marcia, or any future loved one. "If you assume," he wrote, "as I did at 19 and even at 24, that a satisfactory, steady sex-life would be the answer to every emotional problem, the chances are you will run the risk of hurting a lot of people and getting yourself into a deeper rut. The point of the analyst, I need only remind you, is that he infinitely absorbs your fantasies and isn't hurt; that he isn't hurt means that you are not, and, in a curious way, a habit is broken."

Jimmy's letter ended with an appeal to the Delphic maxim. "My real argument is: you are so knowing, how can you resist knowing more?"

With Marcia whole-heartedly committed to me, and with much of my career anxiety resolved, I didn't see my problems in such a drastic light. As far as I was concerned, the two episodes were just that—blips. But I was willing to give Jimmy's suggestion a try. What did I have to lose?

My parents, perhaps because they were paying, were less than convinced. They viewed psychiatry as a direct affront to their authority. Nonetheless, they contacted Charlie Merrill's heart specialist, Sam Levine, who found me a proper Central European psychiatrist from the Harvard Medical School.

Three times a week I now sat before this small, silent, forever scribbling, bald-headed doctor. So as not to have to respond, I see now. But it could, and indeed did, look as if he were gathering evidence. About my sexual leanings—straight, bent, or a monstrous new indeterminacy? And about the rightness of a vocation I had so desperately grabbed. Judge me, I implored him, tell me I'm the man I want to be—healthy, normal, and despite all that, a natural writer.

From the start any transference was marred by the physical aversion I bore to my judge. The feelings emerged in a dream at the end of our first week. I found myself being swept up in the night waters of the Seine. But it's not so much the embankment walls, the stone bridges I was bobbing under I remember as the scary limpidity of the water beneath me. I passed over, first, a reef of vengeful beaver tails (the frontier cap favored by Senator Estes Kefauver), then some middle-European bowler hats.

By then the Seine itself had disappeared in a long underground sewer and I was growing tired and more and more anxious. Where, how, was I ever going to emerge? Finally my hopes rose as, at the end of the tunnel-sewer, I saw a gleam of daylight beckoning. But as I beached on the concrete embankment, so exhausted I had to drag myself forward on my arms, there came ambling belligerently towards me a very large muskrat—the guardian of the sewer and all those hats. I awoke screaming. Yet it wasn't until six months later I identified the muskrat with my psychiatrist, whose bald noggin and deeply set brown eyes recalled the animal I used to come upon browsing beneath our lakeside willow tree. With that, the psychiatry was effectively terminated.

The Muskrat, in good Freudian fashion, kept his lips resolutely sealed, preferring to let me stumble on my own conclusions. Only when I'd get overly riled at the maddening futility of these exercises in pseudo-sincerity, would he bestir himself. It was only when I wasn't telling the truth, he pointed out, that I stammered. On another occasion he had me reinvent the dream I couldn't remember. There's no difference, I asked, between a waking invention and a dream? That's right, he answered, your mind exists to serve you, it has your continuing survival as its mission. In later years I've had occasion to look askance at the promptings of my body. But I've never doubted the messages culled from my subconscious.

The psychiatry failed because of my personal antipathy, but more, I think, because I had no reason to be in analysis and thus nothing at stake. For The Muskrat, though, it must have been frustrating to have to minister to a patient more concerned with the figures of speech, the imagery he was bringing forth, than "the truth." That's why he focused on my dreams—one reality I couldn't doctor.

If The Muskrat would not pronounce me a writer, then it was up to me. For the summer of our junior year, Marcia had secured a job in Cambridge. Not anticipating my father's reaction, I decided to sublease an apartment there as well and try to write a novel.

Given the issues at stake, not least that of Father's authority, my challenge had to be squashed. What, Father asked, was I intending to write—not another tell-all family novel like *The Seraglio*! (Mother was so upset by it, its betrayals as she saw them, that she did not speak to her brother for two years. Whereas Father, for all his citing of it, never read it.)

Faced now with this unintended rebellion of mine Father reacted by turning off what he called "the money tap," convinced that he had me stopped in my tracks. "This," he wrote, "is a direct declaration that I will not finance any adventures that do not meet with my approval. And if I don't pay for them, I don't know who else will—with the possible exception of one of your uncles. If they do that, they risk an estrangement from which I think they would shrink."

On my home Cambridge turf I was not to be budged—not with Marcia radiating courage—and at the last minute Father backed down, restoring my allowance. Why not let me discover what little aptitude I had for such a daunting profession?

Of course Father was right. I had begun a novel on Le Rosey, counting on the exoticism to carry me through. Needless to say, the novel never progressed beyond an endlessly retyped seven pages. And all that staring at the wall poisoned the idyll that Cambridge had been until then.

E N G A G E D

For Christmas of senior year my parents took us brothers skiing in the Austrian Tyrol. I had expected, after graduating, to take Marcia abroad and have her experience the Europe that had bewitched me. Not possible, Marcia explained, not without breaking her father's heart. Nor could she go on living with me in, say, a shared apartment. That left me in a quandary. I didn't want to get married and restrict my exploration of the female sex to my first woman. Yet neither did I want to give Marcia up.

I missed her while in Austria and wrote resolving to not let us be separated ever again. Was this a declaration of a kind? At any rate Marcia, when I saw her in New York, must have interpreted a new seriousness in my manner. When I put my arms around her in the elevator of my family's 69th Street house, she not only offered no resistance, but brought me into her bed.

I must have enjoyed our sex because next morning, even though I had no job prospect, or any identifiable income, I proposed. And a few days later I bought her a topaz engagement ring—because it went so well with her complexion. Selfishness, or rather plain stupidity, an inability to envision a life in separate apartments, had hooked me.

As might be expected, my parents did not welcome my news of an engagement to a fiancée who possessed neither wealth nor the right poise and glamorous looks, and who came from New Jersey. But there must be few parents who would not have tried to dissuade a twenty-one year-old from marrying the first woman he had bedded.

Why, Father asked, if I had to get married, couldn't I be marrying someone he knew, a Liz Mellon, a Cindy Rockefeller? Whereas Mother felt I was too inexperienced to know what I required in a wife. "How can you be getting married," she asked sensibly, "when you've no money of your own and no prospective employment? Besides, when you went away to college, you promised you wouldn't think of getting married until you were twenty-eight. What's your word worth?"

Mother's notion of a promise wasn't mine. But she was right about my not looking beyond my immediate convenience—why cut short an affair before it has fully blossomed?

For the good reason, she might have replied, could we have talked frankly, that a marriage was not an affair. A husband is civilly and legally responsible. Did I really want a lifetime's alimony hanging about my neck?

I was, I think, open to persuasion. But only to an argument pitched to the one choice that mattered—my becoming a writer. But to my father, a writer's career was anathema, far worse than any prospective marriage. By marrying, at least I was being socialized. And there was a good chance that the pressures of an expanded life style would teach me my responsibilities—to my parents and my brothers. If no serious writer, other than Jimmy, had ever darkened his door, there were reasons. It wasn't merely the life style and general bohemianism of the art crowd I was frequenting in Southampton that put him off. Rather, it was the different way a writer viewed and played the game of life.

Father's way was to keep his cards, marked and unmarked, close to his chest. And to play as if his very existence were at stake. "Challenge my card and you're challenging me." It was by constantly raising the emotional stakes that he won. Whereas the writer, in attempting to create a more open society, has no choice but to expose the nature of the deck the businessman is playing with (whose money? whose future?) and call his bluff.

In this clash of views there was, for Father, no room for a compromise. Rather, the wings that Jimmy had given me were to be stripped from my back. Upon hearing of my engagement he had written, "Your personal problem, i.e., marriage, is complicated by your desire to be a writer. I would give anything to think you have a talent in that direction, but I would not be a good father and a good friend if I said something that was not in accord with my belief. There are people with a facility of expression who are natural writers, and I just don't believe you are that kind of person. I thought at one time that you could have fun and satisfaction out of teaching, but here again I think there are limitations. A teacher has to be above all things articulate, and you do have some defects in that quarter."

Going on, Father concluded, "In summary then, there are funds in trust for you to get an even larger allowance than you are getting now. But I have the disposition of those funds. I do not want to be tough and arbitrary, but I do want to try and exert my influence so that the best in you will come out. I do NOT want another Jimmy on the family blotter."

In his efforts to dissuade me from my choice, Father commanded some persuasive allies. I remember my godfather, Jack Straus, confiding to me over a lunch all by ourselves in the great boardroom on Macy's top floor how at my age he had been himself discouraged from pursuing a career as a jazz pianist. That did not keep him from playing whenever he had an occasion. He just wasn't making an ass of himself pretending he was another Earl Hines.

To me, writing wasn't the hobby jazz was to my godfather. Instead it was my one window to liberation and self-knowledge. In the circumstances, all of Jack Straus's talk of the usefulness of his chains, of the good that, as head of Macy's, he had brought about, was not to deter me. To be myself, I told him, I had to get free. And, since writing was the one pair of wings I had found, what choice did I have but to see how far they would take me?

In June, 1958, with a rousing cheer, "No more classes!" I graduated from Harvard, cum laude, if in the lower half of my class. Marcia and I were to be married in September. Enough time to make a trip I could try to write about. To where—Hollywood? No, Haiti, the country of voodoo and possession. Why couldn't I too learn how to be that Emersonian poet, "balked and dumb, stuttering and stammering, hissed and hooted?"

Lack of funds had much to do with my choice. My allowance had ceased upon graduation, one way of underlining who Marcia was marrying, me and not them. With some $500 put aside there was only so far I could venture.

When I told my cousins, Merrill and Alicia Matzinger, of my plans, they insisted on my making a ten-day detour to Cuba. They wouldn't be there, but I could stay in their house, and they would see that their friends showed me the renowned sights.

Under normal conditions, it would be hard to imagine a surer way of not seeing anything. And there were moments in their beautifully crafted home, sweating in my sheets and unable to pry open a window, or paddling about under the eyes of a troop of circling vultures in their frangipani-strewn swimming pool, when I felt trapped in another goldfish bowl.

But then those weren't normal conditions. A clandestine war was being waged that would end, eight months later, in Fidel Castro's capture of Havana. I saw what Castro was up against my first night when the Merrill Lynch branch manager (a former OSS agent who had gotten into the business by running a dummy Merrill Lynch office in Santiago, Chile, during the war) took me to his Mafia pal Trafficante's casino. Deputized to show me around the brothels for a couple of nights was one of his salesmen, a warm, highly educated man of the left. He would be shot in the bloodbath that followed Castro's takeover. And on the urban guerrilla side, there was the ethnological museum curator I met while trying to learn about Bembe, whose lover had been killed in Fidel's failed July twenty-second raid on Batista's palace. The day I saw her she had just witnessed the execution of another of her comrades. Solzhenitsyn remarked that a revolution was not something he'd wish on his worst enemy. From the little I saw, I would agree.

The Black Republic, too, opened my eyes. True, the mere sight of a colored person did not send me, as a small child, into a screaming fit, as it did my brother Mark. But neither my grandfather's servants—they were family to him, not me—nor the few black people I had encountered at school, had done anything to lessen the profound alienation, not to say guilt, I felt.

It helped that early on I was befriended by a painter my age, Hervé Télémaque, who would soon become Europe's most reputed pop painter. In America, I was stymied always before an African American, because I couldn't discuss the different perspective skin color gives; to do so would seem patronizing. With this African-featured mulatto I could. Color—paint, politics, sexual skin tones—was his cross, his heritage. As Hervé questioned me about what I had seen that day and the inferences to be drawn, for the first time I felt part of the range and diversity of the global spectrum. Maybe this is something any French-educated intellectual can impart, as easily as he chews his croissant. But it was different from any milieu I knew where conversations rarely advanced beyond the uneasy staking out of a common ground.

I travelled all over Haiti and, with Hervé's help, I saw a lot. But in a country whose flag is the French tricolor with the white band ripped out, a white kid—that burnt marshmallow of the tropics—could not help but feel like an intruder. And the glare of so many diseased eyes, full of such wretchedness, such undisguised hatred, did not make for congenial traveling. Meanwhile from the other end of my life, Marcia was bombarding me with almost daily, "I miss you, why don't you come home if you're not enjoying yourself?" letters. By now, after five weeks on the road, I was prepared to see her point. And I wrote telling her I'd be back on the first of August.

RUMPELSTILTSKIN'S TRAP

I took a week off to fly to Jamaica and check out the calypso equivalent of Storyville before the Navy closed it down—Milneburg Joys, Marmalade Rag. Their effect was such that the highly tanned youth with the crimson-flowered shirt and unwipable grin who stepped off the plane into Marcia's arms was a considerably different minotaur from the one who had written her from Haiti ten days earlier.

In Summit, I found the wedding preparations well advanced. Marcia had wanted a small wedding—good friends only. But she was overruled by the two mothers, and we found ourselves saddled with a platoon of ushers and bridesmaids, along with a reception for two hundred and fifty, half of them social and business acquaintances of my parents.

But though my parents were putting their shoulders to the bridal wheel, they had by no means capitulated. Marcia suspected that this Rumpelstiltskin, as she saw my little father, forever about to explode through a hole in the floor, could still play us a nasty trick. That he hadn't as yet tried to buy her off bewildered her. Surely she had a price! But so far he had done nothing other than to try to buy time by having me apply to Oxford (a gambit that worked more successfully in delaying Peter and Mark from marrying their Jewish fiancees.) But at the time the machinery for landing a Magowan in one of the lesser colleges still needed oiling. The future Knight's emissaries could not overcome the damning evidence of my grades and my unwillingness to fly over, as my brothers did, for a personal interview.

But Marcia was right in her suspicions. My father did have a plan. Upon my return from the Caribbean, he voiced his amazement that, in my fundless state, I had chosen to visit Marcia and her family rather than avail myself of the "free grub and booze" of Southampton. But, with the wedding less than a month away, a duty visit could not be staved off. I agreed to meet Father in his Wall Street office and then drive with Mother down to Southampton.

I found Father dressed in one of Charlie Merrill's silk ties and a London-tailored, pin-striped blue suit and seated behind a large mahogany desk bursting with family pictures: of the five of us brothers, a team in identical shorts and sweaters, looking up from the grass of the Beach House lawn; of Mother regal in her Brockhurst portrait; of Charlie in double-breasted serge and clutching as always a half-spent cigarette. Beyond my father, two corner windows gave on the harbor, forty flights below.

I took up the chair across from him. "What's up?" I asked.

"Your marriage," Father replied. He went on, "I wish I could tell you the number of people I know who show bright promise as young men and who are semi-failures today because of mistakes they made at the outset. One of those mistakes—and a frequent one," he added, looking straight at me, "was a too early marriage. The very necessity of taking care of a wife and children handicapped the man in making important decisions. He couldn't afford to take a new job to advance his career—perhaps at a lower salary—because he couldn't afford to reduce his family's eating money."

Scratch the threats, the enticements, the leaves out of Thomas Hardy, and there remained his all powerful narcotic—money. "I don't know what plans you and Marcia have made to support yourselves. But if you think you can survive by climbing on my back, you've got another thought coming. When a family lives the way ours does, there's an obvious assumption there's money around. But your mother and I can give it all away, just as Grandpa did. We won't, I assure you, but it's our right."

"You act," I protested, "as if I don't have a penny."

"Well, you don't," he said, looking me straight in the eye.

"What about the portfolio I've heard so much about, the great stocks you've bought. Whose funds are they," I asked, pausing as I looked back at him, "mine or yours? Or is it all another tax scam?"

"Your trust fund exists, but since the money derives from me I can decide when and if you get it. The last thing your mother and I want," he said, fixing me with his small piercing eyes, "is to deprive you of your ambition—the will, the need, to make a buck of your own."

"What about changing life itself by changing people's sensibilities?" I countered. "That's what Uncle Jimmy's about and Grandpa saw no reason not to support him when he made poetry his career."

Father was not about to see our two situations as remotely comparable. "There is much about Jimmy I don't approve of. But at your age he had already accomplished a great deal. What proof do you have that you possess anything like his talent?"

Father had me there. But then comets of Jimmy's precise brilliance do not blaze through the firmament that often. (The last was Alexander Pope.) Instead, I tried to express the encouragement Jimmy radiated, his belief that I had it in me to be a good writer.

"Doesn't Jimmy's opinion," I replied, "count for something? He doesn't give his respect lightly. Not unless," I couldn't resist teasing, "the young man is unusually handsome."

"What!" Father said, darkening perceptibly, "Have you slept with him?"

In another family at that moment the son might have risen to his feet with the remark, "Keep your hard-earned money, I don't need it," and walked out, never to return. And he would probably be a better man for it, and a better writer.

But I wasn't sufficiently emerged from my labyrinth that I could countenance throwing away Ariadne's thread and making a clean break. While I might not be able to lay my hands on all the funds stashed away in my name, I thought I commanded enough leverage to prise out enough to cover my immediate needs.

In our family the memorable confrontations have often taken place one-on-one in a car. It's our canvas-roofed Buick convertible I still associate with Father's joining the Navy; the De Soto with his eye-opening facts of life instruction; Mother's Thunderbird with her accusation that, in getting engaged, I had reneged on my solemnly given word.

So, when, on our drive down, Mother asked how, without a bean, I could be thinking of getting married, I was ready. "How can you prattle on about my having no money? What about the famous trust fund Grandpa and Father set up together the day I was born? Or the account Jack Straus opened the same day at the Riverside Savings Bank? I don't understand by what right, a year after I've come of age, the two of you can go on withholding these funds. Do you want me to take my case to Cholly Knickerbocker?"

These remonstrances worked. Next day, Father summoned me in to announce he was turning over a $60,000 portfolio my grandfather had set up for me. "But I don't want to encourage any misperceptions on your part," he said, measuring his words. "That's the only money you have in your name."

Whether true or not, the portfolio represented an appreciable sum. Enough, I told Father gratefully, to give me a safety net, while allowing us a long trip to Europe. Upon our return I promised I would look for a job.

If Father was unable to cast me into the fundless perdition he thought my rebellion deserved, there remained in the family annals a host of gambits waiting only to be dusted off. Earlier, when a liaison of Jimmy's with his Amherst mentor, Kimon Friar, was discovered—Jimmy was nineteen at the time—Charlie had briefly considered taking out a contract on Kimon with the folks at Murder, Inc. Instead, on further reflection, he convened his trust fund lawyer, Larry Condon, my parents and Hellen for a mid-winter conference in the chills of Southampton.

What did they think, Charlie proposed, when they had all assembled in the great card room, of his hiring a prostitute to initiate the young man into the sweets of heterosexual intercourse; as if a mere plunge in such female honey could undo the eroticism of a lifetime.

To a worshipper of the Almighty Wad, Charlie's proposal sounded eminently practical and Father said as much. But they were stopped in their tracks by Larry Condon who dumbfounded them with a prophecy Father would never forget. "You may not believe it, Charlie, but this boy of yours is going to be as famous in his own lifetime as you have been in yours."

With me, there was no question of anyone alienating, much less fucking up, a future genius. The problem rather lay in coming up with a woman sufficiently persuasive. One can see perhaps the two of them interviewing the various candidates—professionals, demi-mondaine, soi-disant amateurs—before settling on a former beach flame of mine.

I have no idea what form the bait took—cash? a job entree? a bonus if she succeeded in skewering the marriage? But once the particulars were agreed on, I can see the rest of the dialogue. First, the Candidate, "How do you suggest I approach him? It's some years, after all, since we last dated."

"For a starter, I would compliment Robin on his forthcoming marriage." That would be Mother, the mistress of the formal.

"Then?"

"Tell him you need to see him—urgently—and put that urgency in your voice."

An idiot ruse, but I fell for it. I should have smelled a rat when Mother, on our drive down, and then Father, on his own arrival, feigning a new esteem, made a point of letting me know that the Candidate had phoned several times during the past week. But difficult as it was to fathom her renewal of interest, I welcomed the chance of seeing her. "You know," I told them in good sap fashion, "I've always liked her."

I had been at the Beach House scarcely an hour when the Candidate called with her congratulations. How pretentious, I remember thinking, what's come over her? After delivering that part of the script she said, "I have something personal I want to discuss with you—is there anywhere private we can meet?"

"How about our Cooper's Neck house for a drink this evening? It's being sold," I added by way of reassurance, "and there won't be anyone around."

Some hours later I found myself seated on the sun parlor's long lemon-colored sofa beside this fetchingly dressed future fashion leader. For a couple of summers we had met on the beach nearly every night, a sweater of mine under us as we lay in the dunes side by side, or climbed over the wall into the Beach House swimming pool. But for all the roaring of the waves and the brilliance of the stars, neither of us succeeded in overcoming our inhibitions and making the gesture that would have bridged the abyss between us. Must make up for that now, I thought, coiling a predatory arm around her as I drew her down into the plush depths of the sofa.

As might be expected, the Candidate responded, with a warmth that soon had me envisioning more exquisite possibilities. I had a hand in her blouse and was starting to undress her when, with a brusque movement, as if suddenly come to her senses, the Candidate swung herself bolt upright and in an offended tone inquired, "How can you be doing this when you're in love and GETTING MARRIED?"

Under the circumstances, I had no problem explaining the pull of our own unconsummated past. "Besides," I blurted out in my best minotaur style, "Marcia's not around and you are." For much of the next seven years, I'm afraid, that summed up my sexual code. I wanted Marcia, but if she was not available, I would try to satisfy myself with whoever was. I was not marrying Marcia because she was the one and only woman in my world, but because it was the one way I could take her abroad. Getting married, for me, was nothing more than a legal fiction, a bit of theater. I did not foresee that the fiction might mean something else to Marcia; or that, once on the boards, it might take on an extended run.

In Summit the loot, as Mother cheerfully called it, kept rolling in. But among all the bar material, the decanters and silver ice buckets and plate silver trays, the toasters and clocks and asparagus plates, there were some kind exceptions. Larry Rivers produced a painting of Marcia seated in a garden chair in my favorite mustard-gold sweater; less a portrait than summer heat incarnate. Whereas Jimmy contributed a seven-paneled Edo period woodcut of a wedding procession in elegant, billowing, cherry blossom kimonos. But the presents, for the most part, exasperated me by projecting us onto a scale that I knew I would never be able to live up to. Typical was Mother's own offering of a thirty-piece dessert set of pierced Regency colporte; as if I was to rush out and hock everything on the breakfront in which to display it.

Of the wedding I remember Marcia's tiara, lily of the valley decorated veil, and long white gloves; the cautionary dueling pistol my grooms presented at their lunch; Charlie Merrill's much too small tailcoat and top hat into which I allowed myself to be squeezed; one more item in the incomprehensible charade to which I had consented. I had given Marcia my word and there I was. But in that get-up and looking the callow youth I was, I felt an overriding shame. One more male fatted calf. My one hope lay in the temporariness of the arrangement. All the more distinct, therefore, the crack of doom with which the words of the ancient oath descended, "Do you take this woman . . . for as long as you both shall live?" For the first time, the awful solemnity of the bond I was taking on caught up with me. "I'm really in it now," I remember gulping. And I was, differently shackled maybe than in my familial labyrinth, but shackled nonetheless.

These feelings turned to outright dismay when, on our second night on the Ile-de-France, Marcia refused to satisfy my lust. Doubtless, she had her reasons. Post-wedding withdrawal blues? The gray wastes in which we were immured? A sense that this night I wasn't turning her on?

It was one thing to slip my head into a lovingly plaited noose. It was another to be strangled. All the more in that the one adult identity I felt sure of was sexual. (I certainly wasn't a writer.) Now when the minotaur in me should have been regaling himself, I saw my worst fears being confirmed.

Why I put up with it I don't know. All I had to do was to go to the purser and request a room of my own. And take the first plane home. Or gone on on my own. Instead, I was now condemned to be this half-man dragging himself along from one absurd page to the next. When would it ever stop? When would I be me?

More gray days in that floating hotel followed. Shuffleboard, ping-pong, badminton. And I had left Jamaica for this?

AFTER THE WEDDING GUESTS WENT HOME

Yet we did disembark together at Cherbourg. I remember on the boat train to Paris Marcia fascinatenated by the front yard vegetable gardens, the stone farms and spires and turrets, the maroons and acid greens of the Paris streets, textures so different from the wood and brick that she knew. For her, it was as if we had stepped onto a stage set. That we were doing it together, the finding of a cheap hotel, the perusing of a menu where we recognized hardly a dish, gave something of the feeling of a dance. A dance in frozen time because there was a whole ongoing life we could not be part of. But that brought the past all the nearer, the shadowed reflections of a window, of ourselves under an arc lamp in the autumn mist, alone and yet perfectly safe. With unlimited time at our disposal, a half continent beckoned. In an effort to focus ourselves we chose Spain. Marcia had studied the literature and I had never been there.

Unfortunately our boat landed in Cherbourg and not Algeciras. By the time we had crossed the Pyrenees we were thoroughly spoiled. By all the green, twisting, country roads, a vernacular architecture that changed every twenty miles. Spain, by contrast, was still in the aftershock of its civil war and decidedly grim.

For a couple of months we stuck it out, staying outside Madrid in the poolhouse of a friend of Father's while we tried to secure a three-month let. When that proved impossible, we set off for Rome by way of the Provence of the troubadours, my boyhood Rapallo and Stendhal's Parma, checking it all out, three-star restaurant by two-star Romanesque church.

Marcia and Robin wed, 1958

135

Marcia made an appreciative companion, eager, fearless, willing to meet anybody, try anything. And being sophisticated about art history, she retained much better than I what we were seeing. Yet she also gave me the space in which to try to write. But among all the jewel-like masterpieces nothing set off in me the least proprietary spark. Instead I felt the host of eyes who had already stripped them of what I could say. And an ever-growing unease as I saw my financial lifeline frittering away.

Wherever we halted, there would be encouraging letters waiting from my father. "Enjoy yourselves, stay as long as you want. You two will never have an opportunity like this again." Aware, no doubt, that the longer I floundered on the honeymoon line, the easier I would be to reel in on my return. In the Caribbean, maybe, I had sowed what few wild oats I possessed. Here I felt more and more like a dilettante pretending to myself I was a writer. Having nothing to say never stopped Jimmy; I had no such faith in my own personality. By March, Marcia and I were more than ready to return to New York.

That summer in Cambridge, endlessly retyping my seven wretched pages, had been dispiriting. But this was worse. Maybe Father was right and I wasn't cut out to be a writer. Upon my return, I remember asking Jimmy, "Why, when I could make something of Haiti, did I draw such a blank in Europe? We were certainly in enough literary places."

My failure, Jimmy offered, had less to do with the sites, than in the mistake of "traveling with a loved one. One is so intent on having him or her see that one forgets to look for oneself. In all of my three years abroad the only site that actually moved me was Ravenna. It was also the one place I went by myself."

That may be, but on the way to our boat in Algeciras we stumbled on the beautifully tiled alcove bedrooms of the little white palace of Ronda's last Moorish king, each with a balcony looking out on a fountain-loud patio. And in Grenada we were struck by the water gardens of the Alhambra and a joy such as I had glimpsed only in Matisse. We were sufficiently enthused that, with a week to spare, we crossed the straits to Tangiers. There, too, came discoveries: of the Arab yellow (slippers, hassocks, musicians' caps), a smoky gold that seemed joy itself; or the flute-playing snake charmer rising up out of the orange garden of the King of Morocco. If, as Marcia said, these intimations of paradise originated in Persia, it was there, I knew now, we should travel.

Upon our return, to avoid the humiliation of 69th Street, Jimmy and David let us stay in their $30 a month walk-up apartment on First Avenue and 51st. The previous tenant, Kimon Friar, had strewn honeycakes under the plush chairs, and, as a consequence, the apartment was now patrolled by a battalion of indestructible cockroaches. But the walls were a lovely green, the library contained the usual Jimmy trouvailles, and we found ourselves well placed for exploring the ethnic enclaves of lower Manhattan, while trying to pretend the city could be enjoyed as one did a European city.

While Marcia went to work pursuing her own interests as an *Art News* reviewer of gallery shows and as a research assistant at NYU's Institute for Art History, I pounded the legendary pavements. In a time of considerable prosperity you would think that a young man with "BUSINESS" written all over his genes would be employable. But Father warned me that getting a job was not going to be as easy as I thought. "I'm willing to bet you can't land one on your own."

As could perhaps have been foreseen, I found no management training program willing to take a chance on an already overeducated Harvard man. "Why don't you go to work for your pop?" they asked, not implausibly. Or, evoking the post-Korea nitty-gritty, "How do you stand with the draft?" And my efforts to secure more anonymous employment, as an office temp or a ballroom dance instructor, fell to similar wariness and a lack of previous experience.

These main road efforts did, however, succeed in throwing an unholy fear into my parents. A job just wasn't a job I learned. Instead there were good ones and bad ones. After forking out for me the best possible education, they did not relish seeing me, like a former boyfriend of Mother's, becoming a lowly baggage checker at La Guardia Airport.

In that case, I suggested, always conciliatory, perhaps they could use their contacts to find me a job compatible with a writing career. A copywriter in an ad agency? An editorial assistant in a publishing house? But the ad agencies I applied to had no interest in training a person whose heart was set on being a writer. Whereas the one way of becoming an editor was to buy my way in—not my idea of landing a job. Jason Epstein at Random House even suggested that, instead of a career in publishing, I should buy out Miss Steloff at Gotham Book Mart. His superior, Bennett Cerf, laid it out even more flatly, "We try to hire only women—because they are not so likely to keep pestering us for a promotion. If you want to write, why don't you become a university professor. They make the same salary as an editor and enjoy a lot more freedom."

With no real alternative, I took Bennett Cerf's advice and enrolled in Columbia's graduate school. Not that I regarded teaching as a permanent career; rather I saw it as a temporary refuge to tide me over until I discovered what, if anything, I had to say.

More positively, there was the educational side. If the work of the past is a writer's bread, why not share with others what one is feeding oneself? In the late Fifties, this was enough of a rationale to get a great many of us to our sundry degrees. Only later, and by then hopelessly immured, would we discover the incompatibility between the demands of Academe and making yourself into a good writer. Or realized that our classroom satrapies in our cowtown universities were the establishment's way of siphoning off the over-educated and non-productive. It's simply not true, as G. B. Shaw claimed in words that my father was always quoting, "Those who can, do. Those who cannot, teach." A good number of us could have locked horns in any variety of worthwhile arenas. But at a susceptible age, we had fallen for our professors' self-defensive proselytizing—the lure of a "life" of the mind. And where could the life be better lived than at a big university with a well-equipped library?

THE BROTHERS
DUKE IT OUT

Early in the summer my parents, in a conciliating gesture, invited Marcia and me to Southampton for the weekend. They were not able, at the last minute, to join us there. But they made clear we had the run of the house and could stay in whatever bedroom, other than theirs, we wanted.

We drove down with my brother Merrill in the almost toy-sized Fiat Mother had won in a lottery and given to me. After inspecting the available bedrooms, I picked one in the front end of the house. It was the only one with a degree of privacy and its own bathroom; items essential, I thought, to my new marital status.

But Merrill had his own well-honed notions of territory. Once, after dining out with our grandfather, he had, for reasons of his own, refused to thank him. But Charlie refused to let the matter drop and kept after him the whole way home. When the car finally arrived at 69th Street, the eight-year-old leapt out with the parting remark, "This is my sidewalk and you can't yell at me any more."

So now, when I announced my decision, Merrill protested. "That's my bedroom you're taking over."

"How can that be?" I retorted. "You haven't set foot in the house all summer and there's not a thing of yours in the room." And I started to unpack our suitcase.

For Merrill, after a lifetime of enduring an older brother's appropriations, this was the last straw. "If you intend to evict me from my bedroom," he said, "you're going to have to fight me first."

But I felt shored up in my new status. "Mother said we could stay where we wanted. This is the only bedroom with its own bath."

Merrill was adamant. "I don't care what Mother said. She's not here and I am. Are you a man or a mouse?"

In all our thousands of fights Merrill had never defeated me. Even when he had outgrown me I was still fast enough to outwrestle him. But after two years in the military he was definitely the stronger. No sooner did I crawl out from under one piece of furniture than I found myself being pommelled into the next.

One would think, as he stood over his defeated and heavily panting brother, Merrill would have been satisfied with the threshold he had crossed. But victory is not revenge and, for Merrill now, nothing less than my complete disfigurement would suffice. "Don't worry," he said, alluding to the lore he had picked up at the army boot camp to which he had been directed midway through Yale, "I know how to rearrange your face."

The remark touched off a proprietary nerve in Marcia who had been standing nearby. And with a shout she leapt to my defense.

Merrill protested, "No fair, two against one."

A first victory might be thought Merrill's due. But my parents were mortified when they learned about it from my brothers. They responded in true form. The next Monday in New York Father summoned me to his Pine Street sanctum. After a remark about how dismayed he was by Merrill's reception, he came up with the usual distancing atonement. "I warned you that landing a job on your own wouldn't be as easy as you thought. But now that you've decided on graduate school you should have an allowance. I'm turning over to you from your trust fund $500 a month. In return, I want you to sign this paper appointing me your trustee. The trust fund is something I've set up—with my own money. It has grown very nicely and I think I should continue to take care of it."

The moment was crucial. Before putting a pen to that sort of a document, at the very least I should have consulted a lawyer. What exactly was I signing away? (Nothing is less trustworthy than a trust fund.) For the remainder of his life Father would use that legal form to keep me his chattel, forced to bow and scrape for each additional pittance.

My not entering the family business had a ripple effect on my brothers, Merrill especially. Upon graduating from Yale in 1961 there was no question where he would work. Merrill Lynch Magowan was Merrill Lynch, how could they not grin and make way? But the greatest money making machine in the world had become the personal cow of Father's former assistant, Don Regan, and the set of tall cronies, all at least 6'2", this ex-Marine colonel had gathered around him. And they milked it for the company planes and the Wimbledon box, the poison pills and golden handshakes.

At a party for him a few years ago in London I remember the chairman, Bill Schreier, telling me how my father would have been pleased by the way the firm had expanded along the lines he had charted.

"My father," I replied, as Schreier visibly winced, "would have made sure Merrill Lynch turned a profit." Unfortunately Father's shareholder revolt never took off. We taxpayers might have been spared the consequences of Treasury Secretary Regan's deregulation of the savings and loan industry.

As a beginning broker Merrill did well enough on commissions to rake in a $200,000 stipend. A rising star, one would think. But when the man with the unforgivable monicker graduated from the training program Father had started, all he was offered was a choice of running the Palm Beach office or the new one at Carmel, California.

Merrill chose Carmel and its better golf. From there he progressed to the number two slot in the San Francisco office and a corporate vice-presidency. Finally, after some twenty years, Merrill asked Regan if there was some way he could prove himself and move up the ladder. Regan replied that he needed a personal assistant, the job he had performed for Father and the basis of his subsequent rise. But Merrill, who had a beautiful home in the center of an old rose garden in suburban Hillsborough, was understandably cautious about junking everything for the hazards of New York. "What job," he asked Regan, "does being your assistant set me up for?"

"None," Regan snapped. "I just get to kick you around the way your Old Man kicked me around."

That didn't appeal to Merrill. Instead he quit Merrill Lynch to go into business for himself as an investment advisor, specializing in securities trading.

Merrill's going into Merrill Lynch left Safeway open for Peter. Except that Father was still so incensed by Peter's marriage in 1963 to his college sweetheart, a Jewish girl with an Upper West

Side accent, that he wasn't speaking to him. Peter was within a half term of graduating from diplomatic school at Johns Hopkins when he got himself a job with Safeway's Washington, D.C., division. As he put it later, "I realized that I wanted to try to succeed on my own without Father orchestrating my career."

Peter's hunch worked out and he rose quickly through the ranks. At thirty-seven, he was running the company. But then Peter had qualities Safeway needed. He could plan, he could write a coherent speech and he worked prodigiously. Whereas Father worked an eight-hour day, Peter often worked a fourteen-hour day, plus weekends; a sign of how much more complicated running a chain store second in size only to Sears had become. Under Father, Safeway may have become the biggest supermarket chain. Under my brother it became a quality outfit as well.

One might think size a guarantee of permanence. But the bigger the corporation the more vulnerable it was to the raiders; all the more when there was a big disparity, as with Safeway, between its book value and its less than two percent profit margin. The value of its separate parts, when sold off, exceeded that of the ongoing operation.

Peter made out very handsomely in the resulting management buyout; at the expense of some long-term employees, it has been alleged. But for Peter it was a question of either dismantling Safeway and throwing everyone out of work, or taking a chance and trying to save something of a three-generation family creation. Of all the Kohl, Kravitz, and Robert engineered legal buyouts of the mid-Eighties, Safeway has been the only one that has succeeded so far. That had a lot to do with Peter's acumen and his caring about others.

Running Safeway brought Peter close to Father. The two shared the dark side of corporate power—the frustrations, the personal sacrifice, the loneliness of having, as Peter said, "no one I can talk things over with, no friend." But Safeway, with its eight hundred labor contracts alone—it was the Mafia he was negotiating with—and its low profit margins, made for a difficult and, I suspect, insufficiently cerebral business. When it became a choice of directing the Giants baseball team he had helped save for San Fransisco or continuing with Safeway, Peter chose his boyhood idols.

My youngest brothers, Stephen and Mark, evolved out of a slightly different family dynamic than the first three of us. After three boys my parents wanted a girl. Some of that intention went into Stephen's and Mark's upbringing and gave them something to combat. Of all of us Stephen was the best looking, the wittiest, the one with the most personal charm and imaginative talent. But sex—Stephen's acceptance at twenty of his homosexuality—took him over so profoundly that for years he could conceive of no other identity than that of a glamorous man on a barstool, puffing away at a cigarette, studying like a hawk how to move like Gene Kelly.

Stephen's view of a malefic Father was not mine. But seen from eight years further along, the paternal features may have narrowed and hardened. A Mephistopheles with only so many emotional buttons. And Stephen, rehearsing the drama out of which he would make so many of his plays, knew how to push one button after the next to draw the predictable outbursts.

As to why Father regarded Stephen's homosexuality as a personal affront one can only guess. The tears, Stephen remembers, misting Father's face when he spoke of the sailors on his carrier dancing with one another? The shock of recognition I felt when I came upon an early draft of *Cat on a Hot Tin Roof*, of that jealous man unable to brook any female rivals for his son, any life other than that across the tennis net from him? Was there in Father this not so repressed core?

The older we got, the more Stephen and I, the "non-working brothers," as Merrill still refers to us, were drawn together. If I was a minotaur, Stephen with all his major astrological signs in Taurus, was definitely the bull, an obsessive's obsessive driven by the maleness that everything about him gave off.

To escape from my labyrinth I had no choice but to break with my parents and their world. Stephen did not necessarily buy it all either. But as a fourth son, the family glue bound him in a way it hadn't bonded me. (I had my grandfather, my uncles, my cousins to turn to.) When Mother needed him, that handsome, funny extra man at a dinner party, he was willing to drop everything and go to Palm Beach or Southampton, performing his filial duty dance. He kept up with their milieu, their friends, even their friends' children. But he lampooned them too, plays with titles like "See You When You're Better Dressed."

Of Stephen's battles none has been more courageous than the one he has fought, and to this day won, with kidney cancer. The struggle has made him a changed person, with a different life style, a different way of talking even.

My remaining brother, Mark, I don't know as well. He is seventeen years younger. In bringing him up, my parents were determined to rectify their previous mistakes; those gaps, as they perceived them, in the labyrinth walls. We older four shared the same peasant nurse, Eileen, for six years. Mother always regretted that Eileen had not done more to sort out my wretched manners. But Eileen did not want to make us into princelings, but boys who could stand their ground and take a licking. Whereas Mark began life in the charge of a Danish woman who had made a career of ministering to royals.

The older four of us were constructed on the ideal of Father: narrow features, short arms and legs, long torsos. And we were all small—the runt brothers. With his round cherubic face, his dimple under the chin, his taller, thicker body clad in a double-breasted suit, Mark looked very different. And his was not the same metabolism. A potassium deficiency, inherited apparently from Father, made him slower to get started in the morning, slower of stride, legs like jelly after an irresistible meal.

Of us five Mark has been the closest to my parents in his affection and general style of life. And, unlike us, he saw himself as a scion of a princely family. "Why don't we all," he would suggest, "pool our resources and invest together?" As if we had control of the said "resources," or could afford to give up our separate kayaks.

But growing up with Father blasting about the house prepared Mark for what he encountered when he went to work for his wife's cousins, the Abrams family, at Abbeville Press. Whereas the office staff was terrified of the Old Man's rages, Mark was not. As he cheerfully explained, he had already lived through it all, the crashing verbal bolts, the black face and thunderous pronouncements. A mere storm, he knew, and passing. Unlike the four of us, Mark is not a creature of impetuous whim, ready to jettison in a moment everything he has built. His instead is a witty refined sense of life and civilization; an eighteenth century gentleman.

THE ACCELERATING GRADUATE STUDENT

By September, I had begun my graduate studies. In philosophy, as Jimmy, thinking of what he would have chosen, now advised? No, English, but the field of specialization I sought—Modern Comparative Literature—was oversubscribed, and I settled for American Nineteenth Century, which had been part of my undergraduate major. A despised part, I should add, thanks to D. H. Lawrence whose exuberant rants had deeply infected me. I found I could not dismiss high-handedly a whole corpus—not if I was preparing to teach it. Obliged to be positive, I made some discoveries: on the saturnalian masque, derived from Spenser and the Italian commedia, that informs Melville's "Benito Cereno"; on Jewett's adoption of Renaissance pastoral in her Pointed Fir sketches, which I made the subject of a master's thesis.

Columbia's M.A. program was conducted under the French system. Your specialization aside, all you did was audit. There were no tests, no papers, only at the year end, bingo, a two-day exam. (The first day covered the entire body of English literature, the second your period of specialization.) I ended up taking a seminar on Melville just to taste the pleasure of writing weekly reports.

Because of a somewhat generous admissions policy and the continuing need we males had for draft-exemption (I was absolved because of my stammer and the psychiatry I had undergone to try to cure it), the program was overcrowded. Those of us wanting to proceed to the doctorate were encouraged to apply elsewhere.

The year before, on the boat back from Algeciras, I had met Richard Saez, who was at Yale studying comparative literature with

145

the Czech "critic of critics," Rene Wellek. Saez encouraged me to apply there. As a subject of graduate study, comp lit perhaps only made sense in the way Wellek defined it, as a history of criticism interpreted from within the prevailing polylingual context. Certainly there were no jobs at the entering level. But I had a language background of sorts and was attracted by the more speculative horizon comp lit seemed to offer. The last thing I wanted was to be buried in a period cubbyhole.

I was well taught at Yale. So far as English and Romance literature were concerned, Yale's was then the best graduate school in the country. And Marcia secured a great job as the personal assistant to the art museum's oriental curator, describing and dating Persian and Chinese artifacts for a catalogue. But the Dixwell Avenue black ghetto, off which we lived in one of those pink-painted apartments, with its fortnightly murder, was another matter. And, with some five haberdasheries to any one bookstore, it was clear where Yale's undergraduates were headed—Wall Street. A graduate school can take one over. But neither Marcia nor I wanted to spend any more time in New Haven than we had to.

That I managed to fulfill the doctoral requirements in twelve months might seem brisk all the same. But Yale wanted you out and teaching and much was done to speed us over the various hurdles. Among them were the language requirements. Despite three years of German at Exeter and a summer course in Vienna, I failed the exam twice. But rather than re-examine me, Wellek detected, he said, enough improvement to give me a pass. As for Latin, I hadn't studied it since St. Bernard's. But the examiners in medieval Latin saved the day by assigning the passage in which the asp goes to work on Cleopatra's nipples.

At Harvard, I had not taken a French course. At Yale, I made up for it, taking seminars on the medieval Romance of the Rose, on Stendhal and Gide. I relished the luxury of immersing myself in the whole of an author's work. Most literary courses tend to be surveys. The area of concern may shrink as the student advances, but it still remains a map over which one floats like a tourist. Gide may be an over-rated writer; but, thanks to my Exeter tutorial and Henri Peyre's seminar, he is part of my experience. Stendhal is a great writer, and, in the course of a seminar with Victor Brombert, I conceived an affection for both the man and his many commentators. One can read a lot of recent writing (Lampedusa, Savinio, Sciascia, Giono) and recognize a master shared.

Expanding on my interest in American literature, I took a seminar on Whitman and Hart Crane given by R. W. B. Lewis. Critics, I learned, had talked about Whitman's comic epic, "Song of Myself," as registering a mystic experience. But no commentator had ever explained what Whitman's experience actually consisted of, or how he managed to translate it into a poem which marks (with Les Fleurs du Mal) the beginning of modern poetry.

My own travels indicated that Whitman scholars had never made it to Haiti much less their local Pentecostal church. If they had, I maintained, they would have seen that the experience inspiring the transformation of self in "Song of Myself" was one of possession.

This was startling enough to justify a twenty-page elaboration: an exposition of what Emerson—the thought behind Whitman—understood by a poetry of possession; followed by a close reading of the relevant sections of Whitman's poem. Since possession works through an induced schizophrenia, the trick was to isolate the conflicting verbal musics that appear in the early part of the poem and relate them to the corresponding selves in Whitman himself; then show how, through a typical voodoo process of chanting and listening to music—here vocal music, symphonies, and finally opera—Whitman intensifies the schizophrenia to a point where, in the "fakes of death," he falls backward onto the floor, aware of a vice-like clamp about his neck. The spirit mounting him is that of a cow—he refers to "the rest of the herd", to the provokers "straining the udder of my heart for its withheld drip"; to the horrified realization that "my own hands carried me there." As in voodoo, the possessed dance ends in an orgasmic release, "rich showering rain." Fortified thus, Walt sets off to proclaim his new message and realize the god latent in him.

We produced semi-publishable, twenty-page papers like this at a rate of three, even five, a semester; a pace tolerable because we knew the course would eventually end.

The papers were nothing compared to the agony I endured preparing for that September's ninety-minute oral examination. I had picked eight topics in a more or less historical sequence: Old Provençal literature; the Romance of the Rose and the courtly epic; pastoral; Molière; Stendhal; Melville and Whitman; modern poetry; modern criticism. There were gaps aplenty. I knew next to nothing about the courtly epic and almost as little about Molière. My one hope was that my examiners, like the three Graeae, would get so caught up passing about their one eye as to forget the time.

My plan worked better than I had any right to hope. Back and forth, swifter than a tennis ball, the eye flew: Melville and Whitman, Whitman and Melville, the most finicky questioning possible for a goodly half hour. By now, inspired by the array of blinding detail I was batting about, all were in full cry. I sat there at our oval Harkness table letting them chatter on, from time to time stoking a flame with a name or a date or a conversation-rejuvenating mot. Finally, after a seeming eternity, the tiny alarm clock I had been watching rang.

One can imagine the consternation. "But there are all sorts of topics we haven't questioned you on!"

"Too bad," I said, "time's up. What have I earned?"

"A First. Truly brilliant exam, wasn't it?" Chorus of nods, while Wellek could be heard muttering, "It doesn't matter what we give you, since I suspect your stay in the profession will be only temporary. Now are we done with you?"

"Not so fast! I still need a dissertation topic, one that will take me to Paris."

"You don't want to avail yourself of the Beinecke Library and its incomparable facilities?"

"No, I want to go abroad."

"I won't argue for the comparative merits of New Haven. Doubtless, we all pay a price. As for a topic, how about Fromentin?

"The painter and art critic?" I asked, somewhat out of my depth. "Wasn't he a follower of Delacroix and the author of a pair of travel books on the nomads of the Sahara?"

"Fromentin was also a protegé of George Sand, a champion of

pastoral. Under her influence he wrote a pastoral novel, *Dominique*. You'd only have to add a couple of chapters to what you've written on Jewett and we'd be satisfied—hopefully even enlightened."

INTIMATIONS
OF PARADISE

In Paris, I ensconced myself at the Bibliothèque Nationale, copying out all that had ever been written on Fromentin. But Paris in those days was still a city where a couple could walk fearlessly, arm in arm, down the middle of a medieval street. That we had no friends other than the Télémaques, and little access to cultural life, helped to concentrate our curiosity: the American obligation we felt to memorize with our feet the crossword puzzle of an arrondissement.

From our hotel overlooking the Pont Marie on the Ile St. Louis, in the serene, trafficless center of the city, we would saunter forth to gawk at the acid greens, browns, and purples of the shops' fronts and awnings; at the fervently enlaced couples in the wooden metro trains with their magical destinations, St. Lazare, Sèvres-Babylone, Réaumur-Sebastopol, Kremlin-Stalingrad. A city of light that the rain multiplied into millions of specks of desire: the drops on the umbrellas, stockings, and hurrying shoes that expanded, glowed, reminding, as Marcia pointed out, how only in that below sea-level depression of the Seine Valley could Impressionism have emerged so startlingly, with such feminine éclat.

Traveling together on our honeymoon had been a dance of acquaintance. This was more like falling in love. As we drew in the breath of that other life we had penetrated, something began to flow between us. A new closeness, as if we were each other's rapt fingers pointing, each other's dawn.

Robin, Jimmy and Maria Mitsofakis, Piraeus, 1962

By February, however, even Paris had paled, and it seemed time to take up our project of a trip to Iran; discover, as we saw it, the folks who had invented paradise. To ease the logistics there was Uncle Jimmy, conveniently established in Athens. He had recently bought a small house on Athenian Ephebe below the Mount Lykonbetos pine wood and he invited us to come see the "Never on Sunday" style sailor dancing he and David had discovered.

Marcia and I were prepared for Iran. But nothing could have prepared us for Greece—that feeling of having stepped into the morning of the world; a light so sharp that, standing on the Acropolis, there seemed to be nothing in the whole of Athens, not a kite, not a bus turning a hundred blocks away, we could not see. It was easy to understand how, in such transparency, the most rational of civilizations had flourished.

For much of the next five years I thought about little else. Even to descend on Athens's shabby airport caused something to grip and tear at my heart. Any male I greeted like a brother, certain that what made the hair rise on my neck was, if not shared, at least recognized. On a stranger in an airport I'd thrust a stack of 45 r.p.m.'s, knowing with absolute certainty he would contrive to mail them on. Like an archaic statue, I felt enclosed in the life I was taking in. Nothing would ever rob me of my smile.

In this mood I remember once asking Jimmy why this little Balkan country was giving me so much more than a great civilization like Iran. "It may be," he volunteered, "that Iran remains profoundly Oriental, whereas Greece is part of the heritage we all carry in our bones." For one who had studied ancient Greek that might hold. But for me, it was the Oriental aspect, the way Greece so precisely straddled the East-West divide, that appealed: the honey-drenched desserts; the bouzouki-played rebetiko or urban folk dances. And seeing such a dance enacted, spontaneously, in the middle of a taverna, or right out on the sidewalk, could be enough to set one's being afire.

It was the beginning of Easter week when we returned from Iran. With Athens closing for the eight-day holiday, it made sense to seek out an island. "Which of the two thousand would you recommend?" I asked Jimmy when we checked in.

"Paros," he said, pulling a white marble name out of the Cycladic hat. "There isn't much to do, and little choice of food, but it was happy enough. And take a taxi to Naoussa opposite Naxos. The little harbor has all the charm of a run-down Portofino."

To a minotaur an island set opposite the Naxos of Ariadne and Dionysos could seem propitious, and we took a stormy, eight-hour boat there, discovering a distinct Greece: people with not black or red, but brown hair, traveling with their belongings packed in round rush baskets. The thread-like streets of Paroika held a labyrinth more feminine than I had ever encountered; one that made the pirate in me feel I would never find my way back to my ship, nor would I ever want to, such was the beguilement that came with each twist of the head as we peered: through an archway, into a courtyard; over the paving stones daubed in whitewash like hot-cross buns; up a little height to a wall set with columns salvaged from a Doric temple; the whole so perfectly cradled from the winds of the Sea of Icarus we felt rocked by the echoing whitewash. I understood, as we strolled under the vibrant stars of the esplanade, how a cycle of stories had come into being. Arachne had spun a tight web.

On Easter Sunday we took a taxi to Naoussa. We didn't locate Jimmy's Portofino, but in the taverna to which we repaired for a glass of pine-scented retsina, we found a lamb being turned on a spit. Nearby, on a line of chairs, sat an intense, beady-eyed fraternity. No one was speaking, drinking, or doing much of anything but staring. We found the whole rapt scene with its mesmerizing odors so compelling we upped our consumption to half a liter. But the lamb was of a size to feed half of Naoussa. Rather than wait, we decided to walk, while we still could, back to our hotel.

At the time I had never gone on anything as long as a three-hour walk, reason enough to be impressed. And in early April the fields still rippled out in tiers of green and gold speckled with poppies—a red note, it seemed, for each blade of wheat. Ahead, the road spun, high on a waist, through transparencies of sea-whitened olive trees. Here and there shone the white-vaulted cube of a farmhouse, steps aglow like lumps of sugar. What amazed was the visual legato created by the whitewash as the roadway cobbles joined with a house to collect the last rays striking a cove two hillsides away. How sensible on a fuelless island! Suddenly I understood the power of an Orphic flute. On an island where light carries like a note of music, even rocks are capable of dancing.

Further along, at a hilltop crossroad, we encountered a woman on a bicycle carrying some fresh-cut lilac branches. On a sudden impulse she dismounted and pressed a lap-bright bunch of them onto Marcia. "Welcome, strangers, and may you find the joy you seek." A generosity that defines the Greece of the time. We, the two of us walking hand in hand, could still be a possible god in disguise.

Once back at our hotel we eagerly accepted some outer meat from another lamb on a spigot. "For dinner?" I inquired.

"No, a dance later in the evening." That intrigued and, while Marcia retired, I stayed up, hoping to see some local Orpheus dance one of those zembeikikos, "part dream, part prayer," I had read about in the Vista Guide. But the dance was a record hop, featuring the local Cycladic dances; everything but that hypnotic urban warrior dance which the expelled Greeks of 1923 had brought back from Asia Minor.

The chance to see what the Vista Guide was talking about came our first night back in Athens when Jimmy and David took us out beyond Piraeus to a roadside strip in Pérama where the navy sailors came to dance and flirt with the male prostitutes. The cafe we found ourselves in consisted of a few tables and a jukebox. The food served was chicken and, if you wanted it, watermelon. Since the sailors were poor—the average wage was four dollars a month—it was not inappropriate to offer one or another table a round of beer. Now and then in response to a song on the jukebox a tall, cucumber-shouldered youth would stand up and, fingers clicking like a priest lost in a dream of stones, sketch out his dance.

Perhaps after a few steps a friend, flourishing a handkerchief, would rise and join him. Around this handkerchief the dreamer turned, dispersing out of thin white trousers quietude, elation, manna. The two moved, circling, as on the rim of a glass, their hands fat, soft-spinning flowers, their feet spokes in a cycle of prayers. They spoke in a tongue of rain, sensing through the jukebox's din their tablemate's hands breaking in green time like plates.

I didn't know then that the sailors regarded Pérama as their scuola di ballo, all that Wimbledon is to a tennis player. But I couldn't help but be affected by the verve and the witty intimacy of the dancers. Rather than see it vanish, I jotted down some impressions during our taxiride back to Athens. The notes would become, when completed a year later, my first real poem.

Two months earlier, before setting out for Iran, I had come upon an issue of *Time* featuring the 1962 Seattle World's Fair. Struck by the provincial cheek—my parents still talked about the 1938 New York edition which had introduced Belgian waffles and the amphibian car—I read an article about the international dance troupes that would be performing in Seattle. That so intrigued me, I wrote away to the University of Washington for a job teaching English. When I returned from Paros, there was a letter awaiting at Jimmy's from the chairman, Robert Heilman, a former colleague of Yale New Critics, Brooks, Wimsatt and Robert Penn Warren. A lectureship was being held for me, would I telegram my acceptance?

Heilman's offer left me in a quandary. The Washington department, while not Yale or Berkeley, was well respected. At this late date nothing better was going to come my way. But for a writer how much should such considerations weigh? Maybe it was Jimmy's personal spell, maybe it was the very stark Greece of the time, but I had found something I could and wanted to write about, and I was loathe to see it all dissolve in the northwestern mists.

That evening I took my arguments to Jimmy, a very different Jimmy from the one I had known in Stonington. He who had been so spoiled, so shy, so effete, had been transformed by the country of "Essentials: salt, wine, olive, the light, the scream." He spoke

Greek, he cooked Greek, there was little in Athenian life he didn't rejoice in. For the first time he felt joined to people of every class; at one with a culture in which homosexuality was certainly understood, if not accepted.

Jimmy lived in a little two-story house above posh Kolonaki on the last street below Mount Lycabetos. But you saw little of the house, as you were shuttled quickly through the rooms and up by way of a narrow curling metal staircase to the rooftop garden which, at the time, commanded a view all the way to the Acropolis. As I drew up a seat there, I described the job offer I had received from the University of Washington; one I was sorely tempted, in my new mood, to reject. I had, after all, fallen in love with Greece, and, like any amorous man, all I wanted was to move right in and start learning Greek and everything else I needed to know. My five-hundred dollar a month allowance would not go far in America. In the Greek countryside I could live on it well enough.

Patiently, Jimmy heard me out, a slight narrowing of the brows showing his concern, as he said, for the bitterness I might come to feel one day, deprived of a career into which I had already put a substantial effort. He spoke slowly, "Teaching, for you, may be a means to an end. But the confidence that can accrue from it is no small matter. If it hadn't been for the invitation I received on graduating from Amherst to teach at Bard, I'd have gone to work at Merrill Lynch. It was that year which allowed me to see myself as a full-fledged writer."

Jimmy went on to say that, from everything he had heard, Seattle was a lively city, David had old friends living there, and he himself would come to visit us at the first opportunity.

All that, coming from Jimmy, was reassuring. Next morning he and David, after plying me with a pair of highballs, marched me down to the one open post office, under Omonia square, where I dutifully fired off my telegram of acceptance.

MUSHROOMS IN THE RAIN

The wound Greece opened was not easily staunched. But it helped having by me a Marcia who understood from what I had been exiled. "You're thinking of Greece," I remember her saying as she caught my eyes misting over. "I know, I feel that way, too."

But if distance and time cannot quite eradicate loss, they can brush it back, out of sight. Seattle may have lacked the light, the vibrant intensity of Athens, but a city straddling a series of hills, with Lake Washington and Puget Sound within a mile of one another and the snowcapped peaks of the Olympics and Cascades to look out on (not to mention that "watermark on celestial paper" which Louise Bogan called Mount Rainier) certainly had some natural beauty going for it. And, unlike New York or San Francisco, Seattle was unpretentious. Nevertheless, in venturing out to a restaurant, a theater or an art exhibition, you could find yourself surprised and, often enough, actually moved.

The senior English staff had its share of deadwood who would rather be building a boat or fermenting a wagonload of California grapes than trying to expand anyone's head. But among us untenured imports, morale was high. We were all more than willing to read and comment on one another's blue-dittoed essays. We helped each other pack and move, and when the first of the month rolled around we entertained, carrying on as if Seattle was not the isolated Kamchatka it might appear to a less committed eye. And most of us could count on friends from other walks of life: vendors from the Pike Street market; Boeing engineers and businessmen I played squash with at the YMCA; theater directors of the class of Andre Gregory and Ralph Lee; radio people I met conducting a poetry program for America's first community station, Lorenzo Milam's wonderfully ambitious I'll-stop-the-Vietnam War-myself KRAB. (This was 1963 and the American commitment had just begun. Lorenzo was from Jacksonville and his mother and Jimmy's Hellen had been in each other's weddings. This polio-paralyzed man would go on to fund, on a shoestring, a host of stations and write a wrenching, sexy, and very funny autobiography, *The Cripple Liberation Front Marching Band Blues*. Of all my friends, Lorenzo is the one I most admire.)

The spontaneous combustion of all of us exiles, mushrooms, whatever we were, springing up in the months-on-end rainy bleakness could not have been more palpable. And Marcia and I were in the middle of it, knitting people together and doing what we could to animate a community.

Of all the activities, I prized most the ethnic league soccer I played Sunday mornings on the mud fields at Volunteer Park. Upon arriving I was fortunate to find a team of ex-college hot shots who were willing to put up with me while I converted from the forward I had been at Harvard to defense. But playing for them was like playing for the United Nations, and we never knew who would show up. When our team disbanded at the end of the season, I switched to the United Hungarians.

In the Fifties, Hungary was the world's premier soccer power. It may well have been their success that gave a nation of seven million the fantasy it could revolt against the Soviet Union. My teammates had mostly arrived via Canada, lured by the advertisements in the immigrant papers. "If you play soccer well, we'll pay your fare and guarantee you a job." Enough came to form a team, the Seattle Hungarians, which twice reached the national finals.

United was an offshoot, formed by Hungarians who had fallen out, or could not make the more famous team. But that famous slur on their powers of friendship could result in a renegade team that contained some talented players. Some, like our captain, a riveter for PACCAR, had played only once a year in Hungary, at the annual factory picnic. But in America playing soccer was a way of remaining Hungarian, and they all played as if they were still out there with Ghengis Kahn on the steppe, riding the shaggy ponies and surviving on mare's milk.

In the middle of my second year I found myself, for a four-game spell, installed in a position I had never been trusted with—

centerhalf. A centerhalf is the last finger in the dike. To have held out for ninety minutes against an endlessly onsurging tide could give rise to as great an athletic satisfaction as I've known. When the game was over, there would be the fans' hugs and congratulations raining down on me while I sat in the middle of the winter mud, lapping up one spiked thermos after the next. Not so much to get drunk as because I couldn't bear to leave all those incomprehensibly babbling people and drive home.

It was their sense of a tribe I welcomed. Writing, one is so alone. If I kept silent in the locker room, it was less out of shyness than because I hesitated to intrude on their community. And, by not speaking, I preserved something of the wonder of the fall afternoons when I played at St. Bernard's, racing with the ball ahead of me like a waiter's tray on the great lamb of a field.

But there was more than nostalgia drawing me. I remember the painter Kaldis once describing the excitement of watching Matisse paint in his Nice studio, the painting changing with each new stroke—a blue daub here, an explosive red there. It was like watching, Kaldis said, a great end-to-end soccer game. For me, of course, the analogy applied in reverse. It was as if, by stepping onto a field, I had become color myself, those barberpole socks, that flaglike shirt.

The crowning accolade came at a farewell banquet. I had just been presented with a trophy to remember them by when the owner of the other Hungarian team called me over to tell me that, should I ever return, he wanted me to play for them. Admittedly, the likelihood of my taking him up was slim. But to me his offer meant something like what escaping from Chester or rural Florida had meant to my father and Charlie Merrill. I knew now that, had I needed to, I too could have found my way out, the ball a wide rolling grin I followed, from childhood cowfield to illuminated stadium glory.

In Seattle there was no poetry colosseum, but there was a welcome hive of poets. The English department, alone, featured a good dozen of us, mostly Roberts or Robins in honor of our chairman.

Being of a competitive disposition, I found them stimulating. And by now, after many years of Ted Roethke as the resident poet, the locals knew what our ilk needed. My students were forever dropping off prospective inspiration: a collection of local mosses and lichens; sprigs of flowers; even on one occasion a large soulful gray rock; anything to help me grasp a very different landscape, and perhaps themselves, more accurately.

By now I was myself writing poetry. For the first eight months, in what time I could snatch from my teaching and thesis, I worked on the description of the two dancing sailors I had begun in the taxi returning from Pérama.

The anxiety I felt when I finished it—would I ever write another poem?—was such that I embarked on "Paros." Foolishly, not thinking of the violence I was doing to myself, I hurled into its cauldron all my memories, line by line building the flame to where a fisherman could conceivably feel impelled to rise to his feet and dance out his deliverance. With the help of a Gadinis LP, I was able to conjure a slow, spherical zembeikiko, the fisherman's arm pointing like a boom as, eyes on the floor, hissing, he descended, circle by completed circle, through the maelstrom of light, of music:

> ...the sea with him now
> Naming her, the sound a thread downwards
> Through the spool of hisses guiding him as
> He steers over its tilting sundialed frame
> And light pours in swords into him, melting
> The streets into a wax, while, the head, dis-
> Membered, floats over the singing stones.

The poem made a comrade of Ted Roethke—until then decidedly leery of this Safeway heir. Roethke even sent a copy to an unbeknownst Paros resident, the future Nobel laureate Seferis. We were set to lock horns at tennis when Roethke succumbed to a massive coronary.

Over the next couple of years, working with the different dance rhythms, I would write several more such taverna poems. The form was basically pastoral. My dancers were in their own pictorially defined space, and I was the objective outsider, watching from a corner table, deep in my glass, invisible.

But to some there could seem too pronounced a gap between the dancer and the recording scribe. "Aren't your poem's dancers," Jimmy once asked, "really you? That's what the reader of a lyric expects, not somebody else, but you."

I remember being taken aback by Jimmy's admonishment. After all, much of the admiration I felt came from their doing something of which I was incapable. How was I to barge in and shatter such transparency, "Everyone off the floor, the American wants to dance!" But I could see that one might prefer a rhythm not lifted from a record, but generated from within, the bloody fool with each step, each gesture, declaring himself. Like it or not, I would have to learn how to be that expressionist.

FELIX, DOLPHIN SON

In mid-March of our first year in Seattle, my son Felix was born. Conceiving him had not been, any more than anything else in our marriage, my idea. But from the moment I saw Felix, his mouth wide and twisted like a harp, his eyes the color of distant firs and mountains—tilting up at the corners like small pontoons—something new took shape in me.

I was standing some hours later behind the glass of Felix's nursery as his mittened hands trembled in their sleep, like a starfish searching. It was as if, in his own instinctual being, he had not yet emerged from Marcia's womb. I saw him there with his blind heron eyes wading, seeking his length of gum-green water like the answer to some dream of distant raft and sunlight, thistle and cloud-white thigh.

Felix and I were very close those first years. I'd flip on a Greek record and he would spin around alongside. I'd go on a training run and he'd tag along, wanting to dart down every path but the one I was jogging. And, because of the initial vision I had of him, of a being more dolphin than human, there was this unexpected element of earth which I owed to him and had to make good.

Felix was too young to be hauled off to Greece, so we spent the summer in Seattle, renting a cabin for a few weeks on the Olympic peninsula. This water child changed the way I saw the world that surrounded me: the cobra-headed grebes floating, beaks outstretched as they probed the glisten where the moon was salt and they swam under a legend of fishes. From a ferry, islands plunged past, shot with silk and the mahoganies of silence; islands so drenched that only their fir crests were now visible, the "white writing" of Mark Tobey's abstractions. I saw the rain forest where we lived as a vast tenement, trees growing out of other trees and others, skinnier still, waiting behind them, with the uptilted faces of would-be basketball players; trees so numerous that I understood how Morris Graves might have wanted to portray them as a squadron of woodpeckers. In the jabbing fire of their beaks I saw Felix and I turning, our wings shining with the iridescence of salmon as we moved under a glass that we filled with our needles of dazzling, fist-scented rain.

My new fatherhood, the beauty of the city, the poetry I was finally writing, the different world that soccer gave me, all helped me get over the Greece I had cast aside. I was, I thought, reconciled to my life such as it was, when Jimmy came by on his long promised visit. With him he brought an Alexandrian friend of ours, Tony Parigory, to whom he was showing the country; New York which had rather fallen short; Palm Beach, "Ah! that's more like it," and now the northwest before descending on Mediterranean San Francisco. We were returning from an excursion to Victoria and Vancouver when we learned of President Kennedy's assassination. To lift our gloom Jimmy had Marcia and me play with him his new psychological find, The Landscape Game. It was a good way, he said, of breaking through to the hidden self and finding where you stood.

The player begins by describing the dream house he would like to inhabit. But the description of the house, for all it may say about how you see your public self, exists basically as a way of centering yourself for the ensuing walk with its sequence of symbolic encounters: a key; a bowl; an animal perhaps rushing across the path; a body of water; a final wall.

Rather than design a house of my own, I borrowed the little white L-shaped palace of the last Moorish king of Ronda that we had come upon at the end of our honeymoon. For the dining room (one's social self), the only room Jimmy asked specifically about, I adopted that of the poet Robert Graves, with whom we had dined once in Mallorca: a rectangular oak table set for six; bare walls hung with old Hispano-Mauresque lustreware plates.

"Are there any trees about?" Jimmy asked.

"Three," I replied, "in the fountain patio." The trees, I later learned, were my friends, "firmly clasped in the walled bosom of your heart."

I was now directed onto a path and told to follow it until I came to a key. A phallic symbol, I suspected, and I described an intricately notched tool of tumescent length.

"To what," Jimmy asked, "does it belong?"

The one set of doors that seemed worthy of such a key were the ones, I recalled, guarding Charlie Merrill's "Orchard" wine cellar. Within the doors appeared a sloping earthen runway, wide enough for an ox cart, leading to the ten-foot tall cellar that underran the entire length of the house.

Back on my path I proceeded along until I came to the inevitable bowl—a barrel-sized jardiniere as I described it of green and white majolica. And I knew at once what I'd plant in it, once I had had it trundled to a position outside my front door—an orange tree! The notion of the tree's roots eventually demolishing the pot did not displease me.

As the key symbolized my religion, of a drunk, possessed, earthdiving persuasion, "In vino veritas," so the jardiniere with the orange tree planted in it stood, Jimmy explained, for my notion of art. If the winter is what challenges, what better way of keeping it at bay than with one's own planted sun, so resplendently orange in its Arabic bowl? The poet as a gardener rummaging the grounds for containers he would fill. In effect, that's what I was doing with the set pieces like "Paros" I was then writing: taking a landscape that enchanted me and filling it with the rhythms of a dance—that

Orphic movement of the light I had discovered on our Easter walk in Paros.

Jimmy interrupted my reverie. "There's something I forgot to ask—what time of day is it on this walk?"

"Three o'clock," I replied, unaware I was indicating how old I felt. Yet with my new responsibilities there was reason enough, I suppose, to feel in the mid-afternoon of my life.

Next came the sexual body of water. "What is it?" Jimmy asked.

"The Mediterranean," I announced. From where I stood I could see it glowing invitingly far below.

"What do you do," Jimmy persisted, "when you come to it?"

"I'd like to go swimming," I said wistfully, "but it's so late in the day." Obviously the Mediterranean wasn't in itself a sufficient inducement. Or perhaps I needed a rock on which to bask until the sun burned me out of my inhibitions. But I wonder what other response I might have given. True, Greece and Felix's birth had, each in its way, refreshed our marriage. But for one reason or another, Marcia and I seldom made love; certainly nowhere near as often as I craved.

That unswimmable three o'clock, looking out wistfully at the nymph-filled Mediterranean, summed up my conjugal life. At twenty-seven, not only did I feel preternaturally old, but I saw myself living out a grotesque replica of my parents' marriage: the same bourgeois amenities; the same lack of any visceral communication. An entire sexual life had, I feared, passed me by. Lack of initiative? Lack of courage? Lack of luck? But there did not seem to be anything I could do about my sad state. I was certainly not about to walk out on Marcia and Felix for something I had never had.

Past the glimpse of the sea I continued on until I came to a wall— one's conception of the hereafter. "What sort of a wall is it?" Jimmy asked, "and what's on the other side?"

Mine wasn't a proper wall, but a series of fences in a pine forest, sheltering a mixed flock of goats and sheep. An after-life clearly in keeping with the thesis on pastoral I was articulating. Death in the sense of an extinction—that sharp picket fence with rocks and a few trees behind it—hadn't as yet registered.

The Landscape Game threw open some wide portals. But I don't think it would have challenged me to reconceive my life without Jimmy's adding it up for me. The oracle once again setting into motion what has to be. "What I like so much," he said, "is the consistency of this very earth-centered, Dionysiac and Mediterranean self you've revealed." His own bowl, he added, had been a blue-green Chinese celadon. Cupping it in his arms, he had carried it down to his river and there, kneeling, he had proceeded to fill it. "Just enough sex," he joked, "to irrigate one's art."

But we were all humbled by Tony Parigory, a true Mediterranean. "I was out on the dock at Faleron," he related, "it was nighttime and pitch black. But that didn't stop me, I just stripped off my clothes and dove in. Voilà."

DIONYSOS RULES

It seems odd to ascribe to the Landscape Game the role of a catalyst. Wasn't the birth of a son more determining? In the long run, certainly. But for me, it has often been the unexpected remark or dream that has set me afire. All the more, when the remark came from a mentor like Jimmy. In naming my dionysiac path, he was making sure I would not undersell myself.

While in New York a month later for the Modern Language convention, I set in motion the new design. For Marcia's Christmas present I bought her a set of oil paints; a present she remembers gratefully as it set her on her career path. For me, however, the gift was not altruistic. To be sure, I wanted her to develop her talent. But I hoped that having a vocation of her own might help her see she could do without me. Despite Felix's birth, I wanted out of our marriage. But I didn't want to be the one making the decision. Why couldn't Marcia think she was dumping me?

Felix was two and a half now, old enough to travel. "For our summer vacation, where should we go in Greece?" I asked the Greek-American expressionist painter, Aristodomos Kaldis. It was his little painting, seen in Marcia's boss's home in New Haven, of a donkey's ears sticking out of some blades of grass, which had given me a first intimation of what Greece might look like. Kaldis could think of nothing better than his native island of Lesbos. And he suggested we stay in Molyvos, the Mythmna of Daphnis and Chloe.

Situated on Lesbos's northeast coast directly across from the salt-laden, fish-rich mouth of the Dardanelles, Molyvos had long thrived as the last port of call before Constantinople. But the Turkish victory of 1923 ended the prosperity. In desperation, and for much the same reason that other towns turned themselves into free ports or gambling dens, Molyvos decided on an art scene. How the word got about I can't say, but from the far corners of the globe a host of "littles of today—but greats of tomorrow!" had descended, drawn by the assurance that, however they carried on—painting themselves with yogurt, whatever—they would not be persecuted.

To these would-be artists the local life hardly mattered. They had come not for Greece, but for the chance to perform on a stage where life was cheap. They congregated on an algae-ridden shingle beach smack in the midst of the town's discharging sewers. There all day long they sat, their gaze rising from the rampart cafes to the gaudy pink, blue and yellow painted houses that climaxed in an oversized Venetian castle straddling the hilltop.

Marcia did not share my reservations about the dubious art scene or the foul beach. To her, the young artists were fellow pilgrims on the hallowed road. And any beach was a blessing after rainy Seattle, especially one that contained such intense male proximity— beards, towels, shirts, color after color vibrating within a five-to-fifteen foot radius.

With each day, Marcia's enchantment grew. For the first time color was taking her over, saturating her to a point where only a well of red existed, as radiated from one or another wine or watermelon-shirted man. And woe to him who changed his shirt for one of a less fetid hue. He might just as well have turned himself into a stone. For as a painter picked a dominant tonality, so Marcia chose her suitors. And the men clearly admired her in her blue polka-dot bikini, with her wistful enthusiasm, her bursts of shy wit. This Penelope, putting down a first toe in the adulterous brine, must have let on she would soon choose one of them.

What was I to do—acknowledge this was the liberation I had intended with the gift of her oil painting and cheer her on? Or go about, as I did for a week, with an assassin's rock clenched in my possessive fist until the escalating possibilities, of Marcia's suitors all together against me, began to dawn. Was unleashing a vendetta what my "honor" required? No, I had my own curiosities to attend to, those wine harvest panegyris that were beginning to take me hither and thither about the island.

The day before the August fifteenth feast of the Assumption of the Virgin into heaven, Marcia and I had given an end-of-summer party in a valley cafe that could have been straight out of Daphnis and Chloe. With the explosive mixture of elements—Marcia's bohemians and my shepherds and fishermen (I had hired the town barber and his brother, they had brought their rock'n'roll records), it was not a happy affair. Even more when I woke chagrined to discover I had missed the day's only bus.

But I had my heart set on finally seeing an authentic wine festival or panegyri. "I may have missed the bus," I told Marcia as I roused myself, "but I'm still going to the panegyri at Aghiassos, even if I have to walk halfway across the island."

"You're in no condition," Marcia rejoined, "to do anything of the sort. You can hardly stand upright. Why don't you take it easy and go with us to the panegyri at nearby Petra tomorrow?"

I was not to be fobbed off. I pointed out that the mountain village of Aghiassos, right under Mount Olympus, had the best spirit of any village we had seen and that should make for a festival worth attending. With that, I started for the door.

Marcia called me back. "How long do you intend to be away?"

"Both days of it," I replied, "if it's any good. I want to see it all."

"All I can say," she said, looking me fiercely in the eye, "is you'd better be at Petra tomorrow, or I won't answer for the consequences."

Faced with her threat, I did manage to turn up the next evening at Petra and its famous church of the Holy Kiss. On its steps I found Marcia in a strapless flamingo-pink bit of bewitchery that had her rivals reduced to so much furious sulking paint.

"Won't you come sit with us?" she offered, flashing a pleased smile as she took me by the hand and led me off to her table. But her table was not well placed for anything but some inspired crawling by her little goat-bearded Moroccan suitor. I excused myself and soon found a makeshift table of my own. I carried it over my head through the throng before plunking it right under the bandstand next to a table of screaming, whistling, acrobatically somersaulting shepherd boys. That's what I had come for.

To dance, however, as the most virtuoso of the shepherds insisted, required fuel—three small jugs of retsina. As I tottered back up the hill towards Molyvos in the early morning, I was in no condition to notice Marcia under a bush, a few feet off the road.

I learned next morning about those threatened consequences from a genuinely contrite Marcia. The bushes, it seemed, had made for less than inspired copulation. "I wish," she said, "I hadn't been the first of us to break our vows. If you had just taken me by the hand and led me away, I'd have come."

But it was just that gesture I couldn't and did not want to make.

So we drifted apart, I into the wine-harvest panegyri that in late August seemed to come nearly every couple of days, Marcia into a sexual intensity enhanced by the glasses of white sizzling ouzo that concluded their afternoons at the beach. At twenty-eight, she felt she was only now coming into the glory of her body. While one part of her revelled in an appreciation perhaps long overdue, another observer remained standing a bit to the side, as if with a flick of her mermaid's tail she could be safe. She did not want to be unfaithful; it was more that the husband she was counting on to rescue her was himself prey to his own exclusive desire—to behold the dream which is a man, utterly alone, on the round of a moonlit floor, dancing out his zembeikiko.

* * *

Earlier in the summer, as Marcia and I were strolling home past the cafes one evening, through a doorway I had caught a glimpse of an elegant, gray-haired shepherd, George, and his brother, circling, cigarettes in hand, to a zembeikiko's stark, hypnotically pounding nine/four rhythm. When some weeks later George asked if I wanted to rent his mare and make a trip into the hills, I was able to tell him about my fascination with his dance, this wrestling with the eagle as the Zebeik tribesmen of Southern Anatolia originally conceived it.

At first I was content to watch. But now and then, faute de mieux, I might struggle to my feet and attempt to follow George as he swayed, shifted, stamped. There was no dionysiac release in it, nor perhaps could there be. It was more a rapport we were trying to further than some crashing through the wall on my own.

Unlike the so-called butcher's dance or hasapiko, the zembeikiko does not have steps that can be taught. It requires, in the hashish idiom, kefi (literally "head"), something that wells from within and which you can't let out any other way.

My own breakthrough came in the last week of August when George took me to a panegyri in Magdalena, a gangster-exporting mountain village on the other side of the ridge from Molyvos. I was making my way into the parapet-clinging cafes when the rope holding my saddle bag came apart. I was on my knees, picking it all up when the sound of an eight-piece orchestra, more ancient than anything I had yet heard, reached my ears. At ten in the morning, that couldn't have been more unusual and, leaving my effects behind, I set off in the direction of the sound.

Bursting into their cafe and ordering a mug of retsina, I took up a far corner table where I remained oblivious of everything (of George's "What are you doing in this private party? How did you ever expect me to find you?" when he arrived out of sorts, of the anxious-eyed townspeople returning by the window one or another of my abandoned belongings) but the patterns being woven by those absolutely committed dancers. The best of them was the cafe owner, a portly fellow dressed in sombre black and white who moved with the grace, the surprising swiftness, of a great cloud.

On the stroke of twelve they all spilled out of the cafe in a single line, handkerchiefs ablaze, onto the high-walled, steeply cobbled street. In the glare, and before a red-eyed assembly of bemused, whiskered faces, they proceeded to weave an elaborate figure-eight around a man saluting them with a tray of ouzo glasses. Then, the last glass quaffed, they were gone.

Some five hours later, after waking from a nap, I found them again, a wild Serbian jig shrilling from the roof of a house. There was a ladder, so I climbed it to be met by an Australian revenant, the son, as it turned out, of the cafe owner. "What can I do for you?" he asked.

"I love the music these guys play," I said, as if that excused my butting in.

"How about then dancing something with me—a twist?"

A twist, I pointed out, was not part of my repertoire. But I could, given a couple of glasses, dance a zembeikiko. Whereupon a tall fellow, dressed in old-fashioned, long ripply sleeves that gave him the look of an oversized stork, asked me to dance with him. I tried, rather frenetically I fear. Then everyone filed down the ladder and, with the orchestra leading the way, we all paraded from one doorway to the next, to be greeted by one or another smiling, blackdress wife, holding a silver tray and the maximum possible ouzo glasses.

Back at the cafe, on a long table mounted over the street, a dinner of roast lamb off the spit followed, friendly fingers pushing choice morsels into my mouth. Sometime in the middle of the feasting, the Australian brought me into a little room, produced pen and paper and, to my astonishment, asked me to write a note for him to the Australian consul, requesting a year's visa extension so he could attend to his "dying" mother, she of the bewitching smile and the many ouzo glasses.

We had barely returned to the table when his father asked me to dance a zembeikiko. A two-person zembeikiko is, as I've noted, not conducive to self-expression. But opposite this portly man and his luminous melon of a belly, wings of my own suddenly sprouted—dancing down, from every conceivable angle, right into him and his belly. For hours afterwards, in one shoebox cafe after the next, those new wings went on flapping, while across from me, or even over me, George or Stork Sleeves or perhaps the local Idiot danced with a power that I, prone there, helped set ablaze.

Ever since, sufficiently moved by the first notes of a song, I have only to rise to my feet for an initiate to understand what, until then, would never have dawned: that I was one of them; not a Magowan, but a rascal, a mangas, Icarus-like proclaiming,

> Wings walk and melt.
> The fire
> Is the globe I am.

GLORIA

Before going to Greece, Marcia and I had purchased a lake-view home in the central, racially integrated Madrone district; sign, it might be thought, that we intended to batten down for a while. Upon our return in September our first guest was Father. He had come, he announced, to inspect the local Safeway operation and his first grandchild. But his real aim, as it turned out, was to give my provincial complacency a shaking.

The two of us were sitting out on the verandah with drinks one early evening, and I was trying to describe the satisfaction I felt with Seattle, when he asked, "Isn't it every professor's goal to teach at Harvard?" He was puzzled by my obvious lack of a game plan with which to storm the academic heights.

"Harvard," I replied in my professional capacity, "is one of the better appointments, if teaching is your primary career. But I'm a writer first, not a teacher, and I can't imagine a more inspiring place to write than here."

But Father was not about to be sidetracked. "How do you make your living," he asked, "teaching or writing?"

"Teaching," I admitted.

"Well, that's your career."

And with no if's, but's, or in between's, there I was.

Once again the poisoned dart had struck. When, some weeks later, a poet friend (with a wife and five kids) resigned in anger after not receiving an expected summer grant, I decided to resign too in support. Why, with Chairman Heilman absent on leave and several hundred vying for a position, I expected anyone in that bureaucratic forest to hear, much less respond to, a lone crashing oak, I can hardly imagine. But, just as I had given Marcia her oil painting set, so leaving Seattle and the new house she had just decorated may have been another way of making Marcia question her marital assumptions. Then, too, there was a greener pasture temptation. In a highly mobile time a professor wasn't a real success unless he was constantly uprooting himself. In the chess match I was still waging with my father, I may have needed assurance.

I soon discovered that my professional stock, despite a number of publications in prestigious journals, had not risen appreciably in the three years since I had last thrown myself on the job market. As an Americanist who spoke French after a fashion, I did succeed in garnering a Fulbright to Marcia's native Roumania. But of the forty literature departments to which I applied in 1964, only Berkeley, then in the heady throes of the Free Speech Movement (FSM), expressed an interest. And while holding out this carrot, the Berkeley chairman, Mark Schorer, made clear he had a number of more important period slots to fill before he could expect to offer an appointment to an "exotic flower" of my sort.

When in April the funding for an umpteenth assistant professor came through, I declined the Fulbright. For me, almost as alluring as Berkeley, was California's divorce reputation. Perhaps its marital shock waves would sunder my cage.

Why then didn't I seek a divorce? After ten years together I ought to have known what I was or wasn't getting. But that was precisely my problem. Apart from one night with a Jamaican prostitute, Marcia was the only woman I had known before getting married. And the half-dozen beds I had strayed into since had never been given the time to uncup their thousand mysteries. Female sexuality is itself so unpredictable. There are certain furnaces which, no matter how assiduously stoked, will never catch fire. Others ignite at a glance. Where in this spectrum Marcia hovered is hard to say. I don't think she disliked sex. It just wasn't for her the same consuming preoccupation it was for me.

Confronted with a minotaur of my needful disposition, another woman of her temperament might have cast me aside and concentrated on finding an older man to provide the goods she required. But like many Pygmalions, Marcia had become entrapped by what she had every reason to regard as her creation.

As I started to come into my own as a man, Marcia became increasingly enamoured and, by the same token, highly possessive. She would let fly with some crockery, or thrust a suicidal vein through a plateglass window. But all her passionate duende did nothing to alleviate the pain of my wasted manhood.

The more Marcia embellished our marriage labyrinth, the more I resisted, convinced that nothing less than the authenticity of my vision was at stake. Was sex, as I believed, an experience so transforming as to hold the very key to an adult life? Or was it, as Marcia maintained, merely another romantic mirage?

It was May and Marcia was about to go into the hospital for an operation, when I found myself hurled into an affair with Gloria, a petite, green-eyed departmental secretary who had recently divorced. She took me to her favorite haunts, showing me a new unsuspected northwest. And when she turned up on my charter flight to London, I managed to spirit her off to Greece and a week on Paros. Wherever we were, like mating lions, we coupled; perhaps not every twenty minutes on the dot, but more in any twenty-four hours than Marcia and I could have encompassed in a month.

It's easy enough, looking back at those six weeks, to see another instance of the dream that may be anyone's essential life. But a man doesn't immerse himself again and again in those life-giving waters without emerging in some way changed. By the time I put Gloria on her plane to Rome, I had resolved to ask Marcia, when I met her in Athens, for a divorce.

Marcia's response, once she had recovered from the initial shock, was composed. She had, after all, faced my qualms before. "When you left Seattle, we were still man and wife. Now it seems we're not. Have you fallen in love? With whom may I ask?"

So I told her about Gloria and the sexual being she had released in me.

Marcia heard me out. Then, smiling bitterly, she walked to the room's open window and, removing her topaz engagement ring, flung it as far as she could into the gritty beyond. Whence next morning, in a less romantic mood, she retrieved it, some two court-yards away. By then we had agreed to meet at the end of the summer in Molyvos. I could then decide if I still wanted a divorce.

In reality, I had gained very little—at best six weeks' temporary relief. But to me, after so many emotionally strangled years, I felt as if I were now embarked on a life of my own, and I set off on the first of two ferries for the island of Ischia and the hotel address where, I knew, Gloria would eventually arrive.

Ischia turned out to be a Mediterranean Southampton. Rather than wait for her there, I returned to Naples for an overlong week. Gloria was not exactly prepared for this spectre with the room down the hall. And it took another ten days before I had weaned that lizard of the beach from the relaxations of an island summer she had promised herself. But eventually we did clamber onto the train across southern Italy and the requisite three ferries to Paros, the one place in the whole Aegean where I could be her Dionysos.

Yet for all the island's magic a wider reality kept intruding. And the notion of what we were doing to Marcia and little Felix had Gloria "climbing the walls. Your joy," she said, "is so electric and I'm glad I've helped you find it. But what's liberation for you may be something else for them. Believe me, I've been down that road and I don't wish it on anyone."

Our last days were difficult. Gloria seemed always on the verge of booking passage on a boat and sailing away. Again and again I had to silence that ringing ship's horn and somehow bring her back to the reality of not they, Marcia and Felix, but us merged in what we were giving each other. But however I tried to pour myself into that tankard of hers, to be for one more embrace her risen phoenix, there was little I could do to keep the sea of guilt from roaring back. Eventually I had no choice but to return her to Piraeus and the Turkish liner she had booked. I couldn't see the storm of mascara blackening her face as she waved and waved from its diminishing railing. But even I knew that this was adieu.

CRIMES OF THE HEART

The morning Gloria sailed was August 24th, the date of the Magdalena panegyri where I had learned to dance a year earlier. Just the ticket for Jimmy, I thought, who had never taken in a village festival. Gathering him, along with my brother Peter and his recent bride, Jill, I flew off to Lesbos and my agreed rendezvous with Marcia.

It was perhaps expecting too much for the panegyri, when we reached it by Molyvos's one cab later that evening, to live up to the previous edition. But the first shoebox cafe we strolled into had two grizzled shepherds dancing atop a table and a chair respectively. Nor was it long before they had each presented me with a bottle of retsina. For my two amazed rhythm-clapping hands? Or was it, as Jimmy offered, a canny way of getting rid of me by putting me under the table? If so, it would be a good several hours. I still had considerable fires of my own to stamp out. Cafe by packed cafe that's what I did, kneeling, wheeling, stamping, slapping, heel, toe, thigh, floor.

Across, deep in the gloom of an only six-month-away fortieth birthday, sat Jimmy. Backs to the dancing, oblivious of everything but next week's meeting in Southampton with our parents, sat Peter and Jill. Marcia, silent as a sibyl, kept her thoughts to herself.

A month later, though, some quatrains arrived from Jimmy. His version of an evening, of what it was I was doing to myself, to him, to my whole family:

OUZO FOR ROBIN

Dread of an impending umpteenth
Birthday thinning blood to water, clear
Spirits to this opal-tinted white—

Uncle, the confusion unto death!
Last night's hurled glass. On the wall a mark
Explored by sunlight inching blindly
Forth from the tavern onto tree-tarred
Heights of gilt and moleskin, now gone dark.

Thorn needle launched in spinning grooves' loud
Black. A salt spray, a drenching music.
Each dance done, wet hawklike features cling
To one more tumblerful of numb cloud.

Joy as part of dread, rancor as part.
Lamplit swaying rafters. Later, stars.
Case presented, point by brilliant point,
Against the uncounselable heart.

Ground trampled hard. Again. The treasure
Buried. Rancor. Joy. Tonight's blank grin.
Threshold where the woken cherub shrieks
To stop it, stamping with displeasure.

In that stamping syntax, those perspiring "hawklike features,"
Jimmy catches something of my pent-up wrath: the frustration of
an all too young married youth absolutely determined, with the
help of his ouzo glass's "tumblerful of numb cloud" to break his
way free. Yet I see now that "the woken cherub shriek[ing] to stop
it" was as much the divorced child in Jimmy as it was little Felix.
But a similar verdict—my family having long since departed—
could have come from the waiter in the last cafe, pointing to the
upstairs cots. Sign that even in his practiced eyes I had breached
the limits.

In Molyvos the next day there still remained Marcia to be faced.
I had tottered my way down from those heights because I had,
after all, given her my word. And I assumed she could use an extra

hand in getting herself and Felix and their luggage onto the plane. But foolishly, I let her persuade me to stay with her. It was during that final week our sex produced another pregnancy.

I failed to dissuade Marcia from accompanying me to my new job in Berkeley and carrying on as the wife she indeed was. All the same I did manage to return to Seattle and Gloria for a couple of extended weekends. But for Gloria my visits could come to seem intrusive; she had her own sexual life to live. By the time of my third visit, late in the fall, I grasped that any embers I might once have lit were smoldering fitfully. But it was only the next evening, when she failed to show up at her house after a party as promised—I waited in my car until dawn—that I got her message.

That ended our tango. But I can't help but acknowledge the way Gloria brought the minotaur in me forth. To this day my horns shake in gratitude. And in my own being I felt achieved, as if I had stepped through a door, entered a sea-girt home.

In Berkeley, there remained what Jimmy called our "grim final toccata" to be played out. Or was pregnant Marcia to pull off another wifely escape? Try as I might, I could not gain her consent to a separation. And she refused to consider an abortion. It was her last chance, she thought, to bear a second child. That left me all the more desperate, and ruthless. To my new colleagues and students I must have looked like one of those drowning swimmers, wildly screaming and waving my arms as I thrashed towards a perceived surface. To anyone stupid enough to hold out a hand I could be dangerous.

But my need for a more authentic life remained. For a man the erotic quest—for the unknowable in oneself—is an inextricable part of one's ongoing social identity. And with every scrap of his being he points himself to the next coming into being, a woman, a poem.

Women, like Marcia, march to a different gong. From me she had always sought a confirmation of herself as a woman and as a wife. When I refused now to provide it and instead tried to leave her, a self-destructive impulse emerged. After one suicidal episode, I persuaded her to call a psychiatrist. He told her, "Don't do anything until I've seen you in my office." To her question the next day about her frequent hysteria he remarked, "If you get kicked in the teeth you feel pain. You don't commit suicide."

In the house and the bed we still shared, I felt increasingly marooned. Strange as it may seem, I did not understand that all I had to do was present myself before a lawyer. Instead I saw only the accusation of desertion, if not absurdity, in moving to a motel. Then in March, as Marcia was entering her seventh month of pregnancy, I began an affair with Christine, a twenty-two-year-old ex-model who was putting herself through college as a part-time secretary in the English department's typing office.

For the next months I had to keep my affair secret lest Marcia react in a way that might rebound on the child she was carrying. After James was born, healthy, red-haired, the need for secrecy lessened. Finally there came the moment when I could not hold my tongue any longer. Marcia had insisted on a weekend together in a Napa Valley hotel. She and I were lying in bed after having made love for the first time in five months. In the afterglow I could feel her renewed assumptions closing in. We were a couple once again. Our new son was going to unite us. It was now or never. I told her about my affair, making it clear I saw no point in our staying together. By now Marcia was prepared to accept a divorce. All she asked was, "Do you love her?" When I responded, "Yes," I found myself released. The freedom I had so long awaited could begin: dreams, I thought, picturing a horse, on the necklaces of wind.

BERKELEY ERUPTING

The affair with Christine lasted through the summer. A young man is so open to any novelty he hasn't tasted as yet. And Christine possessed a princess-like sophistication that seemed to offer a bridge back into the world in which I had been brought up; one I had perhaps foolishly renounced. At twenty, it is the rare man who consciously seeks his past in a woman. At thirty, the age I was now approaching, my earlier princely options seemed all too willfully cut. Was Jimmy right in insisting I choose between the life of a writer and life in a tuxedo and dancing pumps?

As it turned out, I wasn't quite princely enough for the exquisite tastes that so drew me. And Christine wasn't finally, as she had imagined, pregnant. So, despite myself, I escaped. A year later I remember seeing her in her white make-up crossing the traffic circle near where I lived and experiencing a shudder. I had come so close to marrying a ghost.

My moving out was confusing to four-year-old Felix. "You are Mommy's Daddy aren't you?" he once asked me. And he asked Marcia, after I had removed Charlie Merrill's four-poster, "What was wrong—was the bed too large?"

His confusion came to a head one day when I was helping Marcia pack books for her move into a small house nearer the campus. It was not altruism. I was eager to speed her along. But I must have overplayed my hand because at one point Marcia, harassed by the whole sum of her concerns, turned to me and yelled angrily, "I don't have to put up with you. Just get out of my life."

This was too much for Felix, who was helping me stuff her books into carton boxes. Picking up on her words he said, "Mommy, you get out of my life." Then, aware of the uncanny silence his remark had brought, he repeated it.

At that, Marcia, forgetting she had nothing on her feet but sandals, gave one of the boxes an almighty kick. Next thing I knew, she was hopping about on one foot and shrieking. Thoroughly cowed, I left the house. Next day I learned that she had broken a bone in her big toe.

I had come to Berkeley somewhat reluctantly. The prestige of the university, the so-called Athens of the West, and its nearness to my parents in San Francisco—how some of us long for an impossible rapprochement!—were positive inducements. But for all the beauty of the campus, the two magnificent botanical gardens, the old wood-shingled houses and the setting on a great hill overlooking San Francisco Bay, Berkeley could never be for me the Shangri-la it was for so many others.

I did not arrive in Berkeley until a year after the Free Speech Movement. Thus I missed the opening scene of the decade and the euphoric mood that those participating had of a volcano joyfully pouring out its revolutionary ashes over the entire planet. I missed what, a year later, had now become legend: the campus strike, the Sproul Hall sit-in, the arrests, the marches, the spectacle of a choice few students, ringed in by thousands, dancing on the hood of a liberated patrol car.

By the time I arrived, the authorities had the vents pretty well plugged. Not that there weren't almost daily protestations, rallies, picketings, repeated attempts to burn down an ROTC Quonset hut by attacking it in broad afternoon, several hundred marching strong. (In Berkeley no one ever did anything in the morning or alone at night, with a set of matches.) But, for all the efforts, the revolutionary keg never stayed lit.

My generation did not have a group identity. The baby boomers did, thanks to television. They were the first generation whose buying power was solicited. And it gave them the illusion of having other kinds of power as well. By uniting, they could change the world.

There were different views among them as to the degree of change required. The great protest movements of the era—women's liberation, black civil rights, the various gay and ethnic coalitions— all started out as raids on the establishment in the name of a more just society. They wanted what I had, up to then, taken for granted— the same opportunities, the same perks and privileges—within a merely expanded middle-class America.

Then, towards the end of 1966, something new emerged: a revolution led by the privileged youth of the baby boomer generation, which sought to do away with the constrictions of middle-class life. All too predictably, I fear, I joined in.

The proposed hippie transformation of American values spoke all the more in that I was now comparatively free. Apart from my job, there was nothing to keep me from trying to reinvent myself. And that's what one long-haired satirist after the next asked as he or she swaggered by in the ubiquitous blue jeans, the flag-striped ass, Uncle Sam hat, fringed "redskin" leather jacket and dangling love beads. But for these young Californians the costumes suggested an answer as well. Just where, in the long ride out west, had America come untracked? And what could be done to set her on a less wasteful, more free and sane course?

In the daily spontaneity I saw the makings of a new poetry, an androgynous generation showing me how I could turn on, tune in and, given some help from my friends, get away with it. We shared, after all, a belief in a life of exploration, a climbing out on a limb and, one way or another, letting go: with a shout, a scream, a barbaric yawp; or even a near suicidal plunge, as some psychedelic TNT exploded.

The hippie apogee was the mid-January Human Be-In in Golden Gate Park. Perhaps no more than fifteen thousand attended this "Gathering of the Tribes"—half the attendance of an average baseball game. When I arrived, it was mid-afternoon, and I remember passing a stream of returning celebrants for whom the best was over. But even an event's final moments could bear checking out, and I hastened on until I reached a pair of overturned garbage pails propped up by a chain metal fence. Clambering over, I dropped onto the new revolution's Champ de Mars, a polo field carpeted as far as I could see with squatting hippies, spread out like the buffalo of old prairie times.

Stepping gingerly around and over the blankets, dark glasses and proffered joints, I made my way towards the Be-In's command post: a scaffolded platform at the far end of the field blasting out rock'n'roll from Big Brother and the Holding Company, the Jefferson Airplane, the Grateful Dead, interspersed with an Allen Ginsberg-led prayer chant and hysterical announcements of lost children.

Here lay a paved walkway where progress was somewhat easier. Those sufficiently inspired danced, shirts discarded in the mild air, shoulder-length tresses snapping in a syncopated flail across ecstatic pinkish-red faces. Ah, so that's what *Hair* was about! Old-fashioned daguerreotype faces popped up everywhere, set off by bandannas, sideburns, wire-rim glasses, beards and moustaches of every cut and thickness. When I stalled, unable to move in the surging throng, I had only to fix my gaze on the tribal encampments parked on the far side of the encircling chain metal fence: women in mini-skirts seated on the tops of trucks, silver boots smacking back and forth in time to the rock beat; kids in old-style vests and long granny dresses playing fiddle tunes beside an aluminum Air-Stream camper whose open windows disgorged a cloud of pungent smoke.

The distinctiveness of the Be-In may have lain less in its Seurat "Grande Jatte" aspect than in the anonymous community we all made up. Though everybody I knew, or would know, was there, I didn't bump into a single one of them. I remember a few hours later, as my girl friend and I were sitting at a North Beach restaurant table, being asked if I wouldn't mind sharing our table. As fate would have it, who should sit down but Marcia and her new beau, the best student from my pastoral seminar of the year before and a good friend as well. They, too, hadn't come upon anyone they knew at the Be-In. And yet here we were, buoyed by all that anonymous hope, that enthusiasm, thrust anew into each other's lives.

The Be-In's version of a new flower-powered America was to prove ephemeral. But for a few months more it did look as if the Bay Area was about to become a Xanadu; a wave on which each of our little rafts was caught up and lifted, ever more wondrously, more perilously high. In a single week—and every baby boomer-aged woman can probably still tell you which one it was—all the bras vanished. Did our revolution need an agenda, a political leadership? Hardly, it seemed, when the General Will so sufficed. Not conceptual thought, but vibrations, patterns, rhythms, revolutionary change contemplated from within a million molecules of exploding hallucinogens, that's where it was at among all of us youthfully arrogant, self-righteous dots sitting out there on the grass while Santana, Jimi Hendrix and Janis Joplin smoldered and stomped. An instantaneous transformation, both of ourselves and of the entire planet, as we conceived it from that bend of the Yellow Brick Road, seemed just out of sight, a mere horizon away.

A year later, flower power was another bumper sticker on a Eugene McCarthy VW. The wave, like all waves, had crashed.

MIRANDA DELLA GIOIA

For the past ten years with women I had not had a free hand. Now I saw a substantial bachelor's career stretching before me, night after night by the Bay tossing out the rod to the light of the twinkling waves.

The reality was another matter. Cruise as I did the joints, the dance halls, the singles bars, I did not find many mermaids rising to my offerings. Maybe I was too intense and East Coast, not relaxed and Californian enough. Maybe at that stage I still lacked the cool, single-shot photographic temperament which the one-night stand requires, picking up whom I could and making the best of it. No matter how carefully my antennae probed, running my hands over the bodies on the dance floor, reducing the variety to a type—small, slinky, smoke-maned, mercurial-minded Glorias—there was no way of predicting what intercourse might yield. And my way of withdrawing, after a surge of intensity, without even a phone call, much less a redeeming present, could invite a well-justified response.

I was hardly returned from Christmas holidays in Aspen with my brother Peter when I found on my locked English department desktop a black elbow-length glove. In case the sorcery hadn't registered, it was followed in equally mysterious fashion a week later by a length of stout rope hanging looped like a hangman's noose on the inside door knob. Sign that in some unknown quarter I had given offense.

I had to conclude I wasn't, any more than Charlie Merrill, equipped for bachelorhood. We just didn't feel right in our skins unless we were living with someone very pretty whom we could betray.

But those nights of navigating Berkeley's bachelor minefields seemed to be over. Before leaving for Aspen, I had started an affair with a Franco-Polish ballet dancer plucked from a just concluded seminar. Raised in a New England mill town, she had old-fashioned charms of a sort not often encountered. She couldn't see without her glasses; nor could she swim, drive, or even light an oven. For an insecure man like me she was a palpable treasure.

The Ballet Dancer was still mulling over when to move in when fate tossed up a second sexual mate in the person of Miranda della Gioia, a freshman enrolled in the second half of a required composition course.

The question of an affair with a student, of the violation of a trust in someone much younger, is not lightly broached. In defense, it is usual to cite Socrates for whom sex was an indispensable phase of the learning process. But once sex rears its passionate head, it has a way of taking over. And, since the teacher retains most of the power, the liaison cannot be very equal. The resulting guilt, and the inequity felt in the classroom between the screwed and the unscrewed, can blacken even the most positive relationship.

At Washington and Berkeley, sexual morality was personal and no chairman tried to hand down any guidelines. But in view of the harassment I had suffered at Harvard from my social science section-man, I made it a point to postpone any encounter until the course was over. By then, an affair had much to recommend it. After seeing me spill out my guts for nine weeks, the woman had a fair notion who she was taking on. It left me the pleasure of drawing her out, in whatever guise she chose to present herself.

But I wasn't pure stone and, on the winter term's first day, as my eyes lit on a voluptuous, long-haired, Lady of Shalott seated in the first row, I remember feeling a keen pang about a person, and a hippie world, I would now never know. I also remember catching, as I stepped inside, her gasp of surprise. I was a reasonably young-looking thirty, still required in some bars to produce a driver's license.

Miranda was a third generation Albanian Italian from suburban San Jose. Her oval face, with a trace of baby fat still in her cheeks, possessed the mixture of sensual line and sweetness, the "lucent inwardness" of an Antonello da Messina madonna. Add gray-blue eyes from her Alsatian maternal grandparents, a full, small-waisted body and the most dazzling of smiles, and there was a beauty truly unsettling.

Faced with Paris's choice, I'd have elected that child owl, Pallas Athene. Miranda was as bright as anyone I've met, my Uncle Jimmy aside. In class, she answered my questions, returning with searching ones of her own. She produced papers thought out in a single draft, sentences tumbling as luxuriously as her hair. I saw to it that I alone corrected them, trying to make her feel like a fellow writer.

As I spun my web about her, Miranda reciprocated by staying behind after class, telling me about herself with a spontaneity that I matched as best I could.

But I remember my surprise when, in early February, she appeared on the fourth floor of Wheeler Hall during my afternoon "office hours." She was wearing a beige silk blouse tied with a flopping sailor's bow.

After seating her and taking up a relaxed position on the edge of my desk I asked to what did I owe this pleasure.

"Oh, it's nothing academic," Miranda said, "I'd just like to get to know you better."

"In that case," I said, without a moment's hesitation, "why don't we go up to my apartment. It's on Panoramic, above the football stadium." I wasn't my collection of paintings by friends, my Oriental rugs, painted voodoo pots and vessels, and Greek 45 r.p.m. records. But, amongst them, my past might be a bit clearer.

"What about your office hours," Miranda asked, somewhat taken aback, "don't you have to stick around?"

"In principle, but four flights is a good climb and no one usually turns up except at the beginning or the end of term."

Normally I'd have walked up to Panoramic Way, cutting through

Fraternity Row. But not wanting to be seen with such a young and striking looking student, I chose a more circuitous route, by way of the soccer field on the far side of the stadium. Though I was fit from playing, my heart was pumping so hard that, at one point of our climb, I had to halt to regain my breath. It was then, in an effort to clear the air in the fullest of senses, I told her about the graduate student who was about to move in with me.

"I'm spoken for, as well," Miranda replied. She proceeded to tell me about her high school lover who had followed her to Berkeley, where he was supporting himself by dealing methedrine.

They had lived together in a Telegraph Avenue apartment. "You could always tell it," she said with some pride, "by the unmarked narc car parked across the street." But at the beginning of the present term, unable any longer to bear the sight of his emaciated body, she had moved back to her dormitory.

"Why does anyone take speed?" I asked, unable to fathom the attraction.

"It makes you feel so lucid," she replied. She went on. "Since he's not qualified to attend the university, it helps him feel superior. He's always been jealous of me, and my parents' wealth."

"What does your father do?"

"He heads a ten-man law firm. His specialty is compensation claims. Mostly small farmers whose land the highway people want to gobble up. At fifty percent, it's quite lucrative." After pausing a moment, she went on. "At school, I've always been richer than anyone. My dad would be much happier defending murderers, or serving as a judge. He does it for my mother. She has red hair, so everything in the house is red. She craves the glamor: her Mercedes, the big swimming pool, the five gold-plated telephones stuck all over the house. Christ, imagine what that's like bringing your friends home to!"

The nets were being spread. We were both children of Minos from ostentatious backgrounds, if not quite the same. By now we had reached Panoramic Way, an acacia-lined, single-car wide road that wound from the stadium up to vast Tilden Park. Mine, the second of three descending apartments, lay just below the first hairpin turn. As we clomped down the outside staircase we encountered tubs of marigolds and petunias lining the balcony that leaned out on a pair of sixty-foot stilts over this section of the San Andreas fault. Giving onto the balcony were two rooms: a small bedroom that Charlie Merrill's ebony fourposter filled almost ominously and a somewhat larger living room with an exposed floor, like a raked stage, tilting down toward the far balcony corner. Exposed piping added its prominent curves and took over the hallway's dingy bathroom. At the end of the hallway, banked against the hill, lay the kitchen. At this hour it featured a shaded view eastwards, over a series of gardens where the flowering almonds were in full bridal glory, towards the Oakland docks. There, by the breakfast table, with a gallon of retsina by me on the floor, we sat down.

Miranda had said she wanted to get to know me. Which me? The lonely minotaur with the stammer and jerky hands seated across from her? No, this monster was still submerged in his family labyrinth, unwritten, disembodied. But there was a masked man I could describe, this writer-teacher. To a girl whose family had never strayed outside the seventy-five mile San Jose-Berkeley-San Francisco triangle, I tried to explain the lure of elsewhere, all that comes with the disruption of context.

What Miranda made of those journeys, those over-sized relatives, I don't know, but as the shadows lengthened I found myself more and more captivated. By the sexy way she leaned forward as she spoke. By the butterfly-like quickness of her small, round-fingered hands fluttering in front of her speaking lips. By the genuine goodness and largeness of purpose that seemed to emanate from her. I couldn't bear to think that in a moment she could disappear back into her freshman life, her dorm, her hippie glamor. Just to keep her by, and not knowing she was a strict vegetarian, I cooked her a Greek lamb stew which she had to summon all her politeness to keep poking at.

Afterwards we retired to the living room couch to listen to my Greek records. Finally a zembeikiko new to my feet arose, of such imperiousness I had to try to dance it for her. On the one patch of

Miranda, Panoramic Way, 1967

rugless floor that's what I did, insulating myself in a resonance of clicking fingers and ringing slaps as I dipped and bobbed and wheeled.

Finally, winded by my exertions, I collapsed, panting, at Miranda's feet. At the moment, everything still hung in abeyance: the person I desired; the hippy transformation I could accomplish with her help. To take her in my arms, or not to? If I didn't, would I ever have another opportunity? And how would she regard my lack of courage? Faith in the possibility of recurrence yielded to the impelling need to seize the day.

So I sprang. Or rather, since I was on the floor, I raised myself and, heart pumping violently, put my arms around her and began to kiss her. Miranda's mouth responded with a sexy directness. That left several choices open. Probably I should have resisted. I was, after all, accepted by her. But as the Greek proverb puts it, how do you hold honey in your hand and not lick it?

Moving forward I reached down and slipped my arms under her. Then, staggering somewhat, I hoisted her off the couch and carried her through the doorway and placed her carefully on my chest-high fourposter. Four years later, Miranda called the episode a rape.

But a woman doesn't submit enthusiastically three times without betraying a certain complicity.

Of that night I still retain the passion with which her arms held me as she slept. Next morning, after we had walked barefoot over the acacia-strewn roadway, I remember her dousing her soles in ouzo as she sat on the rim of the tub. (Wasn't there a bar of soap about?) I didn't want to choose between Miranda and the graduate student. But if I had to, I knew even then it would be Miranda, for the possibilities her embracing arms seemed to promise.

For Miranda, the yoking of our unlikely opposites had occurred too quickly. And it precluded the separate stages whereby a young woman normally secures herself in her love. Instead of her petals opening one by one, she became a tight, closed, defensive bud. What mattered now was her pride, keeping me from dumping her. At the heart of everything lay a tawdry canker.

Without considering whether it was really me she wanted, she set out to entrap me. To be sure, a poet professor had his value. He might even make a useful pawn in the ongoing struggle with her mother and her own peer group. But control comes at a price: of a woman's ability to release herself, the ringing wells rising from her sexual vulnerability.

After returning to her dorm Miranda had expected me, this disembodied voice, to phone. When I hadn't after two days (I was counting on seeing her in class next day), she swallowed her pride and rang me up and I invited her over.

As we lay in the dark some hours later, I remember her proffering her silken lures. "How can you expect me to stay with you when you don't want to marry me. Everyone else always has. But they were too young to get married without parental consent."

The unlikely idea of marriage brought a smirk to my face. Why, with two willing lovers, would I want to put myself back in a marital noose?

Yet her dart was planted, and soon enough that preposterous teenage notion became my consuming passion. I'm not sure I knew then what a good marriage involves. But at twenty-nine I could recognize certain longings: for a wife of my own choosing, a domestic life and a more grounded being. In Miranda I saw a child-woman willing to dance in those ancient chains.

When I informed the Graduate Student of my decision, she made a remark about teen-age bodies—how perfect they were. A sign, as I took it, of forbearance. But a few weeks later she left out for the garbage man a big pink-and-blue Télémaque painting I had loaned her. It got trashed.

With my earlier loves, Gloria and Christine, I don't think I penetrated much beyond their sexuality. Miranda brought something more personal: a seeking "I," a human alchemist. And it was a wide, multi-disciplined synthesis she was aiming at, she and her mate, hand in hand.

For all my singularity, I found it flattering to be treated as a prospective mystic, out on some brushy hillside exclaiming at a warbler we had sighted. This childhood fascination of mine—intensity speaking to intensity—proved something I could revive for a girl who knew birds only from a borrowed library book.

Miranda told me of those not so long ago nights when she lay listening to the train whistles blowing in the distance. Only for this six-year-old the whistles were ships. Someone had told her the ocean was only five miles from her home—which it may have been, as the crow flies over the Santa Cruz mountains. So it wasn't altogether implausible to imagine a fleet of ships that came and went in the night. She even thought she knew the shopping mall where they moored. Everything was explainable, even the water that vanished from the cement walkways with the coming of day.

Then there was the time her nurse had caught her making up a second bed in her room.

"For whom is the other bed?" her nurse asked.

"For me," Miranda replied, "to cry on."

How could I, whose life had ticked to little else than the idiot hum of my restlessness, not marvel at a person who claimed that she had never experienced an hour's boredom? From what was I trying to escape? Couldn't I, too, live in the present and try to grow from my own internal space? The incentive to remake myself was certainly compelling. Though I often felt too old for her, too stiff and East Coast, I couldn't help but relish the openings she brought.

Hers seemed a faery delicacy, mounted in green, leaflike, against me. A face of a deer, carved in golden wood, in sun-smile. With big thoughtful eyes of that bluegray the Flemish Patinier employed to dress his fantastic mountainscapes. And like Patinier's, her eyes spoke of a quest, they were she. When I think of them I see one of those favorite days of hers, all rain and emptiness, the fog blanketing the Berkeley hills until only a few textures remained, the brick of some garden stairs, the leaded windows of a dark shingle house. Discomposite effects, but so is a church's rose window. Only hers lay on the ground, fragments for anyone to come upon, pick up and throw away. She wanted to be the alchemist who would find value in society's dross. And she was very fine. With her at my side I saw myself starting out anew, as if she could be for me both mother and daughter, each of us inhabiting the same flesh, the same sky.

It helped that 1967 was the spring of the Year of Love. Here was style, sparkle, hope, Walt Whitman's kids teaching me how to open to the child in myself. Strolling with Miranda down Telegraph I was not a professor now, but a fellow innocent. What, we asked, would happen next? Who would enact what new and needed astonishment? Imagine a horde, all of course on tiptoes, peering out from the Fillmore, or wherever we were gathered, while the red of the sun sank behind the Golden Gate Bridge in polluted glory.

Hope had become a presence high in the branches, singing. And beneath, held in spontaneous combustion, stood our various selves, shapes waiting to be melted, molded. Tomorrow's waves, tomorrow's cut glass.

It was at this height, not long after we had started living together, that Miranda introduced me to the I Ching, the Chinese game of fate. With my five coins I rolled—how appropriately, I thought—the hexagram, "Abundance." It read,

Abundance has success
The King attains abundance
Be not sad
Be like the sun at midday

Though my hexagram was auspicious—abundance does not alight every season—the remaining pages of the Wilhelm commentary dwelled on the impermanence of such bounty. The well I was drinking from, whether I knew it or not, was already poisoned. My comeuppance would come. But until then, I should make the utmost of what fortune had bestowed. Since I had never felt so lucky, or so anxious—by what freak had I earned this grace?—the advice registered. On a mountain climb, the peril often awaits on the descent.

Mastering that descent did not come easy. With Marcia, there had been barriers of background and class, but we spoke the same generational language, of Harvard history and lit, of the travel we desired, of the friends we sought out and entertained. With Miranda, the ties had to be improvised afresh out of the scraps at hand: a record album we had purchased; the balcony's hibachi stove for which I chopped and sliced the vegetables and on which she then cooked our evening pilaf.

Then there was Miranda's native idiom. Her expertise came out one day when we visited Marcia in the hospital. Marcia had gone in for a minor operation, expecting to be released the next day. A week later, the victim of an inappropriately administered laxative, she was still there.

"I knew they were dosing me with the wrong I.V.," she told us, "but I couldn't think of the right expression to make them stop. And I'm still baffled."

"You could have said," Miranda chimed in, "it was against your religion."

Marcia shook her head sadly, "I guess I haven't been in California long enough."

***

In our conversations Miranda spoke of truth as of something ascertainable. I would never have ventured such a leap. For me, life was a series of moments—disconnected ones. Miranda instead, with her more linear, logical cast of mind, saw our every gesture as fitting into an overriding purpose. There was fate, or as she preferred to call it, karma, and we were all, willy nilly, slotted somewhere on its turning wheel. According to her, even marijuana, that seediest of weeds, could provide the gateway to this realization.

We had been living together a year when she finally deemed me progressed enough to be offered this sacrament. I had tried it on a friend's houseboat in Seattle, but not knowing how to inhale had felt like an idiot on fire rushing through a cocktail party, "My kingdom for an ice cube!" Ingested in the form of a brownie, a muddy colored vision flooded over me for which nothing in my life had even remotely prepared me.

My first impression, however, was that this could not be real, this large white male opossum padding warily, to a deafening roar of leaves, by our kitchen window. But the opossum was real, as was the need compelling me to remove an orange and green box of Tide from its longtime site commanding our icebox. Other memories are more visual: of the arabesque of our balcony's arches transfigured by the sunset's pink stilettos; the halos of light playing on our room's overhead steam pipes. I even beheld the goddess herself: not Mary Jane, but a more Mexican Maria: squat and of a dusky complexion, she sat very calmly in a bright red poncho in the corner of our sofa.

By now the aphrodisiac had taken over. Impelled by it, we made love. Slower than had ever seemed possible. Articulation. Response. A staccato of fingers slyly grazing, painting rash-like explosion along the contours of her thighs. Pressing the long syllables of her name into the sheets, I watched as they became chariot horses and galloped away, down a silken river where a magpie tilted high on a branch and somewhere downstream a skiff explored:

> piled, leg over rump, two
> soft pink-green
> alligators
> alligators
> dreamward bent
> smiling

MY EDEN UNRAVELS

Before ingesting marijuana I had always performed on a mental see-saw. Reality was, like my doctorate degree, comparative. I might be down or up, but I was never, so help me, vertical. It may have been my naiveté, or the good luck that somehow or other circled around me, but I believed with Miranda that evil was no more than another illusion. How, we asked, could anyone prefer the cynical, satanic Stones to the enlightened Beatles? Was there a path eluding us?

Then one evening, several months later, I was rash enough to consume half a lid, supposing it mostly harmless twigs and seeds. Twenty minutes later there I was, down in a sea bottom. To this day I can still see the tall angular mountains that closed off the horizon, the penumbral light beating down like rain, a slanting gray blue that tore with a diarrhetic speed. It was the speed I found terrifying. Any faster and I'd go bonkers. All the same I could quicken it by laughing aloud. The laughter appeared in machine gun bursts hardly different from a death rattle. Any longer I knew and I'd be myself no more: a shutter banging in a deserted house.

Under the circumstances, the wisest thing was to forbid Miranda any comment—speech so easily turns to laughter! And I refused to budge from the tossing yacht of my fourposter. Beyond its mahogany planks lay a world of dreaded noise. I didn't dare relieve myself, for fear of the toilet chain's waterfall-like roar. Wherever I turned, I met the same rushing vacancy. And the sign, "No anchoring here."

Everything, from the length of the interval between perceptions to their general banality, deepened my gloom. The Rimbaud of *The Season in Hell* came to mind—ah, a master I could emulate! Then, with more compassion, as I understood the relief with which Rimbaud had turned his back on those evil flowers. "It's all in the mind," I tried to tell myself. Yet I had only to close my eyes to see the jangling mountain chains all over again. The terror lay in the unconscionable speed with which the underwater angles surged, dizzying, frenetic, sweeping all before them as they dissolved me to a tune:

I'm a pig
I'm a gentle antelope
I'm a pig
I'm a gentle antelope
antelope
an-te-lope

At first the repetitions teased, amused. As they persisted, I felt caught up in the schizophrenic glue I had released.

In my terror I found myself bossing Miranda about like an evil sultan in *The Arabian Nights*. I was drowning and I was shivering simultaneously. Afraid to fall asleep, I required a ballroom blaze of lights. I felt an overweening need for space—cool, glassy, grotto blue—while, like the invalid I was, I squirmed about in the sheets, seeking a position that would somehow allay the swarming malevolences.

I looked and the light, I saw, was mine.

With my new awareness I understood how much of my being was predicated on performance, the sentence proudly landing on the very point from which I had started. Did I have to go through such gyrations? Was I that insecure? Somehow there had to be a way of making myself more direct.

There was, "a forest of silk where you, Sun, blazed the dawn," a Tibetan might have worded it. Concentration. Absence of desire. Charity. At the end, maybe, a man speaking from within, relaxed, self-realized and whole.

But any such self-realization lay well in the future. The more I searched that night, the more I found myself staring into a black miring pool. How had the wanton current, its impulses that I had once imagined propelling me free, turned into this? However I squirmed and twisted, I was trapped. Trapped by my father, whose financial serf I remained. Trapped by a teaching job that, however glamorous, no longer suited the writer I had become. Trapped, too, by Miranda and a control that was turning us both into ever more constricted knots of flesh. Only I was so enthralled by my Omphale all I wanted was to be the flames dancing in her eyes.

But as the I Ching had foreseen, any ashes I stirred stayed rarely lit.

The lover is the mourner of what shapes his destruction. Early on, Miranda had contracted chronic vaginitis from some mistakenly given sulfa drugs. Each time I entered her was like a stab. By now all I saw was her pain—salt, crystals, blood.

As her lover my role was to transform her from a girl into a young woman. At first, possibly, I succeeded. No earlier lover had anything like my drive that allowed me, on reentry, to wait her out and bring her to orgasm.

But orgasm never came easily. As to what inhibited her I can only guess. But the current that runs between a couple living together differs from that of an affair. It may be for Miranda, as previously for Marcia, that once she had, perhaps inadvertently, snared me, she became dry. Did her springs need the challenge of the hunt to flow?

Then again the emphasis that men of my generation placed on masturbation did not make for genial lovers. I did not stare, like the Indian of the Kamasutra, for hours into her eyes. I did not appreciate the subtle eroticism of costume, of a prepared meal. Instead everything hinged on a depersonalized coupling that took place invariably in the dark, invariably in my fourposter. And, after twenty minutes or so, my job done, I put on my pants and skedaddled.

Miranda did not want a masked Eros, she wanted, as she said, me. "You're not on some hypothetical page," she insisted, "you're in this room, this bed, with me. If you don't feel like responding, go ahead and I'll leave. It's up to you."

I felt terrified by Miranda's threat to leave. How, without her, was I to pursue the path she had opened up? In my dilemma I tried to placate her, when instead I should have voiced my fear of the narrowing tunnel into which her goal orientation was hurling us both. Moments are to be expanded rather than cheapened; they are all we have.

But as Miranda came to know me better, she must have realized that my reluctance to say what I thought and felt was not merely perverse; it could be I didn't know how difficult I was making any self-expression.

So she set out to disencumber me, focusing on the European "one" with which I referred to myself. From the intensity with which I clung to the pronoun you would think I had merged into the universal THAT. Yet "one" brought a freedom, a way of expressing the inexpressible (and thus the essential) that "I" could never permit. In a certain way it was more true, since it referred to a self who, in the act of consciousness, I still was. I didn't realize that, without rooted boundaries, I had no way of engaging my past, let alone another person.

What held for those two pronouns held for much of my life. I did not rule, obsession did. I have spoken earlier about how Father mistook obsessions for reality. But wasn't I doing the same, Miranda asked, by placing Writing at the top of my private pedestal. This was the idol I had sworn to serve, convinced that art was the sole remaining possible truth.

In line with my new faith, I thought I existed in others' eyes only as the product of my artistic intentions. As with my parents, the promise was backed by a considerable willpower: the ability to sit six to eight hours at a desk, and the panicky fear that, if ever for a moment I stopped scribbling, the edifice would collapse.

Oh, occasionally I looked out the window and glimpsed life speeding by. But I believed with Yeats and Uncle Jimmy that one must make a choice, of perfecting the life or the work, not both, and I was more than willing to abide by what I had chosen. The concentration, the singleness of focus required, was so consuming I never thought to ask what it was costing. Did I have to be, Miranda asked, so intense? Couldn't I, now and then, let a sliver of light chink its way in? Go out, say, and have a good time? Or let myself be teased? Well, maybe, but only on my terms, in the way I had pictured.

The notion of progress, of an accruing expertise with which I consoled myself, could not have been more fatuous. In reality, all I was becoming was more and more deeply split. On the one hand, there was the obsessed fellow who gardened, ran after birds, played soccer and wrote. On the other, there was the sexual obsessive. One hand could not hear the other clapping.

It hardly mattered that the writer was human in name only. Of the two of me, he seemed far and away the more admirable. And the other, that shy, wistful-eyed eccentric, hands stuffed in his pockets, bustling about in the rear somewhere, I regarded with professional contempt. "Come on," I'd admonish him, "let yourself go, have a drink." But the guy was like blotting paper. The more booze poured, the more admirable in my own eyes I became: a quieter, more relaxed fellow. I even looked forward to the hangovers. While body shook and temples throbbed, a pen, suddenly compassionate, watercolored along, borne on the slowed, heavy rhythms of the alcoholic current.

Though I felt strangled by my father and the ceaseless panic he engendered, I never thought to question the straight-jacket itself. It was familiar. Instead I scrunched up my shoulders and cranked it tighter, as if an extra notch was all it lacked. New Haven-Paris-Iran-Greece-Seattle-Greece-Seattle-Greece-Berkeley. A man in orbit, faster! faster!

In rebelling against my father and the Southampton life, I was rebelling against a reality in which money alone determined value. But in rebelling all I did was institute a counter-principle of my own in the pursuit of a woman; as if only her fertile eye could make this writer-man real.

That hyphenated identity was very much at issue, since it was my rare fusion of self and purpose which my every gesture was bent on proving: the four-by-six inch cards reposing, if not like Goethe's on his Frau's broad back, then in a trouser pocket. However zany the situation, a servant of the word never abdicates. How far, after all, is cogito from coitus?

Why I needed the theater of a woman's eyes I don't know. I only know I regarded my separation from the nature embodied by the feminine as the driving force behind my quest for a more realized self. They existed, I didn't; not with anything like the certainty they carried in them. And I saw the whole heaving perspiring tribe of us Sisyphuses as forever engaged in the solemn task of pushing that impossible stone of theirs up and over the orgasmic hill.

Long after I went to sleep there would be Miranda reading for the nth time Jane Eyre, trying to recover the self she was. But each time I reached out to her now I only ended up destroying another piece of our first months when we did nothing, it seemed, but hold one another, she wrapping me in her leafy thighs until, from deep within her forest lake, she could hear me exploding, the woods rocking and the spermflakes one by one floating down. Now, some two years later, that interior forest was no more than so many dead leaves and clinging needles where nothing resounded but the relentless hammering of my prick.

I did all I could. But faced with her unhappiness I finally agreed to a summer's separation. While Miranda worked in the university library and experimented with male Berkeleydom, I would make a trip with my brother Stephen. He was attracted by the comic Iran of my "Persian Notes." Why not pick up where Marcia and I had left off six years earlier? Meanwhile, Jimmy produced a bronze owl of Athena to present to the Oxford-educated chief of Iran's dominant tribe, Yahya Bakhtiar; the friend for whom he felt, as he said, the greatest personal affinity. Maybe Yahya could issue us a safe-conduct to visit the Bakhtiari in their summer pasturage and experience what remained of the delicious tent life depicted in the old miniatures?

WHAT IT TOOK TO MARRY MIRANDA

Our jaunt to Iran in June-July, 1968, did not work out. Feeling my Persian was not up to the responsibility of negotiating for two, I had thrown myself on the mercy of an Iranian engineering student I had known in Seattle. He had brought back a new Impala and wanted to show it off to his countrymen. But the point of traveling does not necessarily lie in the swaths of terrain being raced over. Cooped up in the glass prison of the front seat, unable to get out to sit in a tea house, to shop, to bargain, to talk to anyone but the two of them, I had more than enough time to think of what I had lost in Miranda. In a way different from Jimmy, but no less powerfully, she had taken me over. All I wanted, I now realized, was to win her back. I would do whatever it took.

When Stephen and I arrived on our own in Isfahan, we learned that our prince had died of an old bullet wound in his nape. That left little alternative but to fly back to Athens. At Jimmy's was a letter awaiting from Miranda. It seemed her summer had not lived up to her expectations either. If I wanted so desperately to return, she would rent me a pad.

Miranda was at the airport to greet me. Upon seeing her I was so overcome I did nothing but bawl. And in the back seat of our taxi I went on sobbing and kissing her the whole of our long, clammy ride back to Berkeley. Only several months later did she confide that the man she was kissing with such apparent warmth had become a stranger she barely tolerated. Even my scent was unfamiliar.

As my own apartment was still rented out, she had found me a cottage in Lafayette, east of the Berkeley hills. She would remain in her own pad, a way of underlining the tenuousness of my reprieve. But a month's sobbing away in the Impala's glass prison had brought home how much I had at stake in Miranda. Chafe as I did under the weight of her expectations, she was the very best part of my Berkeley life. My one hope lay in convincing her I was a changed man.

So a pursuit began, one that to this day in my dreams thrills me with the enormity of the feat I saw myself undertaking—an unlikely couple, maybe, but one all the same.

With a month before teaching resumed I had time to reinvent myself. I sprouted a Fu Manchu moustache. I came to like the soft hedge it placed in front of my long bony face, the possibility of being an aware pair of eyes rather than some rubbery-mouthed clown. With the moustache appeared boots and hip-hugging jeans. In this gear I attended the meditation sessions at The Blue Mountain Center, led by an articulate English professor from Kerala, Eknath Easwaran.

From the sexual therapists, Masters and Johnson, I familiarized myself with the technique of the clitoral orgasm. I learned of the undersea grotto lying at the center of a woman's flower-like body. As I entered it now I became a floating harpist. There below a whole ringing surf, among the anemones and corals and waving fronds, the bright fish of my fingers darted and played.

My ministrations must have succeeded, for by April we were married: a big-hearted Italian wedding with bags of sugar-coated almonds, a black ecumenical minister, my brother Stephen in a green velvet tuxedo as my best man and our friends' hillbilly band who went on playing from two until midnight. (Father, to my surprised delight, enjoyed it so much he wanted to stay. But Mother refused to believe that an afternoon wedding would not be over by seven and had scheduled a dinner party of her own.)

For our honeymoon we flew to Frankfurt to purchase a Volkswagen, intending to find a base in the French Dordogne from which to explore. But it rained for sixteen days straight, and in Paris it was so cold we were reduced to buying winter overcoats. But with the rain came a phenomenon one doesn't see growing up in San Jose—lightning! I remember Miranda standing in rapt amazement on our hotel balcony, while the zig-zagging bolts crashed over the mansard roofs.

In an effort to outflank the rain we abandoned the Dordogne and headed south by way of Provence and the Rapallo Liguria. But the rain didn't abate until we reached Stendhal's Parma. By then a maniacal gleam had come into my eye—the sort of thing that happens when a character starts taking over a novel. Far away in Calabria lay the two Albanian-speaking villages of Miranda's grandparents. Further still, in Cycladic Greece, lay Peros. The island held a key to much of my life and, like any infatuated man, I wanted her to experience its spell.

Miranda was game enough, but she found the daily unpacking trying. How she envied those fairytale heroines who had only to stamp a foot for the baggage to follow on its own, underground. In the mountains of Byron's Epirus I remember her being reduced to numb speechlessness when I struck off on the wrong dirt road for a hundred miles. But in Athens, in a cellar taverna off of Omonia, she did behold some authentic dancing, peasant women up on their tables and proudly stomping away. And Paros proved everything I had promised: stars like a thousand rugs spouting stories; a maze of curling streets whitened like hot-cross buns along which we strolled with a serenity that came as much as anything from the car-less town we now inhabited.

With no call to do or see anything, I could sit out on our balcony and read with an unexpected relish *War and Peace*; a novel until now unread by me because of the demands of teaching.

Not that I didn't relish the duels with my students, who were as determined to change me as I was to change them. Or the friendships, however fleeting, the teaching brought. But the teaching was, from the outset, provisionary; something I could do to exist on my own if, as seemed all too probable, I couldn't write. But once I discovered that I did have something to say, then everything else, the round-the-clock correcting of papers, the constant cramming, the keeping up with each new polemical wind that blew by, became extraneous. It was not critical discourse I wanted to reshape, but rhythms, movements, the mysteries of place, of what obsessed me and what I loved.

But any prospective freedom would have to wait until Miranda had finished college and graduate school. At her rate of one or two courses a term—any grade less than an "A" warranted an incomplete—that could take a decade. And I didn't think I could stomach living in a university town as a defrocked teacher.

FIRED, REHIRED AND FIRED AGAIN

The spring of our 1969 honeymoon was the spring of People's Park, an event I regret missing as it might have explained what the agitation at its best was about: a park rather than a parking lot; a university's responsibility to its community rather than some bureaucrat's bottom line.

But most of the issues facing us teachers were not so clear cut. Pincered between the Student Left and the business-dominated Board of Regents, we found ourselves in an intolerable no man's land. Had we possessed a functioning union, or adequate representation on the Board of Regents, we could have played a mediating role. As it was, left and right had every reason to clash, if only to keep their publicity mills churning.

All the commotion took its toll on us. One colleague became a motorcycle racer. Another quit to direct encounter groups at Esalen. Others gave up scholarly research to grind out text books for the mass market. More still succumbed to the seductions of politics, using their research skills to compile tracts for the anti-war campaign and defend the university—and their jobs—against the incessant flow of attacks mounted by the Reagan-led Right.

At stake when I arrived in the mid-Sixties was the principle of a tuition-free university. It was perhaps predictable that shelling out for a free university of Berkeley's cantankerous sort would not sit well with the retired midwesterners who made up a vociferous part of Reagan's Southern California majority. They had stripped themselves once paying for their kids' education and saw no reason to do it again. And on the backburner simmered the same McCarthyite issues that had produced the Fifties' Loyalty Oaths. If Marcuse and Angela could be fired for their beliefs, why not Robin Magowan?

With each new issue the level of acrimony escalated. Finally, with the discovery of the carpet-bombing of Cambodia, the outrage was such that Reagan had little alternative but to close down the university.

I had followed the war in what was then Indo-China even before Father had gone there on a fact-finding commission for President Eisenhower. At college I had repeatedly dreamed about it, from hunting tigers with Emperor Bao-Dai along the Mekong, to recurrent nightmares in which I found myself pursued by small natives riding pig-like motorcycles, or rising anywhere, at any moment, out of a rice field.

I was in my second year of teaching at Berkeley when my brother Peter, who was directing Safeway's Tulsa division, invited me to join him in Aspen over Christmas as guests of the Nitze family. The father, Paul, our chief negotiator in the disarmament SALT talks, was then working under McNamara as Secretary of the Navy. Paul had been at Harvard with Father and had served in every Democratic administration from FDR onwards. With his impeccable liberal credentials and his patrician sense of service, he seemed to be everything I admired.

As we were sitting together one evening I expressed my unease about our getting mired in an unwinnable land war. Why were we in Vietnam, I asked. For its China Sea oil reserves?

Not at all, Nitze replied. It was to contain a virus, Communism, which would otherwise spread throughout Southeast Asia. And, contrary to what everyone at Berkeley was saying, he insisted we were winning the war.

Why I let this cold warrior who had never known any Vietnamese people (as even I had, of all persuasions, ten years earlier in Paris), con me I don't know. Did I so badly need to believe, against all the odds, in patrician competence?

As it turned out, it was not Berkeley's students who were misinformed, but Nitze and McNamara and their CIA sources. However, it took Cambodia to drive it home.

Up to then I had remained apolitical. But the shock of learning that Nixon, by personal fiat, had unleashed 250,000 bombing missions over one of the world's few Shangri-las was more than I could stomach, and I joined in the wave of indignation that swept over the university. I even lectured in a Palo Alto high school in support of the anti-war Republican congressman, Pete McCloskey, in his primary battle. The Vietnamese, I pointed out, had always posed a barrier to Chinese expansion. And I predicted that the future site of the "anti-Communist crusade" would not be southeast Asia, but Latin America.

In our efforts to drum up the support we needed to stop the killing, it was sobering to discover how out of touch we at Berkeley were with mainstream America. To build a coalition requires, at the least, some contact, and a respect for working people's concerns and responsibilities. Now, when we needed the trust of these "squares," we found that our snobbery had discredited us.

In Seattle, other than basic composition, I had taught mainly American lit; a compelling enough subject since it was their identity—who was this new man, an American?—I was helping them discover. At Berkeley, I found myself teaching almost everything except American lit to anybody from freshmen undergraduates to graduate students: Chaucer, the Sixteenth and Seventeenth centuries, the History of Criticism, the English Lyric, the Pastoral Narrative, and Surrealism.

I found the teaching, with the education that it was for me, exciting. Kids who take ideas seriously tend to take their teachers seriously. A number of us had a little cult following us from course to course.

Yet I missed the easy camaraderie I enjoyed in Seattle. In Berkeley, for much of the time, I suffered from loneliness. A certain amount I had brought on myself; Marcia's social gifts were not exactly replaceable. But I wonder how my other colleagues fared. Those professorial houses tucked away on the hill with their decks and big picture windows might just as well have been tower fortresses. The view was out, to what we had each arrived at, not to what we had it in us to accomplish. In Seattle, life was waiting to be invented, a mimeographed poem or essay handed out. In Berkeley, the audience we performed for was a national one: the New York publishers, the fellow specialists at a conference, determining who we were. We had, in some awful way, grown too big for one another.

In my case, working at home and teaching a one or two course Tuesday-Thursday schedule, there was only a fraction of the staff I could hope to bump into and invite out for lunch. That may be why making friends in other departments—the main point, it would seem, of a university—was discouraged. In a department boasting over a hundred members, the priority had to be to get to know one another. In this respect Marcia had supported me very well. But that made my walking out on her—for a departmental typist!—all the harder for my colleagues to stomach. And my subsequent taking up with a teenage student wife, who resented being talked down to, only isolated me the further.

I was in my fourth year at Berkeley when I was fired as a result of a mid-career review.

The verdict stunned me. Berkeley was notorious for its "publish or perish" standards. It was not so much what you wrote as the amount of it, your so-called productivity that earned you tenure. (The only way then of justifying a light teaching load to our pay-masters in the state legislature was the time it allowed for research. And the value of the research was born out in the critical reception accorded to what we published.) By these standards I had, pre-sumably, little to fear. I may not have produced with the distinc-tion of a number of tenured colleagues, but in sheer bulk I out-weighed anyone at my level. I was so confident of passing this preliminary hurdle to tenure that I virtually ignored the new item on my questionnaire asking for my views on teaching.

This new item had appeared in response to the recent firing of my friend and the department's best teacher, Joe Kramer, for his failure to publish. In the spirit of the times, a "Keep Kramer" cam-paign sprang into being, spurred by the vivid esteem Kramer en-joyed among students and faculty. Although the campaign failed to reinstate him, it did succeed in requiring that a teacher be judged both on the prodigiousness of his writing and his effectiveness in the classroom.

In effect, a new standard had been introduced, since none of us had ever received any teacher's training. Teaching was a skill sup-posedly acquired on the job. In a productive career, teaching and writing fed one another.

With the empowerment, unfortunately, there came the eccen-tricities. One nineteen-year-old from a Chaucer class given during my first term remembers receiving a paper back from me with no grade and the injunction (usually reserved for someone suspected of plagiarism), "Please see me in my office." Wondering what was up, she arrived up there at my fourth floor Wheeler office. She watched me motion her to a chair and then, after bolting the frosted glass door behind her, take off my coat. The necktie followed and then, I'm told, my shoes. As she sat, torn between an amused curi-osity and the impulse to flee down the hall, I jumped down from my standard issue oak desk and, to no music other than that of my clicking fingers, started to dance a zembeikiko. I should add that I have no recollection of the incident. But from then on she was not only my student, but my friend, and one I still have. As to what compelled me to such madness I can only surmise. New to Berkeley, and with my heart in Greece, and still married, despite everything, to Marcia, I must have been ready enough to explode.

Not every nineteen-year-old could be expected to hear such an internal music. My efforts to stammer out a course description were enough to send half the class racing to the dean in an attempt to cancel. "What agony for beauty!" one student sighed in her diary. "I've sat here fifty minutes and I haven't understood a word you're saying," was a more common first week response.

It was not only the linear thinkers and diehard note-takers who felt thwarted by this wild-eyed, teeth-baring, foot-stamping assistant professor. Addressing a tenure meeting, the poet Josephine Miles declared, "One starts up a conversation with Robin and thinks that, though the words are English, the syntax came in on the last space ship." She concluded, none too hopefully, "Unlike Monsieur Jourdain he will never discover that what he talks is prose."

Miles's "never" sounds overly pessimistic. It might take a student a few weeks to figure out where on the dial my blurts and squeaks lay. But eventually most did, discovering a more instinctual verbal cast of mind that lies at the core of literature. Historically, poetry preceded prose. Poetry is not an intellectual medium; it is a rhythm-based, image-loaded enactment; one that allows its listeners a moment's heightened awarenesses even before they grasp the nature of the singular place to which they have been taken.

So there I was before the mid-career review committee, this scribbling paragon with the teenage wife. What could be wrong with me?

"His teaching!" I can see some grizzled swain of Marcia's piping up.

"How do you know?"

"One of my student advisees whispered it to me."

"Me, too," the veteran next to him chimed in. "We may have just found the sacrificial lamb we need to satisfy the baying Kramer wolves."

There I was, canned.

My reaction was one of incomprehension. At that age there was so much that escaped me: about the depiction of character, the art of prose, life itself. And with it came a hauteur, a nit-picking arrogance I regret to this day.

But I was clearly giving my students something they weren't learning elsewhere. My classroom was not a mausoleum. Nor do I hold with the saw that teaching can't be judged. In the classroom you are being judged at every moment. And the proof comes in those signing up for your courses—the quality they represent. But what was I to do, challenge the senior staff to a competition, one mot, one flying text against the next? The nature of the charge, based as it was on hearsay, left no defense.

My firing had come in January, 1969, too late to secure employment for the following September. So I was allowed an extra year to sort myself out. By now, the professorial game of ever ascending chairs, funded by the post-war baby boom, had ground to a most unmusical halt, leaving you stuck in whatever place you had landed. In that climate finding a job took a while, and it wasn't until the following December I received an offer, from Bennington in Vermont; all the more welcome in that Miranda could pursue her degree there.

The arbitrary nature of my firing did not sit well with the Berkeley deans. If classroom performance was to be a basis of tenure, then a more objective evaluation was clearly needed. After a number of meetings, the department produced a form consisting of a blank page on which the student could record his or her impressions about the course and its teacher.

I was teaching two compulsory summer quarter courses, freshman comp and the last hurdle before graduation, a senior criticism seminar, when the assessments were handed out. In October, they reappeared in our mailboxes. Mine, incomprehensibly, drew mostly raves. As I perused them, a wave of anger surged up at the ghost I had been for the past nine months, shuffling through the corridors.

My fate, to be sure, was settled. But there were some misconceptions I thought I could clarify and, on the spur of the moment, I dashed off a letter to the chairman and tenured staff.

After reminding them of the circumstances under which I had taught the two courses—I had, after all, nothing at stake—my letter took up the one negative assessment from the criticism seminar, the tribute of a sorority babe who, in the entire nine weeks, had cut all but three classes:

> When a person has been fired, as I have been, by gossip, he has a right to ask certain questions . . . I say this because the one complaint against me, of a student in English 108, seems in so many ways typical: only two or three classes attended in the whole term, an overload problem, etc. But notice the proportion of the class that she is and how the quality of her response differs from that available on any other sheet. There are mountains and there are molehills. Somebody, somewhere, should be able to tell them apart.

To a highly politicized department my letter must have offered an irresistible opportunity. Immediately a cabal formed, who insisted on having my "candidacy" resubmitted. And, for the first time in departmental annals, a cashiered teacher was rehired. The joy on the scholar and future novelist Tom Flanagan's face, as he tramped into my office at the head of a delegation to announce "the start of a new era," would have been persuasion enough. But there were other voices as well, among them Miranda's, who had never wanted to leave, and the presence of my two sons in Berkeley.

Not without a certain regret, I turned down Bennington. But the prospect of tenure, of being caged for the next thirty years in Wheeler Hall's gloomy, asbestos-ridden corridors, hardly cheered.

On the wake of my rehiring, it seemed appropriate to buy a house. What, Miranda asked, could we afford? I had no idea since my father controlled my finances, but I saw no harm in having a lawyer examine my trust fund to tell me where I stood.

Not a wise idea. My shackles, as it turned out, were forged in legal adamant. And Father in his outrage at my hiring a lawyer— was I contemplating taking him to court?—wrote me out of his will in favor of my children.

It was inevitable that from then on everything that happened to me only confirmed the bleakness of his hypothesis. Not understanding what was driving me, I became in his eyes a quitter; one who in any awkward situation would always take the easy way out. And he may also have viewed me as a financial incompetent, incapable of understanding the complexity of investments.

Up to then, the expense of foreign travel aside, I had lived frugally. I roller-painted my own walls, built my book shelves of pine boards straddling cement blocks, and drove a VW bug. My father called me a "hairshirt." But how else could I live within my means?

When now, in a gesture of reconciliation, Father showed me the books of my trust fund, I was flabbergasted to come upon all those items for which I had dutifully thanked him: my graduation car; my airline tickets anywhere; my entire education. I had paid for them all myself.

More welcome was the discovery that the income my trust fund generated was more than double my salary. I could afford to buy a small house with a little uphill garden in residential Kensington, just north of Berkeley. And if I wanted to give up teaching to concentrate on being a writer, I could.

Between me and liberty there remained the tenure decision, two years away. Enough time, one would think, to repair my social fences and find a publisher for "Narcissus and Orpheus," the study of the modern pastoral I had made out of my thesis.

But financial independence can change one's approach and I applied for an immediate decision. Where was their "new era?" Meanwhile in the hallways I maintained a polite reserve before my future judges. If my writing and teaching earned me tenure, so be it. I was not about to charm my way into another lifetime cage.

From what I've learned the tenure meeting was a massacre. The knives were by now well whetted and from all quarters they descended on the flabby corpus of my writings. "Five mistakes of fact on his pastoral essay's opening page," one scholar chortled. Another challenged, "I defy any of you to make sense of page twelve." To compound matters—most of the cabal who had fought to get me rehired were away on deserved leaves of absence—my defense was being conducted by my fellow poet-critic, Josephine Miles (of the Monsieur Jourdain remark). After another gibe at "what he calls his prose," her brief concluded very generously:

> The poems aren't many, but they are exquisite. And that is one reason why I can't think we want to let him go. He works so hard with so much craft to make as he says in his motto to Voyages "Le gong Fidèle d'un mot." A man who loves words so much cannot be obscure ultimately, if we take the time to read him.

But patience was not the long suit of an overstaffed department beset with falling enrollment. My supporters, I was told, comprised a majority, if not the two-thirds required. To those others I must have remained that alien "exotic flower" Mark Schorer had noted on first hiring me.

For all that I had anticipated and perhaps even provoked it, the verdict stung. Yet it was certainly right. I wasn't a Berkeley MLA All Star.

I resigned on the spot. One lame duck stint had been humiliation enough.

BEES, BEES, BEES!

I missed the perks of teaching—the friendships, the public life—but not the tension of performance, made all the keener by the new accountability, the rows of cool eyes checking me out. Yet the regret Jimmy had foreseen never materialized, perhaps because I had done it. Eight years was time enough.

What I failed to anticipate was the unraveling effect of my firing on the basic fabric of my life. This came home one evening as Miranda and I were sitting in the bedroom of the little rustic house we had bought: a compromise between the country life we both desired and urban reality. I happened to be reading Chandler's *The Long Goodbye*; maybe not *War and Peace,* but not the crime trash either that it was commonly regarded in Americanist circles. It spoke to me all the more in that its evil alliances bore out the corruption I had witnessed growing up.

I was congratulating myself, as I read, on my new serenity when Miranda announced, "You know, Robin—or maybe you don't—but I'm really suffering."

"Oh, are you?" I said, failing to catch her drift. "Why don't you go see that psychiatrist you consulted last year about your fear of bees? What was his name?"

She looked at me wildly for a moment, and then ran out of the room. I followed her, thinking only to soothe her. "I think he's a very good man," I said, taking her hand.

"Bees. Bees. BEES," she said, wrenching herself away, "God, Robin, it's not bees."

"What is it then?" I asked, non-plussed.

There was a long silence, then, "Our marriage. You can't see what it's been doing to us, how shrunken, how fearful, we've each become. Why do you think I stay up half the night reading?" she asked, looking straight at me. "It's the one way I have of convincing myself I'm not living with you."

What was I to protest: that I saw her as an invention of God, dropped for reasons unfathomable into my life; that I was hooked, to my very marrow, absolutely incapable of rooting that tenderest of gazes, of smiles, out of my dreams. Poison, Miranda had said, yes, it was quite a draught I had swallowed. For four years I had lain consumed in the carnage and atrocity of that fierce holding as it took me and ferried me into the bounds of sleep, of an ineluctable dream. She within me, I within her. A sumptuous poison and one that to this day still shivers my dreams. Eurydice, for some of us, exists.

But there was only so long I could go on sustaining a poison passion. I just wasn't the mate she needed, who could soar with her on her flights, or, knowing he was not the problem, could lift her out of her black depths. Once again I was alone, in the alleys of my shame, my impotence, my disaster.

How was I to say any of that? What difference would it have made? Instead I asked, "You want a divorce?" too aware of her protracted suffering to attempt a rejoinder.

Amazingly, that was it, four years of a close, perhaps too close, union snuffed out in a single question. *One Flesh, Separate Lives*, Robin Skynner titled his book on marital therapy. And I sometimes wish I had been savvy enough to propose such a therapy. Patterns of conduct do not have to be repeated. But in Miranda's eyes the time for therapy had long passed. A Pierrot might make a welcome friend, but not a husband. Sex, when it clicks, can green over these relational fissures. When it doesn't, each word, each look, becomes a step on ice, over a chasm ever more attenuated, more withdrawn.

The sexual dearth I had experienced in my life with Marcia had rebounded. And I must say I found little solace in the irony. I hadn't delivered the goods—for either of them. Only now Miranda was the marital captive seeking access to a fuller life. To go out, like others of her age, on dates. But not committing herself to anything beyond that. For her, sexual life had come under the sign of the class struggle. She was a "proud Marxist-feminist," unwilling to serve the male oppressor.

I could not bear to watch Miranda's emancipation. And with no college obligations it was easier for me to leave. A week before Miranda's announcement I had received a postcard from my Harvard soccer teammate, Tony Oberschall. He was in Zambia studying the rise after independence of a new class of entrepreneurs. In line with his research he was planning a two-week safari through Northern and Luapula provinces—would I join him? On the spot I accepted.

Two days before leaving for Africa, I took Miranda to see the Alec Guinness film, "The Man in the White Suit." Towards the end comes a sequence when it seemed to me that the sound track was going haywire. People were dashing about, explosions of every sort penetrating the factory yard. Among all the ack-ack was a loudly reiterating managerial voice. My ear drums felt as if they were being punctured. I took refuge in the last row, hands over my ears. Whose was that managerial voice? What was the tumult I was experiencing?

Afterwards driving home I felt my entire life on the point of shattering. I asked Miranda if she would take the wheel. But she refused, not having driven in the last four years. "I want to kill myself," I caught myself muttering. I still remember the distinct sway of the rear motor as the VW lurched from one uphill turn to the next. Unable to grasp the steering wheel with my hands, I remained foetally hunched while steering with my elbows, as if the wheel were located somewhere in my chest.

I got the car home. But for the first time I chose not to walk Miranda to the door. For a while I remained outside. Then I began to walk uphill along the blacktop, Lear's "Why she, even she" resonating in my ears. As I walked, taking in the pools the street lamps projected in the evening silence, Lear haunted me. He must have known all along how much he was paying for his constant self-indulgence. It was all very well for friends to say that Africa would help me. But was I Lear or the Fool? Then came an answer abstracted from the play, "A man who is nothing cannot offend."

WHAT CONTINENT ARE YOU SAVING FOR YOUR NEXT HONEYMOON?

The news I had inadvertently broken up with Miranda, whom Jimmy had come to admire, and was escaping to Zambia on a safari, did not sit well with my uncle. "What continent are you saving for your next honeymoon?" he quipped on a postcard, genuinely dismayed by the Charlie Merrill-like restlessness that he saw operating in me, the need to keep recreating myself afresh at who ever's expense. For a blurb, fifteen years later, he would write:

Vissi di'amore, vissi del viaggio (I lived for love, I lived for traveling) might well be this writer's theme song. He travels in order to love, he loves in order to find himself elsewhere. From deep in this or that interior his reader gets postcards: dissolving views, myth-haunted, radiantly dislocated particulars. Their sender is unlikely to settle anywhere except for a season in the next virgin forest. To be touched, even dazzled, by the results is less a reflex of avuncular complacency than a taste for that precisely not familiar self, that revenant stung by rare insects and laid low by feverish embraces. . . .

From Jimmy's point of view I think I understand: a home is sacred, not to be broken. But there is more to traveling than biting off places of one's own size. I wanted to try to be, so far as I could, my own Matisse. And, despite Haiti, I still had a substantial curiosity about Africa.

After a couple of days in the Zambian capital of Lusaka fitting ourselves out, Tony Oberschall and I set off with an interpreter in a rented Land-Rover for the north. Our second morning we were given something to think about. We had finished packing up the car and were about to set forth when a five-foot green mambo, of the instantly lethal variety, slithered out from under the overhead rack's tarpaulin. It must not have minded watching us pack; being bounced along was not to its taste.

The snake had a point. The driving was everything I loathed. Confined to the spine of a slick, steeply cambered, endlessly straight road, we bounced through interminable bush, rarely encountering anything but the odd overturned truck, or maybe a pair of mallards quacking up from a pothole.

After the sexual fiasco of the last four years with Miranda, I had a sexuality of my own to address. Bored by the bush and the bars, that's what I did, opening myself to an Africa where the flesh is rhythm, percussion timbres, the flash of a pair of earrings, a silver bracelet.

It is possible to deride the superficiality of such one-night encounters. But beyond a mutual curiosity, there could be something a bar girl and I shared, as parents, as fellow aliens. Add the level of danger provided by the thwarted locals and there could be enough to carry us through to the dawn.

My three weeks with Tony gave me the gumption I needed to strap on my own seven league boots and saunter forth. My travels thereafter added up to considerable locomotion: Arusha and a jaunt with a bus full of Masai through Ngorngoru and the Serengeti; Dar-es-Salaam, Zanzibar, Lamu, and Mombasa on the coast, from where I caught a plane to Madagascar.

It was on the island of Lamu, off of Kenya in the East Indian Ocean, that my explorations came to an end in the person of a stunningly featured bar girl. I should have been warned by her protestations of illness. But I wanted to believe her little itch was no more than a little itch.

The cafe she was closing up lay next to the old stone-built Persian palace where I was staying. But she insisted on a detour to a bench overlooking the port. There in her white dress she sat, back to me, making me take, touch everything in my cold and trembling fingers until she was lit, alive enough, to come with me to my room.

I was not able to keep her with me past dawn. But when I showed up later in the morning at her cafe—I had an hour before my flight, why not spend it fucking?—everything shifted into such a passionate key that I promised her a detour on my way north. And I envisioned our taking a cottage on the more remote Indian Ocean side of the island. After de Gobineau, Loti and Gauguin, why not this minotaur?

NANCY LING PERRY:
ENTER THE DARK MUSE

The Berkeley I returned to in the fall of 1971 was a much darker town than the Berkeley of the mid-Sixties. Everyone I knew now felt powerless: powerless to stop the war and powerless to transform the globe; two actions which, only a few years earlier, had looked not only possible, but inevitable.

The earlier Berkeley offered a place in which to reinvent oneself and do "one's thing." For suburban kids like Miranda it was the mecca to which you escaped to let off steam. They camped out in Strawberry Canyon and read poetry. And even if it was poetry of a low burner variety, it was still poetry. Like the hippie movement, Berkeley offered kids a chance to be both smart and sexy—better, as Miranda said, than being dumb and pregnant.

There were all kinds of hippies. But those heeding Timothy Leary's injunction to "Turn on, tune in and drop out" could feel they had "transcended" such mundane concerns as Viet-Nam and Civil Rights, let alone voting. Yet the hippies' effect on some of us who had come of age in the Fifties was political. Here was an intensely lyrical cause, born out of Whitman, out of American affluence and optimism, and doffing what we could of our inhibitions—"anyone over thirty is the enemy"—we jumped right in.

Alas, before our sparks could gather in a generation-spanning flame, there came the inevitable reaction, from those who felt threatened and outraged. By the sexual riot, the gorgeous young harem trailing every handlebar moustache? The rumor of somebody's angel daughter who had never descended from a LSD high? For whatever reason, a pot and psychedelic-powered culture was driven underground, and the illegality bred an understandable paranoia. At concerts you didn't dance any more, you sat. The street carnival moved indoors. How to blazon it out in your mind-blowing togs when you were constantly being shaken down and strip-searched, or photographed by Big Brother's infra-red cameras?

The kids no longer greeted the arresting narcs with cookies and yogurt, but booby traps. The law was now the enemy, and against the threat of two years' incarceration on a first arrest for a mere joint, you defended yourself: with an impressive arsenal of weapons if you were a dealer; with your front door steel reinforced if you resented seeing your precious stash raided; with a slow fade into the anonymity of straightness if you had no better ideas.

But even earlier, when hippies were proclaiming the Summer of LOVE, the more prescient were already leaving the Haight for the rural communes. Whitman had given way to Thoreau.

The crackdown on "drugs," and the commercial appropriation that reduced a visionary movement to a mere youth style, a Haight Avenue freak show, all took their toll. If the same had happened to DADA—the cover of *Time* and all that—would Surrealism have arisen?

But the underlying cause of the hippie die-out was the over-generosity of their embrace. Join us, I remember the Be-In proclaiming, "Make love, not war." Was it possible, let alone desirable, politicians argued, to separate sexual freedom from civil rights, People's Park from Woodstock and the Paris May 1968 uprising? We were all in the same struggle. But were we? The hippie program was not another piecemeal redistribution of the American pie, but a radical transformation of American values. If you can't differentiate, you end up as mud soup.

The day after the Be-In, I remember *The Berkeley Barb* lamenting that the event's political opportunities had not been effectively exploited. Yet it was that Be-In which provided the first cause I ever got behind, one I joined by clambering onto a field. And it was that shining mirror, of differences transcended, the hippies held up to those outside. "Look at yourselves, aren't you one of us?" Or a more ringing, "Why aren't you one of us?"

Well, not everyone can be embraced. And inevitably, as the politics splintered and radicalized, the intractable elements took over: firebombing our English department's Wheeler Hall; roaring, baseball bats in hand, through my class; egged on or controlled, depending on how you looked at it, by squadrons of vizor-helmeted, mace-throwing Blue Meanies who were being directed from Viet-Nam-style spy-in-the-sky helicopters. The war had come home with a vengeance.

The collapse was all the more exploitable in that the music had become so entirely the message. And our Robespierres knew exactly how to target the hippies' musical addiction. Didn't the transformation that we sought represent a distant social goal? Whereas the open running sore of the nearby Berkeley-Oakland black ghetto was crying out in its immediacy. How could we not stand up for the Black Brothers whose blues had paved the way for our Stones and Beatles? Wasn't pop culture at heart Afro-based?

So the hippies gave up Peace and LOVE and took to Action—all that marching about and getting themselves maced and clubbed. Was it only, as my friend Ling Perry insisted, in those moments of fleeing lemming-like down Shattuck Avenue in a window-smashing horde that there ever was a genuinely fused Berkeley community?

Yet the Berkeley of the mid-Sixties was not a mob on the run. You could address a stranger on a street without unduly startling him or her. And it was a community of couples; not fervently clasped Parisians, maybe, but sybarites who shared a style of life, heads turned away from the make-or-break of the East Coast rat race. What the community lacked in grandparents and little children it almost made up for in big dogs. They took over the campus, bounding about in the fountains, gathering by the twenties in the big lecture hall aisles.

But civility is not a flower you can keep trampling again and again. By now Berkeley had become a victim of its notoriety. One saw the change in the omnipresent scaffolding as the old shingled houses were chopped into multi-unit apartments, in the bombed and boarded up shops, in the new fear and loathing on the streets. Where before a woman could walk anywhere at night, she now needed a car. Add the thousands of runaways hiding out in Strawberry Canyon to the tripling in a mere fifteen years of the city's population—the Gold Rush once again—and there was a tableau ripe for Hieronymous Bosch.

The Rolling Stones fiasco at Altamont did not, as claimed, signal the end of an era. It was merely the first revelation. There would be others: the Charles Manson murders, and the one in which I played an unintended part—the kidnapping of Patricia Hearst.

My involvement had come about as the result of the occupational need I had for a muse. Others had known them, why not I? Hardly a month passed that did not find me backing out my VW to go questing for the Lady of the Lake, all blue notes, as I conjured her, in a raven-black field. But muses are not exactly plentiful on the freeways, waiting, thumb out, and a ball of red twine in hand, for a twice-divorced, twice-fired, thirty-six-year-old man.

I was beginning to despair when fate tossed up the very opportunity I needed in the form of a recommendation request. Written in ballpoint on red-lined, lilac paper, it began with an ominous flair:

> time is gone—but if you can dig it—scrawl something
> on here. Why aren't you teaching anymore? I'm writing
> and working but i'm going to become a doctor. my name
> is Nancy Ling Perry. you have taught me all the best things
> about reading & writing . . . many many years ago. not
> having accomplished the Tibetan Ritual of Suicide here I
> am / i'll see you again.

In less than two years after she wrote this note, Nancy Ling Perry emerged as the principal spokesperson and pin-up gal for the Symbionese Liberation Army (SLA). It was this interracial, Berkeley-based, urban guerrilla organization which was to murder Marcus Foster, the admired Oakland School Superintendent, and kidnap the nineteen-year-old media heiress, Patricia Hearst. The revolution Ling's urban guerrillas hoped to set off never ignited; but their transformation of Patty into the shotgun-toting SLA princess Tania inspired the FBI to assign an unprecedented fifty-five hundred men to the case. As a media blitz it more than rivaled anything the entire J. Walter Thompson ad agency ever achieved.

At the time, all that lay in the inconceivable future. Instead Ling called up for me a tiny (4'11") twenty-four-year-old former student who had sparked the most enjoyable course I taught, a Classics of Criticism required of graduating English majors. Their comments on my teaching set off the chain reaction that got me rehired.

Brought up in the Sonoma Valley town of Santa Rosa, where her well-to-do Irish-Italian right-wing parents owned a furniture store,

Ling had attended Whittier, Nixon's alma mater. There she had supported Goldwater, before transferring to Berkeley in 1967.

I thought of Ling as more of a hippie than a politico. But she straddled the divide by marrying in 1968 Gilbert Perry, a jazz composer from the Oakland ghetto.

Ling was proud of the way she had adapted to black ghetto life— she lived at her mother-in-law's—and proud, too, of Gilbert's musicianship. I remember a class report of hers on Blake's songs, enlivened by a tape of Gilbert's setting of "Tyger, tyger, burning bright."

At the trimester's end I tossed an afternoon party for her class in the little house on upper Panoramic to which Miranda and I had moved after getting married. It was the first chance Ling and I had had to talk intimately. We discovered we shared the same thirst for liberation, and for what living together might bring. We were, of course, both spoken for, I by my beloved Miranda, Ling by her equally impossible Gilbert. But there was always the future.

The party was beginning to wind down when there was a fierce rapping at the door. I answered it to discover a small, wiry black man with short, intensely curled hair and very sharp, pointed features. "I've come for Mrs. Perry," he said fiercely.

I looked at him, this black man, for the longest moment unable to fathom to whom he could be referring.

"Mrs. Perry," he repeated, clearly inclined to make whitey work. And in the nick a memory cell beeped—Ling!—and I hustled off to fetch her. That was the one time I encountered Gilbert, but it stuck. A man definitely not to be crossed.

Now and again after graduating, Ling would appear as an auditor in one of my classes, her tiny shoulders draped in a voluptuous shawl and her hair peroxided and teased out in a black streetwalker's Afro. Testing the class's comfortable assumptions? Or, equally plausibly, setting me up? In the light of her infamous list, discovered by the El Cerrito police, one may wonder. Numbered among the "Fascist insects who prey on the life of the people" were my father, Robert Magowan, Marcus Foster and Patricia Campbell Hearst.

Nelson Algren says somewhere, "Never start an affair with a woman who is crazier than you are." Before this woman who hadn't yet accomplished the "Tibetan Ritual of Suicide" alarm bells should have been ringing. But to speak in tongues you need a certain craziness and I wrote Ling that I had recommended her, but could we meet for lunch? I must have added something about having tried to invite her to a party a month earlier.

My note spurred a reply:

1/13/72

hello robin—dear robin magowan,

perhaps i knew that i was invited to your party—altho' of course I did not receive an invitation in the mail. i had been living for a year in San Francisco until recently. oh did the ghetto make me ache—at night you lie down and can feel all around the ghetto as it turns on its side and sometimes sighs. So altho' my husband left me a year & a half ago, i went the day after halloween and stored all of my so many possessions and made an assignation with exile at my mother-in-law's in East Oakland—the exile necessary for the goal of saving $$. which i have—a little—& am looking for a pad in which to be while i pursue this impossible goal which the i ching says is possible. With the i ching i hear its secrets, now must i learn to speak its language—and so do i know i am still "not quite foreseeing the chain reaction."

Next week I am on a holiday, and it would be truly wonderful to see you.

What have you been writing? my lungs are filled with some of it from the fresh sea air at the ocean.

shanti shanti shanti

With the letter came a note about a dream "2 few months ago:"

i spent the nite and day with you in my dreams yesterday. You appeared wearing a black & brown chinese robe. We walked thru a garden, down a path to a tea room & drank & smoked & talked together. I cannot remember anything you said. But i can see you still as you looked & moved then, until finally we held each other & kissed. It was a vast soft moist satisfying kiss. The dream was freedom and you were love. We were happiness. The tea was water. The garden was bliss. Many thanks to you for being in the air somewhere where my dream went. I wish that i could give you love in your waking hours. I would kiss your feet, for i have always been intrigued by your demeanor.

The stage was set in some wonderful never-never land. All I had to do was show up without my shoes and in a black and brown Chinese robe.

***

Ling turned up for lunch, her shoulders draped in a flowery black and red shawl and wearing a white, many-pocketed, breast-accentuating suit that set off her alive brown eyes and shoulder-length mane of glossy black hair.

"You're looking well," she said, getting down to basics.

"Nice suit you're wearing," I rejoined. "A real splash of summer."

"Oh," she said, slipping into her husky, black-sounding voice, "this is some curtain material I ripped off a fabric store in Oakland and sewed myself. I have a certain proficiency in the domestic arts."

"And for the unusual in five-finger discount, I see," needing that bit of lingo to keep my shock-level from showing. "What's this," I said, shifting onto more comfortable ground, "about your becoming a doctor?"

"You see these hands," Ling said, flashing a bevy of rings, three to a hand. "I ran into this Indian guru, Muktananda, who operates an ashram and a vegetarian restaurant. I have what he calls healing hands. He thinks I should put them to some sort of public service. The first step is that job in the med school lab, for which I thank you. From there I'll go on to medical school."

"As a doctor?"

"No, that takes too many years. There's a new short-term program for paramedics. And in the ghetto they are what's needed."

"When does your lab job start?" I asked.

"Either June or September—it's up to me."

"And in the meantime?"

"I'll take my two cats and go live in the country. I've got this old van and some money saved from a year's waitressing at the San Francisco Jazz Club."

"The place on Divisadero?" I asked. I had heard about it, I said, but had never been there.

"I must take you sometime. It's so revered there's no crime within a block of it. That's where I was living most of the past year. All I need now is to find a pad up by the Russian River."

But her going to live in the country, Ling made clear, did not mean that she had renounced her revolutionary ambitions. "I've no police record," she told me, "despite the couple of hours they held me at the Women's Penitentiary at Santa Rita. I took advantage of a mix-up to walk away before they got around to fingerprinting me. I'd like to think a clear record might land me a job as a domestic in the home of a parole officer. Once inside, I can off him. There's no worse scum."

A distinct shiver ran through me. That Ling had turned out as a street prostitute I was prepared to accept. That she harbored such homicidal ambitions was more than I had reckoned on. But over our luncheon table, among our many shared confidences, I could not admit any squeamishness. In winning her acceptance, it helped that I had recently traveled in East Africa and Madagascar (Ling, too, had a valiha disk) and that I had known Gloria, a woman of the selfsame cigarette-haunted, torch-like temperament.

After talking about Gloria, I asked her about Gilbert. "I can fathom the attraction, but why on earth did you marry Gilbert?"

"There was, I suppose, an element of defiance," Ling replied thoughtfully. "Not only you won't marry me, but I dare you to live in the ghetto—and at my mother's? I must have taken to the life all too well, because after the first week of marriage he split on me.

Not that he didn't turn up from time to time and make it impossible for me to be living with anyone else. I have nothing against sporadic sex, but sometimes," she said, raising her head and looking straight at me, "you do want something else. Something more."

After lunch, as a start towards "something more," I took Ling home to fulfill her dream's prophecy. Afterwards, by way of augury, we threw the I Ching, using coins rather than the twenty-seven yarrow sticks she preferred. I drew Ting, the Cauldron, an image of transformation, of what the two of us operating lucidly together might achieve; a cauldron that evoked the engulfing grip of her legs and deeply rounded lower torso, as well as the acrid musky vapors in which I had been immersed.

When I said as much Ling replied, "I was consciously making my legs into a basket. Usually making love I don't see images. You must dance," she added, "marvelously."

Ling's hips weren't her only physical attraction. Emboldened by her dessert of marijuana pie which was beginning to take effect, I said, "I didn't dare tell you about your breasts . . ." trailing off, at a loss to describe such deeply cleaved, wide-slung, pear-like magnets.

"That you liked them," she said kindly, seeing me at a loss.

"Yeah, that's what I meant." And I went on, "You make me feel intelligent—perceptively intelligent."

But wasn't I also making her feel intelligent? Still, after so many efforts to turn me into Joe Husband, I appreciated being taken as the driven man I was. I even suggested our writing something together—wasn't that the function of a muse?

Yet uncertainties remained. Neither of us, after all, had a clue where we really stood. But, rather than voice them, Ling showed her understanding of the man to whom she had fed half a pie of grass. "There'll be a nice silence and then you'll write. Oh," she rejoined, as she disappeared down the kitchen steps, "about two minutes."

She hit it on the dot. Freed of my inhibitions by her "white negro" persona, I scrawled away in dialect for a couple of hours. No muse could have come on more auspiciously.

Not long thereafter, by special delivery from a Russian River postal box, came a missive written on gaudy brown, orange-flecked paper:

1/23/72

he said that he thought of me as a magician/did he say that? he said that we two should write something to-gether—but that was probably bullshit

oh no i am not a magician, not yet—because you do not really believe that i am.

he said to call him sometime when I get a pad

the I Ching under "Ting, the Cauldron" says, "at the bottom are the legs, over them the belly, then come the ears (handles), and at the top the caning rings."

so perhaps i may not call until i get a cauldron. then will i not be the ceremonial vessel into which you may dip?

One truth is she misses her husband; he loves his wife.

A smart girl, that. The second part, written over five days was a bit more of a letter:

1/28/72

dear R—what a lovely lunch we had—you tasted so exquisite to me

1/31

not nails, but talons on my fingertips. i am descended from the owl.

i have been listening again—after more than a year—to the valiha. et puis je suis allée au Voyage Noir. merci

2/2

Hello, i have fallen into a pad on an acre and a half of slightly inclining hill just above the Russian river. So i have decided to take a holiday trip to the forest by the river and not return to Berkeley until June or September . .

I do not know what I may say—so all I want to say is

that i have missed you a thousand thousand times
shanti shanti shanti

I spent the next weekend visiting Ling in her trailer and checking out the surrounding Russian River forest. In the magic of her
bedroom we lay, soothed by sticks of incense, her Chinese cooking pots, a library that included Leroi Jones, *The Serpent and the
Rope* and, of course, the *I Ching*. And our sorties to such primary
forest haunts as Armstrong Grove turned up such flowering plants
as calypso orchid, trillium or wake robin as it's sometimes called,
shooting stars and blue-eyed grass. I remember Ling showing me
a hillside's waterfall of "dragon's teeth," recalled from a childhood book on Samoa. And, shattering the silence, she made me
feel the two sides of the forest leaf, "shadow," "soft."

Her letter, written the following day, shows her growing taste
for her muse-like role:

Wednesday 2/8/72

the moon is opening an orange—slices—all of an open
orange's shapes for you.

Do you believe i have powers of healing? These things
take time as the cosmic forces within the body stir to movement. I will greet you then, on the 13th, if you're still going up the coast. Mendocino would be grand—you could
see benny bufano's statue smiling and waving to the sea.
Naturally I'll be here, yet it seems like so much—maybe
too much—driving for you. I could come to Berkeley, or
meet you somewhere, or something. I think I should try to
call you on Sunday—just a really quick ass call—to ask
where, when, and hear if you still wish. i'll ring in the
morning, and if no answer then again at night.

I have spent some little time looking at the mushrooms
through the Chinese painting we were in, wondering about
either writing something about them (write my diary in
the language of mushrooms) or eating them. how could
this be any more dangerous than any other thing one might
do? i am trying, beginning to see with the third eye. the
tree is green iridescence through the window. the nite rings

with many bells, rattles sometimes like a tambourine, is still, cool as the sea.

As your muse I shall sometimes be foam on your beard.
and i love you so i chant for you and i love you

It's not every woman who can make herself into a chime for the night's mysteries. Ling, like Gloria, had stepped over the shadow line. And it gave her a transparency that made me want to be with her and protect her. Like death itself she rang true.

GREEN DIZZY SCREAMING SUN-ABYSS

In those first six weeks I had seen Ling some seven or eight times. But we had spent only a single night together. If I knew her, it was mainly in connection with the heaping marijuana pies that spiced our trysts. I had weathered them successfully enough, why not see, my muse urged, what a true cerebral powder—mescaline—might yield?

So in mid-March, on the day we were to start living together, Ling arrived with a cellophane bag of synthetic mescaline fresh from a friend's laboratory. I had already put together an expeditionary basket of wine, cold salmon, sketch pads, a watercolor set and two pairs of binoculars. We set off for Point Reyes, a peninsula an hour and a half north of Berkeley which emerged in the late Cretaceous at about the same time as Madagascar and northeast Brazil.

We had been walking on the Palomarin trail about twenty minutes when, at the end of a ravine, Ling took out her stash; three powdery silver piles crinkled on the blade of a steak knife. Then and there we licked them clean. To a geometrically increasing rhythm we walked, more and more briskly, around two more ravines before reaching, in the nick of time, a meadow dressed with bushes of scraggly gray blue lupine.

I had been there before, bird-watching. Taking her by the arm, I guided her up through the clumps of tiny, purple and gold Douglas-iris to the top of the ocean bluff. In the wind roar, for a vertiginous moment we stood, scanning the fire-mist below. Then self-preservation got the better of us: this urge we both felt before the approaching onslaught to jettison everything superfluous—sweaters, urine, binoculars.

Back on the wind-sheltered meadow, we each fell into a separate ball on the ground. "Go, get away from me," I cried out. But even as I yelled my cowardly plight, there she was calmly assuring me that, whatever I might wish, there was nowhere to bail out to, since we'd still be within that imprisoning sky, those chalk-circle clouds tearing us to leather apes in the jungle of our fears.

There, from edge to edge we rolled, edge of sword, mouth, precipice, star, as one, then another dive-bombing phaeton of light unloaded directly over us its green, dizzy, screaming SUN-ABYSS. Electrons the size of golfballs bounced and diffracted against my eyes as I wriggled over to where my Circe sprawled, elbows over eyes, paint-splotched, black-jeaned belly rotating sunwards at a washing-machine frenzy. Before this person who, it seemed, had deliberately poisoned me, I felt both afraid and vengeful.

"Was this what you intended?" I managed to stammer out.

There was a pause. Then from somewhere within the commotion I heard Ling voice her chagrin. "I'm sorry I've done this to you."

I accepted that. And since the explosions were happening in my mind, it was I who was shaping their content. Not everyone, lying on a balmy spring meadow, has to be so terrorized. I wonder now whether, in submitting, I was seeking a path to the desolation of others, Ling included?

If so, the danger lay in the growing likelihood of being permanently disabled. Hard to stretch forth a fraternal hand when all you've got left is a stump. As the rush increased, my fears of the revelations paled before the more imminent prospect of the madhouse. I am not sure what madness is: perhaps nothing more than the over-exuberance with which any word, any concept, can arrive to blacken one's mist with its reality. But I had no way of knowing when and if the accelerating rush would end.

Probing like water from one vulnerable point to the next, my fears kept expanding. If I dodged one, then its big brother slam-banged in all the harder. The waves bore in on me with the speed of an express train. The long rigid trans-Pacific track out of which they appeared gave me time to brace myself. But the preparation likewise committed me. As the self-hatred hurtled in from one, then another diametrically opposite point of view, I became desperate. No point wondering, Do I think? Is it thinking me? when the issue was nothing less than the Blazing Asylum Halls, I and my fellow inmates staring out from our ever more beleaguered windows.

But those childhood days on the beach playing seaweed, pegged walrus-like on one arm to the sand bottom while one tiny wave after the next battered over me and, even more, the no-flag days when we would all inch our way out hanging to the set-lashed barrel rope, had well prepared me. As one monstrous comber after another crashed overhead, I put my head on Ling's navel and hung on, determined to ride it out. Cocooned in exploding infancy—those stars direct, I told myself, to our tongue-lost Babel—I lay twined around her, letting only the most necessary Alahhhh's shower forth their groaning sparks. I saw myself returning to that mother island where, what my heart once knew, my tongue gave out: the words, "beast," "breast;" the meadow's ring, Ling herself, found.

The change in my feelings towards Ling could not have been more consequential. Where, an hour earlier, I was ready to strangle her, I now found myself enamoured of all creation. Ling had brought me this gift and, with her clasping arms, she had pulled me through.

We clung to one another until the same instant's grasslight found us sitting up, rubbing our eyes before the huge blue-streaked blades. Yet everything was, I knew, because it all startled so: the beads of moisture on a flower; the chirpings all around. But was it Ling who was pulling me into sunlight, her touch making my wax solid? Behind the paradise of a bush lupine I stood, relieving myself, my head in my hands, my invisible legs vibrating under me like stalks.

Like a child I saw my shoes stand up, their laces somehow tied.

My jeans were sparkling blue marks on the pink gravel road. My arms limped at my sides, but that might have been because I couldn't focus sufficiently to make out my fingers, suspended somewhere below in the mist-prism. Nor could I see the gravel road, though with a somnambulist's instinct I felt the seablue at its edge curving away like the railing on a church balcony.

Useless to ponder what was mirage, what reality. After all our writhing in wet ghostly grass, merely being upright, heads in the cool delicious air, was blessing aplenty.

We had reached a last blue railing above the thousand foot distant sea and were sitting there when Ling startled me by asking, "Where are your binoculars?"

In an instant I was on my feet, frantically combing the ridge vicinity. I was about to hurl myself into the infested chaparral twenty feet below—couldn't they have rolled off?—when Ling added, "The pair you gave me are lost as well."

We concluded that we must have shed them on the bluff at the onset of the havoc. What should we do: retrace our steps? return tomorrow with a fresh picnic?

Back, Ling sensibly decided. But there on the meadow, barring our way in the twilight, flared a conflagration of orange poppies. While Ling squatted, sketching them, I sprawled beside her, eyes fixed on her fingertip, as if a stroke might reveal the gold of my face beckoning from my lily pad to the swamp's Cleopatra.

But the comparison paled in the waning light and I felt newly apprehensive, remembering the binoculars and the long walk remaining back to the car.

Our groping about on the bluff ledge confirmed only too well my apprehensions: a rolling glistening of wind; a crashing of assassin waves. Then, through the spray, came Ling's dejected, "I can't find them." And suddenly a whole afternoon, two bodies pulling one another through, lay on its back, blown up.

In my panic I heard the stars ringing "Hurry!" in my ears. I felt the ocean's damp fingers tightening about my neck. But in a sheltered spot, at the end of a far ravine, we halted, transfixed by a tiny pool that the light's ping-pong had transformed to an undersea grotto. Below, yellow brass button flowers shivered, glowed. Then, raising my eyes to the far side of the pool, I saw the bare soil merge with the gray of a wind-bent alder. Swaying together over the water, branches and earth rose, making a mushroom-like blowing, before subsiding. Fascinated by the hallucination, I focused on a watery cavern. As that inner eye gaped open, glistening textures beckoned: silken whites of alder bark; satin water into which a cow-parsley bent its cathedral-like frame and my vision, as if pulled on a reel, shuttled from bank to bank.

Where before I had felt disconnected from what I was observing, now I felt at one with my sea-anemone arms that, writhing with each blind pulsation, registered it as "night," the purple barrier beyond which I couldn't pierce.

When we reached the little parking lot, Ling volunteered to drive, "I've more experience in these matters."

I accepted gratefully, finding it all I could do to open the car door, let alone stay seated while she turned around.

My fears calmed when we reached the asphalted road. As on an aerial cushion, we found ourselves being waltzed along, so smoothly that by the time we realized we had taken the wrong turn north on Highway 1, the only eatery operating was a little restaurant bar in Olema: one of those tacky pine-walled joints with a clattering juke box and a couple of ladies in hair curlers holding forth from their barstools.

The restaurant inside was unique only in that the walls, the lampshades and even the plastic flowers were pink. I could hear my heart pounding like a roadside drill.

To sit down and order amid the noise from the bar, the creaking of the enormous menu, took a control neither of us had. Better, Ling must have decided, the bathroom, eliminate rather than ingest. While she was away, I sat upright like a tomahawk, unable even to turn the menu cover and in my fury perhaps understanding what makes the so-called insane opt out, prefer their asylum paths and hedges to these quivering monstrosities. Life's primal necessity isn't food.

The waitress was a social victim. Each item of our order resounded in her face like a slap, "Fraidy cat, last in your class, won't ever land a decent job." I don't think she grasped a word of my order. But how to make her understand what her nervousness was doing to me?

When Ling came back, I excused myself in turn, choosing a toilet seat in preference to a flamingo urinal. Upon my return there was a bowl of crab stew, the one menu item actually available, lurking above pink seat and napkin folder. How much pinkness could I pump down? An entire bowl, as it turned out, much helped by beer.

When we had finished our meal, the waitress laid down the check as one might a triggered mouse trap.

I thought of the different red of tomorrow's sun. I was glad I was free to go.

In our motel bed that night, for all our newfound closeness, neither of us felt up to making love. That would be tempting fate. But with the guiding spirit of the mescaline, Chief Tomahawk, now directing, I found myself picking up some of my unreleased bolts of anger and hurling them at each shadow that spoke of Father and tennis, a whole incarcerating family labyrinth that, for the first time now, I could name and which had begun back there in primal scream one, deb-going, uppercrust New York society.

Eric Rakhonen

MY GIRL, TALKING ABOUT MY GIRL

Before the blast of mescaline I was not in love with Ling. We were two pals on the same wave length who had wanted to try living together. Now I felt soldered to her by an experience that had brought me, horns, hooves, into her, her craziness, her reality. There was no questioning the commitment. I was hers, just as those swine were Circe's.

Next day, on our way to Point Reyes to retrieve the binoculars, I

Nancy Ling Perry, 1973

remember our coming upon a vernal pool that had been taken over by a congress of fire-bellied salamanders: hundreds of joyfully floating, copulating, penis-like amphibians. In my besmitten state I watched as she stood at the edge of the pool peering from under a spring-green willow down at them. As she stooped forward, enchanted by their orgies, her mane all of a sudden plummeted over her head in a blueblack waterfall. An "incendiary explosion," I immediately jotted in my notebook, attempting to combine the shock of the light with the explosive torch that she carried in her. But of what, I asked, handing her the book.

"Chartreuse," Ling wrote. Instantly I saw each inflammable letter hyphenate into the charged, exuberant, light-and-grass-filled feminine liqueur she had become for me.

With the mescaline my psyche had taken a real hit. When I visited Winnipeg for a reading a month later, Myron Turner recorded my lemur-like nervousness, perched in his apartment always on "the edges of things . . . the arm of the sofa . . . the teak buffet, the chest of drawers . . . unzippering toothy visions" of "the same bruised rainbow as your stammered elations." ("The drunken prince of lemurs and all small animals.")

I had always been able to speak about myself; a way, I suppose, of trying things out, poems in the making. Now I couldn't. The dragon lady I was living with, the mescaline, the seriously weakened, much-changed person I had become, it was all too shameful, too unbelievable.

But what I couldn't talk about had to come out and, with Ling poring through my notebooks and starring one or another forgotten phrase, poems began to rainbow out in a profusion surpassing anything I had ever known. Whereas each writer aims at something, his personal facet, I differed, she made me understand, in my vulnerability to female beauty. For me, just as for Charlie Merrill, Helen of Troy existed and those thousand ships had truly sailed. Such compelling power I saw as the fundamental mystery.

And it upset me, much as a beautiful woman upsets a room by stepping into it.

Yet Ling was never home enough to suit me, "Shouldn't I be giving you an allowance, shopping money, something?" I asked early on. "We are, after all, living together."

"Taking money from you bothers me. I can make what I need on my own."

Her frank, independent agenda only increased my own social guilt. "I don't see how I'm contributing to anything sitting behind a desk."

"Nonsense," Ling replied, taking her cue from Mao, "Everyone in the Revolution has his role and yours is to go on being one of the Hundred Flowers. By redefining our relation to things and altering consciousness, you are making something happen."

That soothed my ruffled feathers, and I was quite willing to look the other way when Ling took off for a weekend to the Russian River to earn a few bucks acting in a porno flick. (I often picture the naked cast, all stoned on acid, squatting in a cabin's frigid rain-driven silence.)

In her last "communication" Ling bemoans the "rather dreadful way I betrayed you." But wasn't that kind of sexual betrayal written into the contract—her end of it, descendant that she was of the muse Polyhymnia, open to one and all. Sex was a commodity she could trade for the cocaine that might extend a manic high. And it suited an actress who saw herself as an emissary between the kingdom of death and our brief mortality. What is a movie, Godard once asked, but a man, a woman and a gun?

All the same, she didn't countenance infecting me with a venereal disease. Upon my return from an eight-day trip I found her diary, along with an oval painting, on my desk:

> The man who lives here has been away for the last eight years. Because I love him I was invited to live in his house. I stack his mail and give water to everyone and chant for him. A vaginal infection, inside, developed in the first year of his absence. I cannot imagine that I am infested with

v.d.—too many outrageous, blatant symptoms. So I wish it to be a private, non-contagious woman's malady. The soreness of the symptoms is easily forgotten over eight years of abstinence; but the worry is an unrelenting fervor of fear. Did I give an infection to the god that lives in this house? (How can that be? Is he all right?) Yeah sure I call it nothing but the blues.

But for all her activity, I don't think Ling saw prostitution as more than a means of survival. "When a woman's down and out," I remember her confiding as we lay together in the dark, her voice cracking under her painful memories, "she can always take to her back."

No doubt her suicidal bent was exacerbated by the hallucinogenics, her equivalent of another's eye-liner, or high-heeled boots. Like Circe, she needed the props to bind her lovers to her, make us honking pigs and scribbling minotaurs forget everyone but her. But wasn't part of the attraction between us that I was a junkie as well, a sexual junkie? Weren't we both in our self-loathing feeding off an energy not our own, that warm hand pressed in ours?

And it was dope and sex that occupied the main ground of our time together. A young woman does not try to live alone in the forest with a pair of cats and the I Ching unless she is intent on strengthening her links with nature. At the time, Ling's sexual identity was somewhat confused. And Gilbert's walking out on her hadn't helped. Nor could the succession of "one time sensual experiences" that followed have done much to resolve what she needed in a mate.

That may be why Ling summoned me into her life, as I had all sorts of notions about the transforming cauldron of a prolonged sexual intercourse. My own being was committed to diving into the magic nets which I saw as the nexus of a poet's vision. Yet in electing to become my muse and all-purpose household slave, was Ling making a belated effort to prove to herself she could be a mistress of the "domestic arts"—no grime she couldn't grovel in—rather than another bimbo in a pick-up truck?

What was Ling's physical presence? Patricia Hearst remembers being guarded by Fahizah, this "girl with the thick drawl," as she calls Ling:

> Tiny, only four feet eleven and slightly overweight, Fahizah sat hunched over the toilet seat, wearing a dark ski mask, a see-through black knit top with her breasts clearly visible, and tight corduroy pants with a gun belt around her waist and an empty holster on one hip . . . I thought she looked weird, malformed, like a hunchback without the hump, sort of a small female ape.

A few pages later, Hearst refers again to this "monkeylike girl." Strong stuff coming from a woman barely three inches taller.

But the "tight corduroy pants," with the gun belt and holster on one hip and the magnets of her breasts glowing through the tank top, all that registers: a woman pulsatingly believable, and with the kind of hunger in her womb that could slake an entire Symbionese army.

"Small female ape" that she might seem, hers remained a sexy presence. Otherwise her airbrushed high school photo would not have graced the front page, nor would her fan clubs have sprung into being. Close up, in her sexual presence, my jottings reveal her husky croak-shadow voice saying "feasts," as she drew me into her vagina's beckoning cavern; the eskimo teeth and coal granite of her eyes, with their curved hatchet fingers. Beauty, maybe, but of a decidedly dragon lady variety.

But in my descent into her underworld I was not about to be deterred by masculine squeamishness. Buoyed perhaps by a pie of grass, I would sprawl beside her, my hands seeking out her breasts, the round moans she gave off as I stroked them and, as if from a wall away, her voice responded, a fire in a throat. It was into that chimney I bored: the ripe vulnerability I sensed in her smoker's yellow-tinged fingers; the mane into whose luxuriance my own fingers drifted, each strand a potential serpent to tie to my own springing mount. Until, a serpent myself, head swinging to her incensor, I plunged into that volcano where heart labors and screams sing.

Ling conceived of sex as being rammed: often, hard, that small case "i" of her letters. Just as I wanted to escape into a mythical persona—Orpheus himself!—so she wanted to be blasted into

Woman, Goddess; the exact fulcrum of a male's merciless driving, banging, entering. In the act of blasting I entered the fire ring of her raised, shoulder-propped legs, the vaginal cavity shortened so that any back wall bull's eye reverberated as so many moans scored, so much of a heart bared, opened up, my fingers adding a clitoral obligato until the yeas, "That's so, so good, man," began resonating their focal encouragement. But for a thirty-six-year-old man the ramming was not my idea of bliss.

"THE MORE YOU TAKE, THE MORE YOU GET"

By the end of April, Ling was ready to take a break from the "ghost town of the movement" that Berkeley had become. I had long wanted to see the flowering wastes of Death Valley. When she proposed camping out there—a new experience for me—I readily assented.

Our week's trip fulfilled the make-or-break test so many couples put themselves through. We had each, I think, fallen in love. But for all our intimacy, there was a shadowed side to her that I hadn't reached. I did not want to be a political embarrassment to her. But on what basis could we connect—my long-standing drive for personal freedom? Yes, she had helped propel me forward and soothed my social conscience. Now was the time for her to find out to what extent I could be made over. It was time for both of us to put down our remaining cards.

For the moody person Ling was, the stripped down world of the high desert offered a perfect outlet. As we drove along a sagebrush valley, I remember her intoning, as if from memory, a three-part poem:

> the sad sand song of the desert dunes
> the sharp choir of cacti
> and above the flat drone of the buttes

However transcribed, the lines show Ling's ear for the desolation that so drew her.

The desert brought out its own music in us as we sat under a piñon tree while the last light poured over our hands and our voices came out like stars and we shone back and forth, husks of our dusk-extended quiet as she saw-pressed her hips up and I burst in like sun in a fern forest as I dropped my head and close-shouldered drank. I drank her laugh of clear silver, her tongue which thumped its water, a kettle over my lit, exploding self. Why, I asked, did I need hope so? Wouldn't a clear eye do instead, my door open to a knock from anywhere—that hole under my bed!

But despite our closeness I was becoming with each day more afraid: of the domain of death and criminality that so enclosed her; of the restlessness of her insurrectionary ambition and the armed "action" she was planning; of what I saw myself turning into, an "almost nothing headed less than nowhere, one shrieking car bounce at a time."

Yet if I could not see a way out, I knew that in my dive into her depths I had touched something holy: the secret, sorrowful well of us all.

No wonder that, home from Death Valley, a succession of poems cascaded out: multi-page rants that left me shaking, hoping my head wasn't going to split apart then and there in my hands. It was everything I had wanted and more than a bit scary. I was a cat high in a tree with no idea how I was going to make it down. What more could I do for Ling, give her?

But even as I bemoaned my impotence, I knew the answer. "There's only one thing," I remember Huey Newton shouting at a Black Panther rally, "you white folk can give a black—a gun!" But that's where I drew the line. Not out of any moral conviction, but because I knew the gun would go off in my face.

Back from Death Valley, and more besotted than ever, I had written:

> If my writing were lead frosting and stars
> Were anything other than unbelievable anguish
> I'd give some of it to you
> Like a gun to silhouette those stockings

You take off each evening to lay beside me
In that place that does not lead anywhere
But back to your heart . . .

My quandary was more than resolved a couple of weeks later in
June when I dipped into the magic pouch for a second time. I had
intended no more than a light hit of the mescaline, perhaps enough
to clarify the new Hans Hoffman paintings in the university museum. So far they had eluded me.

My mistake lay in measuring out the powder from a blade broader
than the original steak knife. Ling was reading on the sofa, as I
hesitated after the second lick. "The more you take," she remarked,
"the more you get." And there I was, reembroiled in the madness.
Only this time I had only myself to blame.

A writer works to prepare himself for the rare moment of vision. This is what I'm about, he tells himself, as he paddles his
bâteau ivre into the forbidden waters. Fine, so long as the boat
cleaves to the rational surface. But what do you do when the reality you are encountering is a hallucinated one and what you are
seeing and what you are transcribing are not one and the same?

Imagine a twilit river at the onset of what one knows is going to
be one helluva storm. Only I was the eye in the middle of the river,
a purple lit with the stormlight's rattling yellows, down which I
found myself being propelled.

As the waters geysered from under me more and more powerfully, I realized I had to switch the locale. Summoning my remaining powers, I managed to change the river into a quiet, moon-
pierced lake out of a northern tale. As I stood on its banks I beheld
out on the water a series of revolving, ghostly gray wave-castles
that my pen named

the silver dishes of the radiators of the soul.

By "radiators," I meant irradiators, a term that encompassed the
churning cyclones of the castles and the bone-chilling cold generated by a

lake whose least wish was ice.

But such a lake was, by its very labials, Ling herself. In the next

238

instant there she was in all her romantic enticement, the shining bangs of her hair translated into a stream flashing frogloud in the black and silver setting. By the mouth of the stream there was even a stone lantern. I could be in a Japanese garden. But was a garden made out of eyes? For it was the eye-like lake's lathering waves that were now drawing me down into their

dins of silver lather,

only in the next breath to launch me skywards, by way of a rhyme, into a far more beautiful

rims of silver night.

I felt I was watching a stellar ballet, yellows pirouetting, reflecting, qualifying one another. Like Ling and I dancing I thought. And I saw us on a little tree platform overlooking the Lorelei lake. Only we, in our romantically clasped

tree-and-tongue-enclenched

unity, had taken the form of a pair of embracing cobras. What sort of cobras? Cobras of night

and of ourselves!

I found myself scribbling. Carried along on a wave of exultation, I grabbed her and together, hand in hand, we dove from our projecting bough into the water, fully expecting to be reborn there in a quieter medium of fish-silvery becoming.

Instead as the letters

d r o w n

bubbled up around me, I experienced something very different from the breast-of-the-waters in which I had expected to be soothed and transformed. Instead of the mothering tent of that great breast there were now two tits, or rather two temples in which to rest, however permanently, our now

twin-parted, twin-brushed

caught alone spreading & engulfed shadows

The vision might have profitably rested there. But much as the aesthete in me might have liked to live out my remaining moments there, another "I" beckoned back from below the waters. To have dived headfirst out of a tree had required a certain trust and courage. But to remain in that female element, submerged for all eternity, lay beyond my powers as a man, an earthling.

But decisions are rarely unilateral; nor do we live in a static universe. As I surfaced, gasping for breath and fearing the vengeance of spurned feminine spirit, at that moment the moonlapping element turned threatening. The forest boughs now writhed with actual cobras. And the Ling I had been living with took on the attributes of the Ling of her self-legend. Only now she was a black stripper-singer, because that was her wish and, much as I regret it, my racist-sexual fear and desire.

I found myself back in the lakeside forest. Only now this was the forest interior, a glade of everywhere echoing eyes, raised hoods and snaking, forking tongues. As before, the lights and darks of the vision alternated. If at one moment I beheld the forest's hooded branches, at the next I saw the spiritual forces controlling them, out of their spidery being generously spinning a fiber pathway, this

moonlight-of-the-hands

along which, quick like a mat-rider between waves, I scurried fast as I could.

As I did, the hope that held me was the lifeline of a path I saw myself, with the help of my spider accomplices, weaving, or rather gardening, back to my beloved. But Ling was now the Ling of her past, a black nightclub stripper

dodalesquing her tentacle-pulpy breasts

as she flounced, snake-like microphone in hand, dressed in a pink body suit adapted from the sheets where I lay transcribing.

The sight, and the reminder of the poisonous "cyclamates" leaking out of her restored breasts, summoned up in me a tide of revulsion on which I now found myself zooming away, out into the night sky's satined, if not satanical, moon-shudderings.

I was out in the zodiac at its Spinal Nerve Reverberator Zone Center, shuddering with maniacal laughter, when the earth's gravity caught up with me and, like a yo-yo, started to pull me back. I saw the earth looming, then the eye-like lake. But as I infernoed through the transparent layer, I found myself on a vertiginous incline. What was to keep me from crashing into the abyss of madness that I knew lay at the end of it? I was approaching the final edge when I glimpsed an unexpected ray of hope—a blossoming

Japanese cherry branch. But my momentum proved too much as it snapped off in my clutching hands and I found myself

petaling

or was it pedaling a brakeless bicycle down the hall of a decibel-loud movie theater. Its lit marquee bore the name of my adventure

INTRUDER IN THE ABYSS

while, below it, a second horror feature proclaimed

BEAST WITH THE CHOCOLATE FROWN

With my Orphic greediness I had offended the infernal powers and there I was being served up as spectacle for their delectation.

To all intents, I had crashed through my psychic walls into insanity.

It was one thing to be zinging about the moonlake/forest glade of a mythic encounter. It was quite another to be trapped in a sordid, X-rated movie. But the visionary comedown explains the peculiar limbo we insane dwell in. It is only people with actual souls who can go about a mythic landscape. Instead, with the dereliction of one's sanity, one enters a world inhabited by people who are no one. This world of

the living walking dead

is what public spectacle caters to: the crowd at a ballgame; the eyes staring from behind their drinks at a nightclub show. There, no different from any man-jack of them, Joe Publick to a "K," I now found myself.

I had crashed through the walls of a movie theater. Into the snow? No, not yet. I found myself stunned, unable to stir, and racked by a fit of coughing that inevitably pointed to the

coffin

that I inhabited. What was I to do, stop the transcribing that was perpetuating my stricken condition? But no sooner had a tearful whimpering, "Let it alone then" appeared than it was answered by a booming Whitmaniacal

LET IT OUT THEN!

To that exhortation I struggled to my feet. Insane I might be, but that did not mean I could not rationally denounce the author of all my woes, this former tender love whom now, in my blasphemous state, I called the

Tendril-Vipered Goddess

I might have been castigating one of those wooden snake-haired effigies of matriarchal antiquity. Except this was a billboard displaying a circus's star attraction, a prone-dyed-blonde voluptuously bikini-suited Ling. Under it, like some red-faced street corner prophet, I stood exhibiting the marks of my enslavement as I pointed out to one and all the unseemly details of her private person: the ape-like hairs tendrilling in their swarming thousands from that nest of vipers; the glorious eyes which I saw readying a next blast of hot brown lead for the ogling circus throng of us, her berserk cheering fans.

The effect of my hectoring far eclipsed anything I had intended. Not only did I succeed in bringing an effigy to life, but as her outsized movie queen face with the re-touched curves and peroxided hair bore down on me and my audience, I realized that I, this raving misogynist, was still Ling's slave, willing to put up with any humiliation for one last crack at her beauteous lips. Yet the crack itself, the much-awaited detonation when her billboard lips collided with my own in a cataclysmic kiss, could not have been more terrifying.

As I braced, from inches away, a veritable sun in itself, there approached a close, ever-expanding voluptuousness. Then with a searing bang, the cosmic CRACK! of her kiss's exploding rays turned to

cosmetic

a disgusting butter-colored goo I could feel covering every inch of my skin as it slathered down me.

But I wasn't the only one thus touched. Wherever I looked in the seated circus into which her kiss's explosion had propelled me were those other horrid male mace-yellow faces. They terrified me with the delved sameness of their eyes, their unappeasable

aloneness.

Only this was not mere paranoia. It was I who had been singled out for public sacrifice. As the voices wailed and the pandemonium rose, there was this honored man being led into the middle of a flameyellow sawdust ring. There I was, as within a bubble, sundancing over her vagina while, from somewhere up in the rafters, her mouth blew a sea wave's diamond curl of cool skittering kisses to our battery of howling fans. With each added moment, I could feel my knees, my entire being, turning to water. Caught, trapped

in the jam of the squares

the cosmic lances of the cigarettes

all I had left was the rocket-like capsule of a word

final

that was now enclosing me. One after another, like mournful bells, the finals rang out:

final breath spraying

final cigarette

swirling

Then, at the last minute, as the knights, cigarette lances in hand, were girding themselves to charge, there came a reprieve of sorts: I was gathered up in vapor fountain of breath spray and tobacco smoke and catapulted onto a trapeze bar. Far away, on the other side of the great ring, I saw Ling in a snazzy pink-and-white Uncle Sam outfit waiting to catch me. So this was the moment of truth, the "final leap" of me,

costumed breath

to her

costumed breast?

But there was no choice, what the script called for had to be and, with ecstasy in my heart,

final love shim

shimmering

I leapt.

" M Y   D A M N A T I O N   I S   Y O U R   B L E S S I N G "

The trapeze leap was indeed final. For both Ling and me. For much of the next year I was a psychic mess. My Uncle Jimmy was convinced I had suffered some brain damage. To his brother Charles

243

he wrote that I looked ghastly and my speech was heavily slurred. Yet worse than the lines down and the broken glass I saw strewn all over the place was the uncertainty. I never knew when the ground under my feet would open up and plunge me back in the maelstrom.

Before there had always been a well into which I could reach and find renewal: the well of a foreign encounter, of birds, a sport, a woman; wells that were all, in some way, the writing they would give birth to. But now the only words that mattered were fixed in an inalterable glue. It was as if I had touched the skin of death.

Nonetheless the vision had brought a phenomenological clarity. If the lake was Ling in her role as a Lorelei, a sexual transparency enticing and consuming me, it was also, in its sexuality, an eye, a means of perception. For a man who had always confounded writing with diving, one can see the magnetic attraction that a Lady of the Lake offered. To realize my deepest dreams, seemingly, all I had to do was take the plunge.

Instead, upon diving in, I discovered to my dismay that the vagina-lake was her element, not mine. In ordinary life a man can usually negotiate an exit from the sexual waters; he has something of himself he can return to. But for me, whole-heartedly committed as I was, there could be no way out. I was Ling's slave, this thing at the end of her attraction/revulsion yo-yo. No sooner had I been enticed into the nightclub where she operated as a jazz-singing sexual magnet, than I was being ejected into the equally terrifying mental stratosphere. At the next flick of her wrist, as I reentered the lake, there I was propelled into a version of the front-page circus spectacle with which Ling and her SLA sidekicks regaled us all a year later.

To cooler heads it could look as if I had merely been catapulted onto the set of a sleazy horror film. But I was the sacrificial figure being held up to public ridicule and the sight brought home, as nothing else had, the reality of the dragon lady I was living with. I just wasn't cut out for an SLA circus existence: leaping through a flaming Watts hoop; diving from a netless trapeze bar towards a fetching Uncle Sam costumed and butter-fingered Ling; swimming about prettily in a media-bright glass bowl, "Look whom we've caught!" There had to be another end awaiting me than that of a prize fool.

***

For Ling as well, the second blast was our coup de grace. She had only to read my "Take me, I can't survive, I'm here with you," to realize the pall she cast. And the fear she inspired as I lay beside her must have been palpable. Within a week, to my considerable relief, she had moved back to her mother-in-law's in the Oakland ghetto.

All the same, our four months together must have added up to something more than the "business relationship" by which she had explained me to her accomplices. She had needed to get away from the ghetto and recharge. And I provided the necessary distance. Just as one can discover one's native roots by moving abroad, so Ling, while living with me, had come to see her life in the ghetto as more than a sordid failure. One of the Sixties' achievements was to destroy, at least temporarily, the myth of inherent racial-sexual boundaries. You could be the person you wanted to be, so long as you put your whole self into it and acted authentically. In accepting her "assignation with exile," Ling had done just that. When the marriage failed, she stuck it out in the ghetto, determined to make herself into someone Gilbert could forgive one day for being white.

While living with me, Ling had come to miss the ghetto's street vitality, the broken bottles and vivid cussings; the hawk-eyed addict following her home from the Safeway, intent on the shopping cart she had borrowed. It appealed to her sense of irony in the way its life mirrored the W.A.S.P. society. Only now it was gangsters and not businessmen adorning the social pyramid. They, not I, were her chosen audience.

The ghetto might seem an insufficiently advanced revolutionary seedbed. But Ling had taken heart from the 1967 Watts rioting in Los Angeles. People don't burn down their homes unless they are pretty angry. Rather than misfits and losers, she saw a storehouse of guerrilla knowhow, aces who could put together a bomb as well as pick a car lock. She hadn't yet discovered that you pay for such short-sightedness by being turned into ants and made to run in smaller and smaller circles until some oaf poisons you or sets you on fire.

245

I suspect that Ling and I suffered from a similar need for excess which we confused with imagination. In Ling the excess took a kamikaze form. She wanted to be the spark that cleared the air, that made things explode. And from the TNT she planted in our two heads to the public fireworks of her death seems a logical enough trajectory.

For much of our affair Ling was I, and I was she. An interchange of selves, based as ours was on a set of parallel needs and drives, may conceivably climax in an interchange of futures. But as individuals we remain, as Lily Tomlin put it, "in this thing alone." To think otherwise is to succumb to those black moonlit waters described in so many tales. There's nothing, of course, to keep one from plunging in: man into woman; woman containing man. But it can't last without one's discovering that this so-called muse was, as a friend remarked, "a BAAAD, BAAAD BITCH GODDESS who will come out of the grave to eat you, to close up your eyes to the dawn and inveigle you into that blank cave where albino plants whirl in the dead current."

Yet at the time all either of us felt, I think, was an intense mourning for what in each other we had lost:

> i fell asleep while waiting for my brother to come
> & dreamt that we all had our heads shaved & went
> swimming on angel island. i love you
> (maybe we went swimming in a pool of tears.)
> you are beautiful

There was after all nothing, other than her compassion, compelling Ling to give me up. A sacrifice all the more real in that I was, she knew, the one person in her life who had come close to understanding her.

After Ling moved back to Oakland, we continued to see each other once a week. She knew I needed the sexual reassurance that she was still there for me. Afterwards, we might drive up to Tilden Park and clamber onto an outcrop, enjoying the view.

I must have been looking pretty forlorn as we were sitting out there one afternoon, because she asked, "What's wrong? Your eyes look so sad".

"The view?" I hazarded. "Actually it's the light that bugs me, the smudged, low-ceiling sky. Nothing has any edges, any definition. Perhaps that's why we leap into our all-encompassing abstractions? When was the last time," I asked, turning sharply to face her, "you saw a shadow?"

Ling cackled, "If that devil with the bag of gold were to come by, he'd better pick the morning after a storm. Otherwise no one would have anything to sell." She paused a moment, taking a long puff from her cigarette. Drawn perhaps by the connection she went on. "They make all that smoke over there in San Francisco and let the winds roll it towards us. Then they wonder why, in the East Bay, we've got all these drawn blinds—why we're so unhappy. There are reasons."

"That's part of it," I replied. "Then there's Berkeley."

"All those students!" Ling exclaimed. "No old people and few children. The ghetto has all kinds of people, but you wouldn't care to move there?" She went on, suddenly serious. "It's not the light that disturbs me. I've known, after all, nothing else. But for years I've wanted to travel—see what's out there. Not like you've done, but a couple of months in India or Japan would suit me just fine." She paused, as if I were about to say something. Then she went on, "But much as I'd like to split, I'm afraid it's not to be—not in this life. What I've got to do is right here."

From the wistfulness of her tone it was clear she did not see herself surviving any fuse she would light. But I was myself too disheartened to believe I could influence the fatality looming above her. Instead, I asked, "Do you mind my writing up our mescaline experiences"?

"Far from it, it's something you should get out in the open. But please leave me out. It's not the kind of exposure a guerilla needs." But she didn't elaborate further. We were together and that sufficed.

* * *

Life at Gilbert's mother's did not pan out any better this time around. And whatever the satisfaction of smoking the local yellow poppy (I remember her voice wheezing on the phone, so husky I could barely make out what she was describing), she now found herself faced with an intolerable commute to her lab job. A Berkeley pad made sense, and I gave her the wherewithal for a downpayment, glad to have her in my vicinity.

Shortly thereafter Gilbert must have asserted his marital rights. A note came listing a different "expensive ass" apartment in the flatland below the campus. The very same afternoon I appeared on her doorstep, a large housewarming box swaying awkwardly between my knees as I knocked. There was no answer. But through the blinds I caught Ling's silhouette moving about. Secure in the value of what I had collected, I kept rapping away until finally she asked who it was and peered out, as if unable to believe there could be such a madman about. Then in a horrified voice, unlike anything I knew, she pleaded, "You mustn't come here, please." I dropped the carton and skedaddled, convinced I had done enough to get an explanation.

Sure enough, at seven next morning, banging on my kitchen door, was Special Delivery:

July 28, '72

trillium—you goddamn tender flower

i guess i have no real basis for saying i thought you knew what i am—a whore, a dope addict—i hussle out of habit
. . .

you'll probably really despise me for saying it's a good thing that last nite was the second day of the new moon for surely nothing else could have saved you. dig, baby, i have clap—not to mention that Gilbert is living at that pad. he was out when you came. he wouldn't have killed you, he would have cut off your penis. he controls the mail box & doors & everything else.

I wish i could say with complete assurance, "i'm sorry when you offered me yourself i took it." i wish there wasn't this anguish.

it's very dangerous for you to come near me—that's the

truth—don't please.

the last point of irony is thank you for the box of things. i open myself to whatever spirits may come from it. also thank you for everything.

can you dig that my damnation is your blessing?
love

Seeing Ling came at a price, but I had always been willing to pay it. But the cold chill of Gilbert's threat echoing through my vitals was such that the glimpse of Ling outlined behind her blinds was the last I ever saw of her.

Yet I still cared about Ling and, a month before leaving Berkeley, I wrote informing her of my plans. Ling replied the next day:

Friday, February 9, 1973

dear robin—hello—hi hi hi

Finally after one year i feel like i have the privilege to write to you. I don't want to keep living in this world without seeing or hearing your poems sometimes . . . i feel like that's too much.

after about 7 weeks of the fall quarter i was just finished—spent a couple of hundred on cocaine, went through an acting routine, & took an incomplete, and the fellowship at the lab ends in a few weeks.

things with Gilbert in our expensive ass flat went from worse to worse. i tried every kind of old routine to make him leave until i finally got the guts to leave myself. did on the first of the new moon this January, renting a room with refrigerator sink & hot plate in oakland by the lake.

I was a mad invalid—frequently—from november till january.

oh my newest goal is to travel to Brazil, which is why I'm still hanging around—to save money. and my most rare fortune recently has been to purchase a several months supply of hash oil.

I feel very out front & for real now that i've walked out on Gilbert. Course i've been trying it one way or another for years, but shit this time at least is very direct—like i didn't say i was going away on business or nothing—i just said i'm leaving.

Berkeley's good for one time sensual experiences—that's what my love life consisted of for most of the time i was with Gilbert

oh, i am actually very very happy to have heard from you & hope you come to have dinner before you leave Berkeley? or you should phone me? or make a deal to write sometimes? or drop by the orange juice stand at college & bancroft any weekday afternoon?

> shanti
>
> love

Included on silvery flower-leaf paper was a warning:

> Far greater the poet's obligation
> To Crime
> Than merely to rhyme.

On still another page, from no doubt the same "mad" period, came another of those all too cosmic images:

> and sometimes i am the ocean
> upon which float
> many troubled rocks

A Ling infinitely older and sadder than the jaunty twenty-five-year-old who had written me a year earlier. Blake, I fear, has it wrong. The road to excess does not always lead to the palace of wisdom.

I did not turn up for a meal on her hot plate. Nor did I call on her at Fruity Rudy's juice stand. Something about her letter's tone put me off. It's not the rhyme in crime that makes it poetic. But Ling felt otherwise. Eighteen months later, I learned of the list of Fascist insects she had drawn up. A slighted goddess can be dangerous.

Determined as I was to go abroad I could not risk seeing her. The only Berkeley ties still holding me were my two sons. But Marcia had finally married the man we had shared a table with in North Beach, after the Be-In, a deeply caring step-father to Felix and James. He made it clear they would be leaving Berkeley as soon as he secured a teaching job or traveling grant. Rather than stick around, savoring my custodial pittance, it made sense to go where I might see my sons less often, but in a more rewarding way.

I make it sound as if I hated Berkeley. The place may have been an aberration in a life that has turned on a more private axis, but it had a spirit I could not have found anywhere else. Political reality, I now knew, could be changed. You just had to work at it and persuade others to get behind the wheel with you and push.

But after eight years on the crater's edge I had had all I could take. And the re-election by a crushing majority of Tricky Dick as president did not bode well. If ever a year cried out for travel, 1973 was it.

Where to go? The far opposite of Berkeley: up into the rawest mountain air, the rocks and scree. I was set to fly to Katmandu, the first stop of a projected trip through India and southeast Asia, when one evening over dinner my doctor, a veteran of the first successful American Everest expedition, announced he would be leading in April a month-long trek along the seldom visited Rowaling Valley and across the 18,800-foot Tesi Lapcha Pass to the Everest area Sherpa highlands. Would I consider linking up with them in Katmandu?

To my admission of never having climbed, the doctor did his best to reassure me. All I needed, besides a broken-in pair of boots, were knee gaiters and high altitude goggles. Porters would carry our personal effects. Here was a chance to learn to live on my feet and I signed up.

AN INFRA-RED BEAM IN
THE SNOWS
OF TESI LAPCHA

Yet in Katmandu on the eve of the trek I remember how afraid I felt of what I might encounter in the mountain wastes I had to cross. If travel is a challenge, then mountains push it to an extreme. All the more when they carry the solemnity of the Himalayas, the millennia staring you in the eye, asking whether you can make it up to their level. Was I really ready to step off the planet? And into what in the way of a life on the far side of Tesi Lapcha, when and if I got there?

In Nepal I was halfway around the world from my father, Jimmy, Ling, Berkeley. But for most of the next three weeks I gave scant thought to the life I had left. The walking absorbed all my attention. I had expected a pleasure stroll, with time to raise my binoculars to a passing lammergeier, a flock of laughing thrushes startled around the bend of a descent. But there was little time for ogling birds. We had to keep moving to reach Tesi Lapcha before the first monsoons. And we had to keep together for fear of getting lost. I found that out the hard way our first day. I had struck out on my own, wanting to put enough distance between myself and this sixty-person-strong expeditionary force to see some birds. Unfortunately, I took the wrong path at the first tree fork. By the time I had been found and had finally caught up, I had had dinned into me the difference between a stroll and a trek.

It may have been the jangled state of my nerves, but I found the Himalayas very impressive. Every time I looked up at a snow-capped divinity I felt elated. And never have I encountered a people more vibrant than the Sherpas. But before setting out, I had unknowingly damaged the ligaments in my left knee cap while demonstrating a sliding tackle—not my forte, clearly—on Rob Wilson's carpet. With my bad knee, and on terrain that rose or fell with nearly every other stride, the walking was painful. I would regularly limp into camp a half hour behind everyone else.

Throughout the first sixteen days there remained the disquieting obstacle of Tesi Lapcha. In the Sherpa village of Bedding, near the top of the Rowaling Valley, we parted with our bare-footed porters, hiring in their place the booted locals, nearly every able-bodied villager and even a monk. After a brutal hike in their summer pasturage, and a couple of days spent there acclimatizing, we set off over the final stretch of moraine.

I had never walked on such precariously poised rocks, and it took a while before I mastered the quick-striding scamper moraine requires, never sure when a stone would blast out from under me like a game bird. Our porters fared less well and twice overhangs sent our gear tumbling down a slope. While they were retrieving it, we stood about, unable even to converse for fear of launching an avalanche. But without the stoppages I'd have been left far behind. Not helping was the unbalanced sneaker-boot combination I had adopted—the sneaker, in effect, on tiptoes. But my first-day blisters hadn't healed, and I couldn't risk reopening them a day before Tesi Lapcha.

That evening we dined in falling snow at 16,000 feet. Everything from the kerosene we were now cooking with to the doubled gloves with which we ate, made it seem as if we were on another planet. My knee—I had had a useless shot of cortisone earlier in the day—had our two doctors worried. But with only another day's supply of kerosene left, we had to get over Tesi Lapcha or face an eight-day detour.

It was dark when we arose, so many pieces of stamping, shivering expectation. Ahead was a several mile walk across the valley floor before we reached the mountain proper. I remember being impatient for us to start while there was still firm snow underfoot. The earlier we were off, the better our chances.

Fortunately, the valley floor turned out to be less hard on my knee than I had imagined. And, in the rising light, more beautiful too, the eeriness broken here by a great powdery rumble, there by a shimmer of cerulean icicles.

At the valley's end we scrambled over a small forest of red and tan boulders. Halfway up, our Sherpas had to cut a traverse across the steep ice with their axes. This was followed by a somewhat more perilous groping along the inner face of a cliff. But if my knee was suspect, there was nothing wrong with my arms and shoulders, and I climbed the way I had as a child when I shinnied up a tree on our place in Southampton; a tree, for once, adult size with no branches to tear out an eye.

Despite their heelless boots and our great crates held by a tie around their foreheads, our porters performed better than we. Their tongues protruded and their heads bobbed as they advanced, necks bowed, goggled eyes lowered against the glare, bodies spread out under their burdens like turtles. I watched them, stopped in a huddle to gossip, or comfort someone sunken onto knees as if never intending to rise again. I envied them the black-red-and-green shifting carpet of their boots. I looked at their wide-set eyes in their fire-stained faces and prayed that nothing would hurt them.

By now my own eyes were burning and my feet felt like stakes as I struggled to shift them forward in the howling gale. But if I couldn't see where I was planting a foot, I could hear the red-beaked choughs piping encouragement. Then, spectral in the rarifying gloom, I made out an elderly porter, his long arm draped protectively around his wife. A few more steps and I found myself on the ice of the summit rim. I had made it.

The electric howl of the gusting currents affected me so that merely watching our guides hopping like foxes on an overhang had me in tears. A life force so surpassing my own.

The ice on the way down on the other side of the mountain proved too much for our heelless porters. At two different points rope lines had to be set up. Even so the valley was chock full of runaway crates. For me, though, with my great boots, the descent was a dance in which I had only to balance my arms to the sides and, two feet together, hop, a "bird in flight through the forest." That high, that floating. Something in me had taken wing.

Just past the last of the snow, in a wind-shrieking dell on the moraine, we set up camp.

Later that afternoon, in accordance with the grant that had helped fund his trip, our other doctor, an eye specialist, checked our pulses by shining an infra-red flashlight into the back of our eyes. In a verbal flash, as the infra-red flooded me, I saw my deliverance:

from the stocking of moonlight, the sexual-visionary temptation I associated with Ling; from the dripping, red sweater of the dawn, one linked in my mind with the terrors of menstrual blood and Larry Rivers' portrait of Marcia. But with the images came the realization that, in crossing the feared pass, I had done it: tunnelled my way out of a life-long incarceration. Imagine the amazement of the child who, digging in the sand, actually reaches China on the other side.

The labyrinth I had escaped was fear. The corridors of that labyrinth were diverse as the silver bonds of patrimony, the icy cords of matrimony, the quixotic quest for myself in women. I had looked to others to accomplish something only I could do. Now, over on the other side, I was my own master with my own life, my own life, to achieve. I could fly, I could jump, I could shout. And no one was going to take that breath, that cry, that joy from me ever again.

FATHER, IN PERIL, REACHES OUT

That night on Tesi Lapcha, while winds ripped at my tent flaps, for the second night in a row I saw my father in a telepathic dream. From the recurrence I knew he was in mortal danger and was reaching out with all of his remaining will to those he loved. Later, I learned that, while in Europe for a board meeting, he had contracted rheumatic myalgia, a painful, debilitating disease from which he never recovered.

Father's brush with death left him an enfeebled man, hanging on by the slenderest of threads. At any point he knew the sword might descend. In the face of that threat he changed. Life itself now interested him, flowers, a dragonfly on a pond. Despite his swollen ankles and the difficulty he had in merely breathing, he took his male folk (sons, grandsons) on a safari to the East African highlands. He sold the Beach House and moved to one on a creek at the edge of Southampton, opposite the Indian reservation. And he bought a Boston whaler to putter about with at high tide. You must come down and see the birds, he would write, genuinely appreciative of the hovering tern plunging like a coin, yellow-beaked, into a ripple off the jetty. Even his politics changed. He who had been a Reagan avant a letltre—so much so that I could instinctively predict the President's every utterance—could now be heard muttering his incomprehension at the folly of our Central American interventions; the bankrupting waste of our arms build-up; the never-ending brinkmanship of the last throes of the Cold War. He didn't want to see the global keg explode; not while he was alive.

How deep this went is hard to say, because there were interludes of returning health when he would let fly with the old vitriol. At other times, I sensed he was refraining from rebuking me only out of fear of sending his blood pressure sky-rocketing. Probably his will, the $33 million piled up in net worth, expressed whatever it was he had arrived at. And like any man who is his testament, he was constantly tinkering with it, lopping off a divorcing brother here, restoring him two years later. For the excised there would be an odd favor, a $1,500 check in his horribly enfeebled handwriting given with a hug in his London hotel room, or the $100,000 cabled to each of us brothers on the very eve of his final attack.

I saw Father for the last time in September, 1987, three months before his death. Mother had some meeting to attend in London and, sick as he was, he insisted on accompanying her. As he said, he might as well die there as anyplace else. His week at Claridge's was not easy. Every other day he seemed to spend entirely on his back, rising only by a supreme effort of will for dinner at a restaurant. But on one of his better days I invited him out for lunch. If he was up to it, I said, we would go afterwards to The National Gallery. The lunch went unusually well. As always there were memories I wanted him to probe, that forbidden terrain of his father, Chester and his boyhood there. But then our probable last time together did not seem the occasion for biographical gathering.

At the meal's end, however, he reminded me, with a shock of The National Gallery. Gambling a bit, I steered him to the Dutch rooms, little landscapes, a Vermeer or de Hooch interior, and finally a room of Rembrandt portraits. Everybody on those walls, I pointed out, looked even older than he. For a few rapt minutes he looked at them, all these wizened, pain-gnarled faces captured with such compassionate tenderness, as if suddenly understanding what art, a life's involvement, might be about. Then he asked to be taken back to his hotel.

His last evening, with all hell breaking loose in his chest from a ruptured aneurysm, required all his courage. He could have undergone an operation, which would probably have left him a vegetable. But mortally afraid as he was, and with only Mother in attendance, he resolved to wait it out. Six hours later he was dead.

Now that Father is no more I find myself every now and then missing him dreadfully. That he loved me at the end I don't doubt, but I wish he could have understood me, too. And I sometimes think that a book of mine might have given him enough to fill in the missing pieces. But a man to whom I could rarely speak was hardly the person to discover me in my autobiography. I see now that the great rift between us was one of truth. I wanted it in respect to his self, his past; Father did not. His life, the achieved version he had set out, was very much his confection and no question of mine was going to take it from him. Put another way, he did not quite trust me—nor I him. So there was always an edited gap between us, of what in me he did not know and, consequently, feared.

MONTARNIS

For years I had found myself being pulled this way and that. Towards my father. Then away from him and his labyrinth, his devouring ocean. Come what might, I told myself, I had to become my own creation. Once across Tesi Lapcha, all the yearning stopped. I was free. And I did not have to go on, as planned, into

India and southeast Asia. Nor was I capable of it. I had lost a lot of weight on our trek, and my efforts to put it back in the restaurants of Katmandu only succeeded in disrupting my digestive system. Instead I used my return ticket to stop off in France, a good place to fatten up. Thanks to the writer-draughtsman, Virgil Burnett, I had a house to repair to in the walled medieval village of Montarnis in western Burgundy.

When I arrived in Montarnis during the second week of May, 1973, winter had barely receded. Each day, as I walked under the apple blossoms, I felt a frosty threat at my heels. But the very fragility brought a burgeoning forth, of self into the earth, the skies, the life in which I found myself.

On two previous occasions I had visited Montarnis without succumbing to any enchantment. To my turn of spirit, spoiled as I was by memories of wine-dark sea and sharply rising hills, by the incitements of violin and clarinet enlivening the nights, all of Montarnis's remarkably intact medieval heritage—convent, abbey, turreted counting houses, gates and fortified walls with their devoutly carved sculpture-set niches—had not seemed replete enough. Now after the rocky barrenness of the Himalayas, I could appreciate a hilltop village surrounded in steep, mist-laden greens.

Here was a once substantial medieval town—the religious center of imperial Burgundy—that had reverted to the same subsistence farming community it had been when Julius Caesar had camped there during the siege of Vercingetorix's Alésia (the victory that had encouraged Caesar to declare himself emperor and made Latin the new world language). Unlike most "preserved" towns, Montarnis was unspoiled. There were no yellow parking lines, no hotel or souvenir shops, and only once in a while a tourist bus pulling up to disgorge its prying horde.

The three hundred person village was so situated that I could emerge by one or another gate and always discover something: a votive stone, a new moth or lichen or damsel fly. The longer I sat, the more aware I became of the depth of presence. Monks, magi, druids, had all contemplated there, bringing an attentiveness I tried to capture.

As I sat by the message richness of a steep descending wood, I understood that the notion of stillness needed to be enlarged so it contained all of an instant's rustling secrets. Or that there was a dance in the movement of any succession of sunlit leaves; even in my own feet treading, catlike, the ivied rhythms of a wall. Walls, walls, in a prospect so steeply pitched, they sang as hedges did back home. Only here the masonry shedded light, vibrations, different grays, blues, pinks for each turn of the day.

The more I sauntered about, the better I understood the extent to which the landscape was the peasants' creation. If it was a soft, lingering countryside, it was because those working it had contrived to keep it full of cows and hawthorn hedges and wooded hilltops. Their tender concern for the world they had molded could influence a visitor into thinking he had been flying all his life toward their still center.

When the long day finally ended, moonlight took over, lighting turrets, gates, ramparts, with the spectral authority of another age. Squares and ruined walls sang. Blood throbbed. To write I had only seemingly to listen. After being for much of my life a prisoner of one sort or another, I was in a setting I had always yearned for. Hopefully, I could start putting myself through those common paces that make up a path: working with my hands; learning in whatever loneliness to be content. A person making the transition from erstwhile victim to more complex exponent.

The transition, I sensed, required that pool of healing green into which I plunged my face and began to breathe with something other than the rushed, frightened exaltation of my last Berkeley year.

In coming to Montarnis, there is no question that I was fleeing, for my sanity, if not my very life. I had no wish to end up nailed to a wall. Or if I was, only I was going to do it and in my own manner. That, it may be argued, is what this kind of writing is about—nailing oneself to the wall. Only it was now I who was choosing the when's and where's. In the choice there is, as I keep learning, a true freedom. In becoming focused, I was more alive. And my fate was finally in my own hands—not a parent's, a lover's, an organization's—each exploiting me for what I might symbolize.

It was not as if I wanted to write about myself, but I had to.

Provided I could see myself, I could see the world. It's the dancer who, alone on the taverna floor, gives back to the company of those watching their space, their freedom.

To anyone the least objective I could see now how foolish I must have appeared. No sooner had I extricated myself from one job, one marriage, than I was enmeshed in the next. My life was my writing; my writing, my life. Whichever way I wriggled, I turned, I was trapped. And, given my coordinates, all I could do was keep repeating myself. The wanton current I was caught in was eternal, and I was being sucked into its maelstrom.

But at the time I didn't see my labyrinth in as dire a light. It was more, I thought, that I hadn't descended far enough. To reach that fabled palace of wisdom down in the muck at the bottom of every-thing, all I lacked was a guide. And I approached each new woman as if she were the Ariadne who would deliver me from the vortex in which I found myself.

I forgot to reckon on the danger lurking in those depths and the pursued becoming the pursuer. Violence and sex are not mere ca-sual bedfellows. Nor can one traipse from one would-be muse to the next, taking everything from her—all the inspiration she has to give—without incurring a vengeful response. In a society where women are pushed to the wall, a gun has a definite relevance. Along the ladder of violence how much of a leap was it from Ling's sui-cide attempts to her becoming a murderous terrorist?

Finally, with the second blast of mescaline, the obsessive pur-suit came to a convulsive end. Staring, on the one hand, insanity in the face and, on the other, a drone's life in a terrorist scenario I did not believe in, I had to admit something was drastically wrong.

With the admission came the possibility of emerging from the current that had usurped my life. And the recognition I experi-enced on Tesi Lapcha, that I did not have to be beholden to any-thing or anyone, effectively thrust me into a new freedom. I now had a story and, through that story, a life. As the proverb puts it, "You can't take from me what I've danced."

THE SYMBIONESE
LIBERATION ARMY

In mid-June the Burnetts arrived to reclaim their house. Shortly thereafter I left for Athens where I was to meet my sons. From Athens I conveyed them to volcanic Santorini for a month of island life. After they left, I lingered in the cooler north, moving to the forests of Mount Pelion to check out what remained of that first of the mythic dance bands, Pan and the Centaurs.

But I returned to Montarnis the first day the Burnett house became vacant in early September. At the time I had no thought of making the leap and becoming an expatriate. It was more that the daily changes I had witnessed in those six weeks in Montarnis had made me curious as to what a year spent there might reveal. Up to then I had lived in a country setting only sporadically, summers in Southampton, two months at a time in Greece. Here was a chance to experience the long undressing of a Burgundian autumn and a spring that, beginning in February, would still be progressing when I returned to California in June to visit my children.

My thoughts that fall kept circling back to Ling. That I knew now where I stood politically and what had to be changed—any patriarchal system that seeks to coerce us—seemed very much her gift. Without it I don't think I could have sustained the balancing act living abroad entails.

I was also involved in writing up my two mescaline experiences of the previous year. I had a draft of *Looking for Binoculars* ready for her comments when a last bulky packet arrived from her. It contained, along with her letter, a twenty-five page prison diary kept by "a young white male." The letter began awkwardly:

> i wish i could come up with whatever could disguise itself as the correct manner and right words to present what i am about to say; it would be a disguise, though right on, and so i really won't even consider trying. there are probably several reasons why i am endeavoring to communicate with you.

1. because if nothing else i think you will appreciate this very brief "manuscript" that i enclose.

a. that is because i carry around this intellectually vague idea that you'd like to get at some of the white roots of this country besides the ones we all, and perhaps you especially, already know so much about; that means something about "country and western" as well.

2. because certain things i was doing mentally while staying with you last year have brought me here to this; i remember (among so much) that you once said to me something like you hoped i would be able to actualize my militancy both by being a little more verbally clear as well as make some kind of tangible connections.

7/9/73 11 p.m. BEGIN AGAIN? and for the last time so bear with me:

Yes, another writer who could not bear to throw away a first draft. And how ironic, in rereading her, to realize that I may have revolutionized her as much as she did me.

dear robin, greetings.

Realizing, perhaps more than i can make you believe, the rather dreadful way in which i betrayed you, realizing this because i've been betrayed many, many times myself:

1. i am very intense and serious these days and when i do just take it upon my mind to relax i get higher than any drug has ever taken me—ANY DRUG—and for that reason i have finally come to the place—as i'd heard and seen so many others do—where i don't touch NOTHING i even kept a lot of acid, oil, and weed around for the 1st month cuz i just couldn't believe it until finally i threw most of it away—along with the handmade sterling silver coke spoons—and then gave the rest away—and all i wonder now is why it took me so damn long to get here?? i mean, you dig, i know i had this outrageous intake due to the fact that i thought i needed to blur the miseries of this reality we all live in. Now I've found in these last months a way

to direct my rage and work at ending these miseries instead of trying to alter them all around and accept them. So there are some of our brothers—white, black and brown (not too many asians it seems just now) with whom i correspond and visit and send money orders to and work at legal aid with AND THEY ARE ALL IN THE PRISONS OF THIS STATE OF CALIF. FOR ONE YEAR TO LIFE And there it looks like they will stay unless I can generate more financial support than the $400 a month i make at this orange juice stand.

And then now HERE'S THE HARD PART (I'm sure you've seen it coming); naturally there must be at least 2 reasons for everything including letters to you. This man whose letters I send is in desperate need of a retainer to get his lawyer on his job and i, as usual, am in desperate need of a little assistance to keep me on mine (i mean hitching up and down the street soliciting blow jobs at $10 a shot just isn't making it). So how much to ask you for???? Accepting the fact that you may just not be able to bring yourself to give—give—give me any more money, let's just say anything from $500 to $50 would be welcome (not that i expect you to believe me, but i really don't do drugs no more, and i'm really sorry—maybe even more than a little—that i whipped so many onto you, really. . . .)

hoping that you'll get this soon—and really wishing you well even if I never hear from youyouyou

love

No doubt, I should have seen Ling's desperation and coughed up the needed $500. But the notion of a lover's alimony bothered me, as did the threat of yearly blackmail. So I responded with a $50 check. But I added I would buy the beautiful pastels she had done during my second overdose, while sitting out in the garden, for the remaining $450—a way of suggesting other lines of work than soliciting blow jobs. But my check was never cashed and to this day is probably lying in some FBI file, part of a government theory that saw me bankrolling Ling and the SLA.

Ling's is a fascinating letter, not least for what it reveals of the disjunction between her private and public selves. The middle-class jargon with which it begins, "endeavouring to communicate," "correct manner," "tangible connections," "actualize my militancy," strains credulity. How many of them are peering over her shoulder? What do they want of me? And the subtext, "perhaps you especially," "rather intellectually vague idea," "brief manuscript," does not seem very friendly.

Whereas the second part, written in her nitty-gritty slang in a more private hour, brings out the Ling I knew. Even so the warmth of her response has to grapple with the "RAGE" of the addict struggling to kick her habit cold turkey. What Ling really needed was not some magical gun's cyanide bullets, but a halfway house.

From the I Ching to the Koran might seem to require more than a hop, skip and a jump of a few months. But these "children of the wind" were as much a mystical brotherhood as anarchist extremists. To attest their revolutionary seriousness, they needed blood on their hands. But why that compassionate Afro-American superintendent from Philadelphia who was giving the Oakland schools an unexpected human face? Were there no other targets available?

I suspect that the schoolboard's proposal for a photo identity card (to distinguish the genuine students from the schoolyard pushers) struck a raw nerve in Ling. Her terrorist availability was based, she had told me over our first lunch, on never having been fingerprinted. And she did not want to see a vast potential revolutionary cadre being thus declawed. Ironically, Foster was himself opposed to the ID card and on October 9, two days after Ling's letter, had gotten it scrapped in the course of a stormy schoolboard meeting. Unfortunately no one had informed the SLA!

Ling was one of the three masked assailants who gunned down Foster in an alleyway; an inexpiable act that, any way you looked at it, made no sense. When this action, as even Bill Harris admitted to Patty Hearst, "sort of misfired," the SLA became the Left's pariahs. To relaunch themselves, they needed something big. Why in those pre-PLO, pre-Red Brigade times they chose body-snatching, I don't know. The relative safety with which it could be pulled off? If America was, as they claimed, an oligarchy, then one way for the oppressed to strike back could be to target the ruling elite.

Among her other roles, Ling was the SLA's archivist. She kept her documents boxed in a cabin-like safe house north of Berkeley in the El Cerrito hills. But when, shortly after midnight on January 10, 1974, two of the back-up crew to the Foster murder, Russ Little and Joe Remiro, were arrested while driving a van nearby, she panicked. The prospect of a police search so alarmed her that she tried to burn the cabin down. In a tinderbox where not even Fourth of July sparklers are tolerated, the arson attracted attention and Ling barely made it out, zooming in her stolen gold Buick Riviera past the incoming sirens.

Among the score of cardboard boxes was Ling's green spiral notebook with its list of prospective victims that included my father and a note reading, "Patricia Campbell Hearst—nite of the full moon." But with the information in police hands, the SLA's revolutionary timetable was moved forward. They needed to find bodies they could trade for the imprisoned Little and Remiro. And among the bodies was my own.

The SLA's decision to try to find me was prompted by Rob Wilson's article, "Berkeley Inscape: The Poetry of Robin Magowan," which appeared in the *Daily Californian's Arts* magazine the day after the bust of Little and Remiro. Why would the student newspaper run such a piece if I was not part of the local scene? But the business of phoning Wilson and the English department was left to the SLA's other actress, Angela Atwood. Had Ling betrayed me enough already? Or did she fear having her cover blown?

I'm convinced the rumors the SLA fed Patty Hearst on the night of her kidnapping, of hers being but one of a number of similarly conducted events, was no more than wishful thinking. Yet it seems unlikely that the two million dollar ransom "to the people in need of food" (PIN) was conceived only when the original prisoner exchange was thwarted by the feds. For what it's worth, one may speculate what a Safeway-managed giveaway might have achieved, conducted without the distribution foul-ups that bedeviled the Hearsts. (Patty's father, by the way, came to mine to ask if Safeway could help. But Father, unaware of my involvement, turned him down.)

While Angela Atwood phoned, Ling was also spreading her nets.

She wrote Norman Mallory, with whom we had spent a couple of days in Reno on the way back from Death Valley. (Norman recalls my awed exclamation, as Ling dove off a canyon bridge into an icy green hole, "She has powers no man would contemplate.")

Ling's note to Norman read:

> dear brother,
> i am sorry i can't tell you who i am or what i'm doing. if you can get this to robin or know where i can get in touch with him just mail this postcard so i'll know. it's very important.
> i love you and remember our days together warmly and am sorry i have to stay so mysterious
> love
> your sister

The intercepted postcard brought Norman a scary, guns-drawn, investigation from a huge, well-muscled FBI agent in a blue shantung silk suit. The first thing he wanted to know was whether Ling and I were "cozy?" When Norman looked baffled by the euphemism, the agent proceeded to illustrate his meaning by forming his left-hand thumb and index finger into a circle. Then with his right hand's straightened finger, he thrust repeatedly in and out. After his visit, Norman's phone, like so many others, was tapped for several months.

On February 4, 1974, Patricia Hearst was kidnapped. From the moment I read her fiancé's description of the break-in—the white woman's voice on the apartment intercom—I assumed Ling had struck. A course or two in dramatic art seemed to be a prerequisite for the modern revolution.

The kidnapping put me in a double bind. Ling had betrayed me by placing my father on her list of victims. Yet we could still consider ourselves friends, with an obligation to stick by one another. But there are limits, and I didn't like seeing myself cast as a class enemy for their propaganda mill.

My role, so far as the SLA was concerned, became that of a latter-day Actaeon. I had seen the Moon Huntress naked, and for that crime I was to be turned into a stag to be devoured by her baying hounds. As revolutionary history keeps demonstrating, the former sympathizer is dangerous precisely because he incarnates doubt. In a cause as beleaguered as the SLA's, nothing less than the blindest faith would do.

But it was not only the SLA with whom I was reckoning. There was also the FBI. I had come under surveillance when Ling listed me as her reference in renting the tract house at 37 Northridge Avenue in Daly City where Patricia Hearst was to spend fifty-two days tied up in a two-foot deep closet. If I was offering such support, couldn't Ling be holed up with me in Montarnis? A Laurel and Hardy-sized pair from the Sûreté were dispatched to check me out.

While Laurel rummaged about the Burnett house, Hardy asked the questions that would inspire my later dreams of Ling: turning on a landing to shove a razor-sharp white piece of cardboard against my throat, "See here, you're coming with us;" or, machine gun in hand, from the top of a double-curved chateau staircase, mowing down this possible blabber; or, in a poignant reminder of our former intimacy, appearing on my doorstep on the lam, naked under a tattered fur coat, a blue prison-tattooed NANCY LING visible on her nape despite clearly strenuous efforts to efface it. But even as my spirit leapt at the unexpected privilege, another self was already foreseeing the blunder that would put her back in the penitentiary. Was it because I possessed what my troubled conscience needed I awoke? Or because I could not bear to see my Eurydice snatched away and returned to her ghostly realm?

I remember Hardy asking whether I thought a piece of street theater like the Hearst kidnapping could succeed in France. Probably not, I heard myself responding. A Frenchman may not care for a particular law, but he obeys it for fear of the civic consequences. An American, I said, is more anarchic. We regard ourselves as having our own social conscience. It is up to us to decide when and whom we obey. To such free spirits the law often seems a code imposed by usurpers, by the banker class "funding" fathers, say, of the Constitution.

A citizen may not be able to reroute such a conservatively rigged society. But he can stop it in its tracks, by exposing the underlying mythology. And the SLA did exactly that, by holding the media hostage by way of their prisoner, Miss Hearst.

The kidnapping of Citizen Kane's granddaughter has been called a "metaphor of America;" of its new, post-Viet Nam vulnerability, presumably. If so, it may explain why the authorities over-reacted: from the Attorney General who, for the first time in a kidnapping case, instructed the police to shoot on sight, to the FBI who assigned half the Bureau's manpower to the case. Why, for her part in a ten thousand dollar bank robbery, did Hearst become The Most Wanted criminal in the United States? Why, when the police had the SLA (but not Hearst and the Harrises) surrounded, didn't they wait them out?

But the authorities feared the contagion of a trial and instead blasted the SLA with some nine thousand bullets and lord knows how many firebombs. How deliberate the fire bombing was is a matter of dispute. The police maintained that the wooden structure caught fire from the ammunition poured into it. But Norman Mallory learned from one of the newsmen present that the house had been sprayed with gasoline from a point outside the range of the television cameras. A charred corpse provides no phoenix.

By the time the firemen were allowed in, all that remained of the body I had loved was her charred hand, about to reload from the bullet bag that contained her make-up kit and perfume—a cheerleader to the end.

A few hours after learning of Ling's death I happened to be in the Montarnis convent getting some xeroxing done. The nun who was helping me knew about the SLA and the Hearst kidnapping. After hearing me out, she remarked that Ling struck her as a genuine saint. The ways of the Lord, she said, precisely because they can't be foreseen, exist to astound us.

Astound me Ling did, by the manner of her death as much as everything else. But it was not a flick of the dice that brought Ling to the SLA and the SLA to Watts, but something intensely willed. Death, for most of us, cannot be completion. There are too many unturned corners, unfinished chapters, flapping about. But for Ling, pausing to reload, I think it was.

Ling and I were constructed of very much the same intensity. And though our experience came from such different domains, we shared the same compelling curiosity: about the transforming effect of the sexual cauldron; about the Orphic leap into the abyss and what it might yield in the way of vision. With her a quest ended; one that had enlisted the deepest part of my psyche. After years of largely futile efforts, she enabled me to crash through my walls in a way that only someone as fear-driven as I could understand. And by the time her personal cyclone had passed, I was in a different hemisphere, determined to make for myself a different life. Sure, I still had a lot of work to do. But the lonely, desperate groping around, the destroying of myself and others in the pursuit of an overheated illusion was terminated.

Yet for all the richness of the "life of uncommon thread" we shared, it is the absences, the things we didn't talk about, that still haunt me. Her suicidal yearnings, for one. How many attempts were there? What had gone wrong? The affliction of the ghetto was not the source of her pain, but a disease was, and it could and should have been treated.

And I wish I had expressed my feelings about those masculine street values of hers—guns and the poetry of crime and all the upside down dead end rest of it. As for helping her "actualize my militancy," well, maybe; but robbing a bank and kidnapping and killing people was not what I had in mind. Nor would I wish on anyone the torture the SLA inflicted upon Patricia Hearst in that tiny airless coffin of a closet.

All the same, the bitter comedy of the Hearst kidnapping threw off some potent sparks. The unlikely transformation of Patty into Tania, the cussing, vindictive, Symbionese rifle-toting princess, certainly spoke to me; it was what I had so narrowly escaped. So, too, did the food ransom "to the people;" a cruel fairy tale that the SLA visited upon the Hearsts. Yet it was illuminating, in what we were being told was the richest country on earth, to see a hundred thousand citizens braving the public ignominy, and untold hours in line, all for a ten dollar frozen fish handout.

Wherever one looked, rifts in the social fabric opened and lives and reputations were wrecked. Five years after she was kidnapped,

Patricia Hearst, the daughter of an influential father, would receive a presidential pardon. In 1976, after forty years of marriage, the Hearst parents divorced. My father, who had no knowledge of my affair with Ling, could not imagine why anyone would try to ransom a semi-retired, seventy-one-year-old businessman—didn't we all want to inherit?—and carried on the same as ever. But both the Safeway chairman and president took so personally the threat posed by Father's name in Ling's green spiral notebook that they sold their lifelong Oakland residences and hired round-the-clock bodyguards.

The author with James and Felix, England, 1988

POSTSCRIPT

Write on what you know, the ancients advised. What else but my life, I thought? Well, as it turns out, nothing is darker, more finally resistant, than the self. Fortunately, I have benefited on the way from the help of many friends who know me and what I have been through, or who are simply better read than I. A bald list can't acknowledge the nature of each contribution, but here, at least, it will have to do: Virgil Burnett, Andrée Abecassis, Richard Howard, Murray Ross, Michael Beard, Norman Mallory, Lorenzo Milam, Gerard Van der Leun, Laurie Lister, Ed Smallfield, Walter Perrie, Julia Casterton, Ann Arensberg, and Victoria Wilson. All generously provided their reactions, and gave me something to cannibalize.

John Ryle saw my work shortly after I moved to London in 1978—not an autobiography at all, but a vast collected ME. John suggested I make a separate book of the travel contents. That became *And Other Voyages*.

Some years later, *Maya Revisited*, as I then called it, turned up on the desk of an agent's reader, Robert Mabry, a former chief editor at Putnam and Dial. Bob could have merely delivered his report. Instead, he was kind enough to call on me. In the process he explained that an autobiography (as opposed to an over-sized prose poem) has to involve a more consistently introspective prose in the way of a narrative voice. Better yet, he was willing to work with me, and show me how to make myself over from a poet-critic into a more disciplined chronicler.

When I returned to America, and a house in rural Connecticut, in 1991, Bob had long since moved to St. Paul, Minnesota. A few years later, while in Berkeley, I happened to show my work to a former student and friend, Susan Hesse, a professional writer and editor. Susan knew much of my milieu first hand, and seemed to know instinctively the expansions, the insights, and the portraiture my story still needed. She made the whole process an alive one, a true burgeoning forth. If this memoir is dedicated to Susan, she certainly deserves it.